MONTESQUIEU
AND
THE PHILOSOPHY OF NATURAL LAW

ARCHIVES INTERNATIONALES D'HISTOIRE DES IDÉES

INTERNATIONAL ARCHIVES OF THE HISTORY OF IDEAS

37

MARK H. WADDICOR

MONTESQUIEU AND THE PHILOSOPHY OF NATURAL LAW

MARK H. WADDICOR
Lecturer in French
in the University of Exeter

MONTESQUIEU AND THE PHILOSOPHY OF NATURAL LAW

MARTINUS NIJHOFF / THE HAGUE / 1970

ISBN 90 247 5039 3

PRINTED IN THE NETHERLANDS

TABLE OF CONTENTS

ACKNOWLEDGEMENTS

This work[1] was begun under the supervision of the late W. Folkierski, whose invaluable guidance and unforgettable kindness helped me to complete its early stages. That it has eventually been brought to completion is in no small measure because of the painstaking and sympathetic assistance that has always been afforded to me by Professor W. Mc. C. Stewart, for many years head of the Department of French at the University of Bristol. I should also like to thank other members of the staff of the University of Bristol, particularly Professor R. Grimsley, Dr. S. C. Gould, and Mr. J. K. Grodecki, for the advice they have given me on certain aspects of the work.

A special debt of gratitude is owed to Dr. Robert Shackleton, Bodley's Librarian and Fellow of Brasenose College, Oxford, both for the encouragement he has given me personally, and for the profound contribution he has made by his researches to knowledge of Montesquieu and of the eighteenth century.

Thanks are also due to M. Jean Brethe de la Gressaye, formerly Professor of Law at the University of Bordeaux, to M. Joseph Moreau, Professor of the History and Philosophy of Science at the same University, and to M. Paul Vernière, Professor of French Literature at the Sorbonne, for the interest they have taken in my work.

Finally, I should like to express my gratitude to the University of Bristol for having enabled me to undertake this research by the award of a University Scholarship; to the Ministry of Education, for enabling me to continue it by the award of a State Studentship; and to Professor R. Niklaus and my colleagues at the University of Exeter both for their advice and for having provided me with time in which to finish the work.

[1] Originally presented, in a different form, as a dissertation for the degree of Ph D in the University of Bristol, in 1965.

INTRODUCTION

In the last hundred years, the philosophy of natural law has suffered a fate that could hardly have been envisaged by the seventeenth and eighteenth century exponents of its universality and eternity: it has become old-fashioned.

The positivists and the Marxists were happy to throw eternal morality out of the window, confident that some magic temporal harmony would eventually follow Progress in by the front door. Their hopes may not have been fully realized, but they did succeed in discrediting natural law. What is often not appreciated is the extent to which we have adopted the tenets of the philosophy they despised, both in the field of politics, and in the field of personal and social ethics, which Barbeyrac called "la science des mœurs" and which the positivists rechristened "social science". Consequently, though we live in a world whose freedom, such as it is, is largely a result of the popularization of the philosophy of natural law, and whose conscious and unconscious standards, such as they are, are a result of that philosophy as it became combined with Christianity, the doctrine of natural law is itself forgotten.

In view of the oblivion into which it has fallen, natural law is a concept which means little to the average reader. All too often, Montesquieu scholars have traded on this oblivion in order to give an exaggerated picture of his originality.

In claiming that he usually neglected the principles of natural morality, they tend to assume that his religious critics represent the doctrine of natural law – perhaps simply because the fulminations of the Sorbonne are very short and the articles by the abbé de La Roche very readable, and because a knowledge of both can be acquired merely by looking at Montesquieu's replies as printed in his complete works, whereas the treatises of St. Thomas, of Grotius and of Pufendorf, which give a more accurate picture of the various kinds of natural law, are rather long and are written in unfamiliar, often tedious styles.

The Jansenist abbé's conception of natural law was very narrow, and the same applies to his conception of Christianity. Just as Voltaire cleverly implied that Pascal's attitudes were those of orthodox religion, so Montesquieu's commentators give the impression that Fontaine de La Roche spoke for the Catholic Church.

Another erroneous assumption made by Montesquieu scholars is that the *philosophes*' idea of natural law was based on a full understanding of the doctrine, and that the criticisms of the *Esprit des lois* made by "Helvétius", Voltaire, Rousseau or Condorcet would always have been endorsed by Grotius or Pufendorf.

There are many other ways in which the concept of natural law has been misrepresented so that it can be used as a foil for Montesquieu's originality: critics talk about "Grotius and Pufendorf" as if these two jurists always held identical views; they make vague generalisations about the School of Natural Law without giving precise references; or if they do refer to the text, it is to quote some statement regarding method which (as is the case with Montesquieu), these jurists did not necessarily put into practice; finally – and this is perhaps the most serious distortion – they assume that natural law is only a political philosophy, whereas in reality it is primarily a moral and legal philosophy that has certain political implications.

In view of the present trend towards a more balanced view of the Enlightenment, the time has surely come for a less prejudiced and more detailed study than has hitherto been attempted of Montesquieu's debt to the philosophy of natural law. Only then can his contribution to the history of ideas be properly assessed.

NOTE

All books in French referred to in this work were published in Paris, and all books in English, in London, except where otherwise stated. Dates given in square brackets after the titles of works indicate the date of publication (not of composition) of the first edition in the original language.

The spelling of quotations has usually been modernized, but the original punctuation has been maintained. Italics have been omitted except where they are in accordance with modern usage.

ABBREVIATIONS

Dg. = Grotius, *Le Droit de la guerre et de la paix.*
Dn. = Pufendorf, *Le Droit de la nature et des gens.*
Dv. = Pufendorf, *Les Devoirs de l'homme et du citoyen.*
Lois = Montesquieu, *De l'Esprit des lois.*
L.p. = Montesquieu, *Lettres persanes.*
M. = Shackleton, *Montesquieu, A Critical Biography.*
N. = Nagel edition of Montesquieu's Works.
P. = Montesquieu, *Pensées.*
Pl. = Pléiade edition of Montesquieu's Works.
P.R. = Hobbes, *Philosophical Rudiments Concerning Government and Society.*
S.t. = Aquinas, *Summa theologica.*
T.T. Locke, *Two Treatises of Government.*

See Bibliography for details of these works

CHAPTER I

INTRODUCTION TO NATURAL LAW AND TO THE WORK OF MONTESQUIEU

I. The History of Natural Law

The doctrine of natural law is one of the most important elements in Western thought. It flourished in Greek and Roman times, and again in our seventeenth and eighteenth centuries, when it became more or less divorced from Christian theology. In the nineteenth century it declined as a result of the triple influence of Marxism, positivism and nihilism, but it is still a considerable force in our own time, especially in the doctrines of secular and religious humanism, and in international law.

It is difficult to give a short definition of natural law, because the concept was not exactly the same for the Greeks and for the Romans, for the Scholastics, for the seventeenth- and eighteenth-century jurists, for the seventeenth- and eighteenth-century scientists. However, a possible definition is: certain rules derived in various ways from the supposed characteristics of God, of the universe and of man. Though this definition covers almost all the meanings of the term *natural law*, it would probably not please jurists, who would perhaps prefer a definition such as that of Frederick Pollock:

> an ultimate principle of fitness with regard to the nature of man as a rational and social being, which is, or ought to be, the justification of every form of positive law.[1]

How the latter narrower meaning is reconciled with the first, more general definition, will, it is hoped, become clear in the course of this survey.

These two definitions correspond to two related yet distinct currents

[1] F. Pollock, *Essays in the Law*, Macmillan, 1920, p. 31. The best short and yet general work on natural law, written from a sympathetic and yet not uncritical point of view, is: A. P. D'Entrèves, *Natural Law, An Introduction to Legal Philosophy* [1951], Hutchinson, 1957.

of thought: natural law as a certain order of events in the universe, and natural law as the moral order that should govern men's actions. The first can be called empirical, descriptive, or *a posteriori* natural law, and the second can be called rationalistic, normative, or *a priori*. These two currents are to be met with in varying proportions throughout the history of natural law, and it is essential to bear the distinction in mind if the prejudiced and unhistorical approach to natural law characteristic of the nineteenth and early twentieth centuries is to be avoided.

Comparatively little is known of the thought of the earliest Greek philosophers.[2] However, it seems that the Milesian philosphers (VIth. century B.C.) belong to the first, more empirical current of thought: they believed that a more or less material and immanent principle governs the rhythm of events in the universe and its changes of state.[3] Yet they drew nearer to the second current of thought by linking this rhythm to a certain order of justice.[4] Xenophanes of Colophon (VI-Vth century B.C.) and more especially Parmenides the Eleatic (VI-Vth century B.C.) exemplify the second, more idealistic current, by denying any basic changes in the state of the universe and by postulating an eternal transcendent principle which governs all things.[5]

The Sophists (second part of Vth century) seem to have belonged to the empirical current of thought, but they were concerned with man, not with the order of the universe. They denied that any link exists between the physical order of the world and man's justice; they contrasted the impulse of nature with the restraint of law; they identified justice with convention and with human laws, and perhaps identified human laws with the will of the strongest.[6]

It was in reaction to such views that Socrates (470–399) and Plato (427–348), developing the second current of thought, postulated a universal order created by a transcendent intelligent principle,[7] and emphasized, as did Aristotle (384–322), the existence of an immutable natural law of justice, opposed to the often varying laws and conven-

[2] It is not the purpose of this chapter to give a comprehensive survey of Greek philosophy; its purpose is simply to define those of its trends which concern natural law. Much of our information on the early history of natural law is taken from E. Bréhier's useful *Histoire de la philosophie* [1926–32], Presses Universitaires de France, 3 vols.: vol. I, 1926–8, vol. II, 1929-30.

[3] *Cf.* Bréhier, *op. cit.*, vol. I, pp. 44–7.

[4] Bréhier, *op. cit.*, vol. I, p. 47.

[5] *Ibid.*, pp. 60–65.

[6] *Ibid.*, p. 84. Plato appears to have believed that the Sophists equated might with right, but he may have distorted their teaching, *cf.* F. Copleston, *A History of Philosophy*, Burns Oates and Washborne, vol. I, 1947, pp. 81–95.

[7] *Cf.* Plato, *Laws*, X, 892a–899d; in the Loeb edition, vol. II, pp. 323–51.

tions of man. One of the most famous examples of this contrast is in Aristotle's *Ethics*.[8]

The philosophers of the Stoic school, and notably its founder Zeno of Citium (335–264), interested themselves in the laws that govern the universe as well as in those that govern man. They seem to have believed that the universe is a living being made up of two principles, the active and the passive. The passive principle is unqualified matter, the active principle is reason, which pervades that matter, causing it to become qualified (as stone, plant, animal, man, for example). This immanent reason, the Stoics also called *god* or *nature*, and they identified it with fate, the law governing the necessary sequence of events between one universal conflagration and the next. Man's aim should be to live a life according to nature: nature here means the eternal law common to man's specific nature – he has more reason than the animals – and to the nature of the universe. This law is the expression of god's reason, so to follow nature is to follow god and reason.[9] The Stoics, like Plato, thus identified law and nature, which the Sophists had tried to separate, as Epicurus was later to do (341–270).

Especially after Greece had become a Roman colony (146 B.C.), Greek philosophy enjoyed great popularity with cultured Romans, though it did not have official approval.[10] The philosophy of the Greek Stoics is for the most part known to us only through the fragments of it and commentaries on it found in the works of later writers, especially Cicero (106–43), Seneca (4 B. C.– 65 A.D.), and the Roman Emperor Marcus Aurelius Antoninus (121–180 A.D.).[11]

It has also been claimed that Greek Stoic philosophy influenced the development of Roman law.[12] About a hundred years before the Roman conquest of Greece, Roman law consisted of *ius civile*, a body of complicated and ceremonious laws regulating transactions between Roman citizens and promulgated by the *Prætor urbanus*; and of what eventually became known as *ius gentium* (in English, *law of nations*, and

[8] *Ethics*, V, vii, 1–4; in the Loeb edition, pp. 294–7.

[9] *Cf.* Bréhier, *op. cit.*, vol. I, pp. 284–331, and J. Moreau, *L'Ame du monde de Platon aux stoïciens*, Les Belles Lettres, 1939, pp. 158–86.

[10] *Cf.* R. W. Leage, *Roman Private Law* [1906], ed. C. H. Zeigler, Macmillan, 1954, p. 22; (the latest edition of Leage, by A. M. Pritchard, Macmillan, 1961, is not so useful in this connection, since its account of the *ius naturale* and *ius gentium* is much more sparing).

[11] Bréhier, *op. cit.*, vol. I, pp. 291–2.

[12] See the following works on this complex subject: W. Buckland, *A Textbook of Roman Law*, Cambridge University Press, 1950, pp. 50–52; W. G. Friedmann, *Legal Theory*, Stevens, 1960, pp. 21–5; H. F. Jolowicz, *Historical Introduction to the Study of Roman Law*, Cambridge University Press, 1952, pp. 100–105; H. J. S. Maine, *Ancient Law* [1861], Murray, 1930, pp. 52–91; B. Nicholas, *An Introduction to Roman Law*, Oxford University Press, 1962, pp. 54–9; F. Schulz, *History of Roman Legal Science*, Oxford University Press, 1946, pp. 69–73.

in French, *droit des gens*), those laws which regulated transactions between foreigners who were in Roman territory, and between such foreigners and Roman citizens. The *ius gentium* was promulgated by an edict issued each year by the *Prætor peregrinus*, either confirming or changing the existing *ius gentium*. It is uncertain whether the laws of the *ius gentium* were culled from the institutions of various Italian tribes, whether they were a simplification of the *ius civile*, or whether they were drawn in some measure from the doctrines of the Greek Stoics. What is certain is that the *ius gentium* contained laws that were simpler, more equitable, and more universal in application than the laws of the *ius civile*. Consequently Roman jurists, if not the Prætors, tended to identify the *ius gentium* with the universal natural law of the Stoics.

The fact that the *ius gentium* was more equitable meant that the *Prætor urbanus* was under pressure to incorporate some of its laws into the *ius civile*, and such incorporation occurred from about 150 B.C. onwards. Gradually the *ius civile* fell into desuetude, a process which was practically complete after Caracalla's edict (*ca.* 212 A.D.) extending Roman citizenship to the inhabitants of many provinces. In the end the only important point where the *ius gentium* was in accordance with the old *ius civile*, and in contradiction with the natural law of the Stoics, was on the question of slavery, which was said to be against nature, and to have its origin in war.[13]

The change from *ius civile* to *ius gentium* brought inevitable confusion with it, so that an authoritative and comprehensive selection was required, in order to separate the dead legislation from that which was alive and in use. This was the aim of the Emperor Justinian (483–565), who commissioned teams of jurists to systematize the law into certain compilations now known collectively as the *Corpus iuris civilis*. From the point of view of natural law the most important works of the *Corpus* are the *Institutes* and the *Digest* (or *Pandects*) (both 533 A.D.). The *Corpus* tended to fix the content of Roman law, but it was not free from contradictions: natural law is variously defined in it as animal instinct, as a universal standard of fairness, or as the equivalent of the *ius gentium*.[14]

The fathers of the Church continued the tradition of natural law as they found it in Aristotle, in Cicero's interpretations of the Greek Stoics, and in the Roman jurists. Natural law was also used by Medieval

13 See the *Digest*, I, i, 4, Ulpian, vol. I, p. 1 of the Mommsen edition of the *Corpus iuris civilis*, Berlin, Weidmann, 1899.

14 Compare: *Digest*, I, i, 1, Ulpian, p. 1; *ibid.*, I, i, 11, Paulus, p. 1; *Institutes*, I, ii, 11, also in the Mommsen edition, p. 2.

jurists as a weapon in political controversy.[15] Medieval theologians argued about various points of natural law: one vexatious question was that related to the contradictions in the *Corpus* – is natural law common to man and the animals, or peculiar to man? St. Thomas Aquinas (1225–1274) tried to reconcile the Roman jurists with themselves and with Aristotle, by accepting both kinds of natural law.[16] His *Summa theologica* (begun in 1266), which is generally regarded as representing orthodox Roman Catholic doctrine,[17] attempted to incorporate natural law in the framework of Christian theology. For St. Thomas, natural law is subordinate to divine law (*S.t.*, II, i, Q. 91, Art. 2, vol. VIII, pp. 11–12), and the same is true for the majority of Medieval theologians.

However, some theologians tended to emphasize natural law at the expense of divine law,[18] a trend that was later taken up by certain secular jurists and philosophers. From the beginning of the seventeenth century till at least the end of the eighteenth, they secularized and codified the natural law of Antiquity and the Middle Ages; their efforts were successful in promoting the wide diffusion of the doctrine, which was given a place on the syllabus of several universities. These writers differed on many important points, but they were united in according an almost autonomous position to natural law, and in claiming (with only partial justification) to believe almost exclusively in the rational kind of natural law, to the exclusion of the empirical kind:[19] hence they are known collectively as the *School of Natural Law*.

In the following pages, reference will be made principally to the following "members" of the School of Natural Law: Grotius, Pufendorf and Burlamaqui, together with certain philosophers who shared to a

[15] *Cf.* J. Touchard, *et al.*, *Histoire des idées politiques*, Presses Universitaires de France, 1959, vol. I, pp. 278–80.

[16] *Summa theologica* [hereafter *S. t.*], II, i, Q. 94, Art. 2, in the translation by Fathers of the English Dominican Province, Burns Oates and Washbourne, 1913–42, vol. VIII, p. 44. For a short but comprehensive introduction to these aspects of St. Thomas's philosophy, see D. J. O'Connor, *Aquinas and Natural Law*, Macmillan, 1967, pp. 57–79.

[17] *Cf.* D'Entrèves, *op. cit.*, p. 39, and *The Oxford Dictionary of the Christian Church*, ed. F. L. Cross, O.U.P., 1957, p. 1353. In the absence of any indication to the contrary, we have assumed that the *Supplement* to the *Summa theologica*, prepared by Fra Rainaldo da Piperno from an early work of St. Thomas, can also be regarded as having represented orthodox Catholic opinion.

[18] See A. Esmein, *Éléments de droit constitutionnel français et comparé* [1896], Sirey, 1921, vol. I, pp. 276–8.

[19] *Cf.* Hugo Grotius, *De iure belli ac pacis* [1625], *Disc. prél.*, xi, vol. I, p. 10, and I, i, 11–12, vol. I, pp. 52–4, in the translation by J. Barbeyrac, *Le Droit de la guerre et de la paix*, Amsterdam, P. de Coup, 1724 [hereafter *Dg.*]; and Samuel von Pufendorf, *De iure naturæ et gentium* [1672], II, iii, 2–15, vol. I, pp. 169–98, in the translation by Barbeyrac, *Le Droit de la nature et des gens*, Amsterdam, P. de Coup, 1712 [hereafter *Dn.*].

greater or lesser extent their outlook and principles: Hobbes, Locke, Cumberland, Domat and Gravina. They are representative of the various currents of natural law as they were known in the seventeenth and eighteenth centuries, and particularly in France.

Hugo Grotius (1583–1645), a Dutch philosopher, jurist and diplomatist could well be called the founder of the School of Natural Law. Taking as the basis of his theories natural law as propounded by the Greeks and by Cicero, and the quasi-universal *ius gentium* of the *Corpus*, Grotius developed the science of international relations, in his *De iure belli ac pacis* (1625), a work which enjoyed great popularity.[20]

Samuel von Pufendorf (1632–94), a German jurist, and professor of the law of nature and of nations at the Universities of Heidleberg and Lund, wrote a comprehensive treatise of natural and international law, *De iure naturæ et gentium* (1672); a year later he produced a popularized version of this work, *De officio hominis et civis juxta legem naturalem.*[21]

Grotius and Pufendorf were the two principal philosophers of the School of Natural Law, but there were other important writers who also put forward various doctrines of natural law. Richard Cumberland (1631–1718), Bishop of Peterborough, in his *De legibus naturæ* (1672), developed, in opposition to Hobbes, a theory of natural law supposedly deduced by a scientific method from the principle of universal benevolence.[22] In France, the philosophy of natural law was represented by Jean Domat (1625–96), a Jansenist who, in his *Les lois civiles dans leur ordre naturel* (1689–94), set out to arrange Roman law, as it was used in France, in a logical order deduced from the principles of natural law.[23] He emphasized the place of religion in natural law more than did the Italian Gian Vincenzo Gravina (1664–1718), but Gravina nevertheless had aims similar to those of the Frenchman, since his *Origines iuris civilis* (1708) is an examination of Roman law in the light of certain natural laws.[24]

Among the less important members of the School of Natural Law, mention should also be made of Jean Barbeyrac (1674–1744), whose fame rested mainly on the fact that it was through his translations and

[20] For details of this work, see previous note.

[21] For details of *De iure*, see p. 5, n. 19; *De officio hominis*, in the translation by Barbeyrac, *Les Devoirs de l'homme et du citoyen*, Amsterdam and Luxemburg, Chevalier, 1708 [hereafter *Dv.*].

[22] *De legibus naturæ*, in the translation by Barbeyrac, *Traité philosophique des lois naturelles*, Amsterdam, Mortier, 1744.

[23] *Les Lois civiles dans leur ordre naturel, le droit public et legum delectus*, Cavelier, 1705, 2 vols.

[24] *Origines iuris civilis, quibus ortus et progressus iuris civilis, ius naturale, gentium et xii. tabulæ legesque ac senatusconsulta explicantur*, Leipzig, Gleditsch, 1708.

annotations of the works of Grotius, Pufendorf and Cumberland that the French public became acquainted with the doctrine of natural law. Finally, there is the Genevan Jean-Jacques Burlamaqui (1694–1748), whose *Principes du droit naturel* (1747) is in many respects a summary of the ideas of the School of Natural Law.[25]

All these writers had important differences of approach to the question of natural law. These differences were often a result of their political views,[26] and are nowhere more apparent than in the works of the English philosophers who used certain theories of natural law, notably the hypotheses of the state of nature and of the original contract, for the corroboration of political doctrines. In his *De cive* (1642) and his *Leviathan* (1651) Thomas Hobbes (1588–1679) used these hypotheses to prove the necessity of political absolutism.[27] Sir Robert Filmer (1588?–1653), in his *Patriarcha* (1680), attempted to prove a similar theory by examples drawn from the Old Testament.[28] Their doctrine was refuted some years later by a more orthodox version of natural law from the pen of John Locke (1632–1704), in his *Two Treatises of Government* (1690).[29] The theories of Hobbes and Locke became famous throughout Europe and exercised a considerable influence on the development of natural law.

These trends in moral and political philosophy cannot be considered in isolation from those taking place in natural science, because in the seventeenth and eighteenth centuries it was often the fashion to express theories of morality in scientific terms. During the period, an important subject of debate was the question of which method should be employed in scientific investigation, the empirical or the deductive, though the difference between the two was not always as clear-cut as used to be thought.[30] In England, it was with Robert Boyle (1627–91)[31] and Isaac Newton (1642–1727) that the theory and practice of the empirical method came to fruition. Newton claimed to establish his physical

[25] *Principes du droit naturel*, Geneva, Barrillot, 1747.

[26] *Cf.* Esmein, *op. cit.*, vol. I, pp. 281–2.

[27] *De cive*, in Hobbes's own translation *Philosophical Rudiments Concerning Government and Society* [hereafter *P.R.*], in *The English Works of Thomas Hobbes*, edited by W. Molesworth, Bohn and Longman, 1839–45, vol. II; *Leviathan*, in *ibid.*, vol. III; also *Tripos, Part II: De corpore politico* [1650], in *ibid.*, vol. IV, pp. 77–228; and *The Questions Concerning Liberty, Necessity and Chance* [1656], in *ibid.*, vol. V.

[28] *Patriarcha and other Political Works*, edited by P. Laslett, Oxford, Blackwell, 1949.

[29] *Two Treatises of Government*, edited by P. Laslett, Cambridge University Press, 1960 [hereafter *T.T.*].

[30] One of the latest works on this subject is: R. Blake, C. Ducasse and E. Madden, *Theories of Scientific Method*, University of Washington Press, 1960.

[31] *The Works of the Honourable Robert Boyle*, Johnston, etc., 1772.

theories solely by observation and experiment, without making any hypotheses.[32]

By the middle of the eighteenth century, Newton's method had more or less replaced that of Descartes in French scientific circles.[33] René Descartes (1596–1650) had tried to deduce *a priori* the laws of motion, which he called "lois de la nature", from a few general principles.[34] Descartes' mechanism was taken up by some religious writers, notably Nicolas de Malebranche (1638–1715). It was also from Descartes' mechanism that Benedictus de Spinoza (1632–77) evolved a theory of absolute physical and moral determinism.[35] All these theories, both deductive and empirical, were to influence the moral and political doctrines of the age.

We began this historical survey by saying that there are two related meanings of the term natural law, the rational and the empirical. In the seventeenth century, as natural law was divorcing itself from religion, the two meanings tended to merge together. The jurists, and especially Pufendorf (*Dn.*, I, vi, 4, vol. I, p. 89), claimed that natural law is a command, a statement of what should be, but at the same time they saw it as a statement of what is, based on the nature of man (*Dn.*, II, iii, 14, vol. I, p. 192). This second interpretation had been made quite clear by Grotius in his controversial statement that the truths of natural law would still apply,

> quand même on accorderait, ce qui ne se peut sans un crime horrible, qu'il n'y a point de Dieu (*Dg.*, *Disc. prél.*, xi, vol. I, p. 10).

Like Pufendorf, the scientists claimed to see their laws of nature both as the commands of God, and as statements, based on the nature of things, of what does happen in the physical world.[36] In fact, both the

[32] *Principia* [1687], Book III, pp. 398–400, in Motte's translation revised by F. Cajori, University of California Press, 1947; *Opticks* [1704], Book III, Innys, 1730, p. 380; *cf.* Blake, Ducasse and Madden, *op. cit.*, pp. 119–43. For a brilliant account of the *a priori* elements hidden in Newton's philosophy, see E. A. Burtt, *The Metaphysical Foundations of Modern Physical Science* [1924], Routledge and Kegan Paul, 1949, pp. 223–99.

[33] See J. Ehrard, *L'Idée de nature en France dans la première moitié du XVIIIe siècle*, S.E.V.P.E.N., 1963, vol. I, pp. 21 and 125–78, for a general and up-to-date discussion of this question. For more detailed information, consult P. Brunet, *L'Introduction des théories de Newton en France au XVIIIe siècle: avant 1738*, Blanchard, 1931.

[34] *Principes de la philosophie* [1644] [hereafter *Principes*], II, xxxvii–xl, pp. 84–7 in vol. IX of the *Œuvres de Descartes*, edited by C. Adam and P. Tannery, Cerf, 1897–1910. Reference will also be made to the *Discours de la méthode* [1637], in vol. VI, pp. 1–78 of the *Œuvres*; to the *Méditations métaphysiques* [1641], in vol. IX; to the *Traité de l'homme* [1664], in vol. XI, pp. 119–215.

[35] *Tractatus theologico-politicus* [1670], in *Œuvres complètes*, Bibliothèque de la Pléiade, 1954, pp. 653–964; also *Ethics* [1677], in *ibid.*, pp. 357–652.

[36] See below, Ch. 7, IV, for a fuller discussion of this question.

jurists and the scientists helped to undermine the voluntaristic conception of natural law based on the command of God.

Since, in the seventeenth and eighteenth centuries, philosophers and scientists were wavering between the two conceptions of law, the empirical and the rational, there was more than a little confusion in their use of the term *natural law*. Such confusion was an historical fact, and though it is important to try to elucidate the ambiguity to be found in the term, and to understand its causes, it is impossible to accept D'Entrèves' advice that it should be confined to moral phenomena: to do so would be unhistorical.[37] Both kinds of natural law have their place in the history of ideas, and both are relevant to a discussion of Montesquieu's outlook.

II. Montesquieu's Life and Works[38]

Five years before the death of the acknowledged leader of the School of Natural Law, Samuel von Pufendorf, which took place in 1694, Charles-Louis de Secondat, baron of La Brède and later of Montesquieu, the man who, we are so often told, helped to cause the decline of natural law, was born. His education took place first at home, in the village of La Brède, near Bordeaux, then at the famous Oratorian collège de Juilly, near Paris (1700–1705), then at the moribund Faculty of Law in the University of Bordeaux (1705–1708). After graduation, he went to Paris, probably in order to gain legal experience, although he seems to have concentrated more on making contact with many of the important social and intellectual figures of his day. However, neither these activities, nor his inaptitude for legal procedure, prevented him from starting a career in law: he became a counsellor at the Parlement of Bordeaux in 1714, and in 1716 he inherited from his uncle the office of *président à mortier* at the Parlement, as well as certain lands, including the hamlet of Montesquieu.

Apart from his duties as *président*, he also attended meetings of the Academy of Bordeaux, to which he was admitted in 1716, and of which he became *directeur* in 1717; here he indulged in his interest in the physical sciences. He also found time to make frequent visits to Paris, where he kept up his acquaintances and at the same time gathered material for the *Lettres persanes* (1721), a satire of France at the time of the Regency that created intense public interest, and hostility from

[37] *Op. cit.*, p. 7.
[38] Montesquieu will be referred to as M. in the footnotes.

conservative quarters. This hostility was not strong enough to prevent his election to the French Academy in 1727.

To give himself more time and money, he sold his office of *président* in 1726. From 1728 to 1731, he travelled in Europe, visiting among other countries Italy and England, where he met many important figures and interested himself in political and constitutional questions. When he returned from his travels, he divided his time between La Brède or Bordeaux, and Paris, and was engaged mainly in the preparation of the *Considérations sur les causes de la grandeur des Romains, et de leur décadence* (1734), a wark remarkable for its anti-providentialist philosophy of history, and of the *Esprit des lois* (1748), a study of the laws of different countries in the light of their constitution, history, and geographical position. His last years were spent mainly in defending the *Esprit des lois* against his critics, such as the Jansenist abbé Fontaine de La Roche,[39] as well as against strictures made by the Holy See and the Faculty of Theology of the University of Paris.[40] Montesquieu's opponents accused him of putting forward a deterministic philosophy that undermined religion and natural law; though his religious and moral beliefs will always be a subject of dispute, it has been established beyond reasonable doubt that when he died in 1755, he confessed his belief in God and in the moral teaching of the Gospel.[41]

In the past, study of Montesquieu's work was inhibited mainly by two factors: critical prejudice and lack of documentation. As regards

[39] Fontaine de La Roche, *Examen critique de l'Esprit des lois* [hereafter *Examen critique*], first printed in the *Nouvelles ecclésiastiques*, 9th and 16th October 1749, reprinted in É. Laboulaye, *Œuvres complètes de Montesquieu*, Garnier, 1875–9, vol. VI, pp. 115–37. M. replied in his *Défense de L'Esprit des lois* (February 1750), and the Jansenist counter-replied in the *Réponse à la défense de l'Esprit des lois* [hereafter *Réponse*], first printed in the *Nouvelles ecclésiastiques*, 24th April and 1st May 1750, reprinted in Laboulaye, *op. cit.*, vol. VI, pp. 209–37. See also the milder attack probably made by the Jesuit, le Père Plesse, *Lettre au P.J.B. sur le livre intitulé l'Esprit des lois* [hereafter *Lettre au P.J.B.*], first printed in the *Mémoires de Trévoux*, April 1749, reprinted in Laboulaye, *op. cit.*, vol. VI, pp. 101–13. M. made no public reply to le Père Plesse.

[40] In spite of M.'s efforts at conciliation, the *Esprit des lois* was put on the Index in November 1751: see L. Bérard, '*L'Esprit des lois* devant la congrégation de l'Index', *Revue des deux mondes*, 1949, pp. 608–33. The Faculty of Theology of the Sorbonne examined the *Esprit des lois* twice, in 1750 and 1752. The comments made by the Faculty on various propositions drawn from the work have been reprinted in an invaluable article by C.-J. Beyer, 'Montesquieu et la censure religieuse de l'*Esprit des lois*' [hereafter 'Montesquieu et la censure religieuse', *Revue des sciences humaines*, 1953, pp. 105–31. The Sorbonne condemned the *Esprit des lois* in 1752, without taking into account M.'s *Réponses et explications* (reprinted in N. III, pp. 649–74, Pl. II, pp. 1172–95 [see below, p. 11, n. 47 and p. 12, n. 48]), but its condemnation was not made public. The clearest accounts of the quarrel of the *Esprit des lois* are to be found in Jean Brethe de la Gressaye's edition of the work, Les Belles Lettres, 1950–61, [hereafter Brethe de la Gressaye, *Lois*], vol. I, pp. lxii–lxxxv, and in R. Shackleton, *Montesquieu, A Critical Biography*, Oxford University Press, 1961, pp. 356–77 [hereafter *M.*].

[41] See Shackleton, *M.*, pp. 392–98.

the latter, many documents were withheld from publication by Montesquieu's family till the beginning of this century, when H. Barckhausen was given access to them, and helped to secure their publication, thus giving a new stimulus to Montesquieu studies.[42]

A further obstacle to our knowledge of Montesquieu's work, namely a lack of good critical editions of his main works, has now been partially overcome. The *Lettres persanes* have attracted many able scholars, and the latest critical edition, by Paul Vernière, is outstanding.[43] The *Considérations* have not been so fortunate in recent years, and the best critical edition is still that of Barckhausen.[44] The *Esprit des lois* has recently been edited by Jean Brethe de la Gressaye:[45] his notes and analyses are very well-informed and stimulating, but the edition cannot be called fully critical, since it does not give all the important variants found in the manuscript.[46]

These critical editions will be referred to where necessary in the following pages, but the bulk of the references will be made to the recent *Œuvres complètes de Montesquieu*, edited by André Masson and others.[47] The completeness of this edition and the fact that it contains many essential introductory articles, make it the obvious choice for the study of Montesquieu. For the convenience of the reader, references

42 See in particular: *Montesquieu, L'Esprit des lois et les archives de La Brède*, Bordeaux, Michel et Forgeot, 1904; and *Montesquieu, ses idées et ses œuvres d'après les papiers de La Brède*, Hachette, 1907.

43 Garnier, 1960.

44 Imprimerie nationale, 1900.

45 See above, p. 10, n. 40.

46 For details concerning this manuscript, see Shackleton's article in N. III, pp. 567–77. Note that the manuscript does not represent the definitive version of the work. It is nevertheless very important to its understanding.

47 *Œuvres complètes de Montesquieu*, publiées sous la direction de M. André Masson, Nagel, 1950–55, 3 vols. Vol. I is a facsimile of the 1758 edition of M.'s works, which is generally considered to be based on the author's final revisions, and which had three volumes. These will be referred to in the footnotes and in the text as N. I, i; N. I, ii; and N. I, iii, followed by a page number. N. I, i, contains Books I–XXI of the *Esprit des lois* [hereafter *Lois*], together with D'Alembert's *Éloge* [. . .] *de Montesquieu* and his *Analyse de l'Esprit des lois*; N. I, ii, contains Books XXII–XXXI of the *Lois*, and the *Défense de l'Esprit des lois* [hereafter *Défense*]; N. I, iii, contains the *Lettres persanes* [hereafter *L.p.*], the *Considérations sur les causes de la grandeur des Romains et de leur décadence* [hereafter *Considérations*] and two minor works. There is, owing to the limitations imposed by the process of photographic reproduction, no critical apparatus in N. I, so the appearance of the critical editions of the *L.p.*, by Paul Vernière and of the *Lois*, by Jean Brethe de la Gressaye, is most timely. Vol. II of the Nagel edition, which will be referred to as N. II, contains the *Pensées* [hereafter *P.*] here published in the order of the manuscript for the first time, the *Spicilège*, the *Geographica* and the *Voyages*. Vol. III, which will be referred to as N. III, contains among many other works, M.'s contributions to the Bordeaux Academy, rejected drafts of parts of his major works, and his correspondence.

will also be given to the *Œuvres complètes* edited by Roger Caillois.[48]

Among other recent important aids to the study of Montesquieu there is the bibliography by D. C. Cabeen;[49] the catalogue of Montesquieu's library at La Brède, lost for many years and rediscovered by Robert Shackleton;[50] and the list of works to which Montesquieu made reference, compiled by F. Weil.[51]

Another major contribution to the understanding of Montesquieu was Shackleton's painstaking examination of the handwriting of the *président*'s many secretaries. As a result of this examination, the approximate date of composition of some of his works, including the *Pensées* and many chapters of the *Esprit des lois*, has been established.[52]

The bicentenaries of the publication of the *Esprit des lois* and of Montesquieu's death resulted in many important studies of various aspects of his work.[53] Finally, Robert Shackleton's recent critical biography, incorporating the results of his discoveries and of his original

[48] In the Bibliothèque de la Pléiade, Gallimard, 1949–51, 2 vols.. These will be referred to in the footnotes and in the text as Pl. I, and Pl. II, followed by a page number. When the text of the Nagel edition is at variance with that of the Pléiade edition, the reading of the former will be followed, except in the case of obvious misprints. The *Œuvres complètes* edited by D. Oster, Seuil, 1964, also suggested itself as a primary source of reference, but the Pléiade edition was preferred as it is more widely available and more scholarly. Apart from the fact that they do not contain the correspondence, another disadvantage of these two editions is that their editors have chosen the arbitrary Barckhausen classification of the *Pensées* rather than the manuscript order. This makes the dating of the *Pensées* impossible without reference to the Nagel edition. *Pensée* numbers in the Barckhausen order will be preceded by the abbreviation: Bkn.

[49] *Montesquieu: A Bibliography*, New York Public Library, 1947; see also Cabeen, 'A Supplementary Montesquieu Bibliography', *Revue internationale de philosophie*, 1955, pp. 409–34; and for later information, Brethe de la Gressaye, *Lois*, vol. III, pp. xi–xxi and vol. IV, pp. xii–xxiii. More recent summary bibliographies are to be found in J. Dedieu, *Montesquieu*, ed. J. Ehrard, Hatier, 1966, pp. 219–23 (the title of this work is misleading, since it is in fact a reprint of Dedieu's famous *Montesquieu l'homme et l'œuvre* of 1943); and in J. R. Loy, *Montesquieu*, New York, Twane, 1968, pp. 183–5.

[50] L. Desgraves, *Catalogue de la bibliothèque de Montesquieu*, Geneva, Droz, 1954 [hereafter referred to as D., followed by the catalogue number only]. See also Shackleton, 'Montesquieu: Two Unpublished Documents', *French Studies*, 1950, pp. 316–21.

[51] 'Les Lectures de Montesquieu', *Revue d'Histoire littéraire de la France* [hereafter *RHLF*], 1957, pp. 494–514.

[52] See Shackleton in N. II, pp. xxxv–xliii; then, for dates of composition of chapters of the *Lois*, see Shackleton in N. III, pp. 567–77. For the dates of writing (though not necessarily of original composition) of the *Pensées*, see Desgraves' article, N. II, pp. xlv–lvii, together with Shackleton in N. II, pp. xxxvii–xxxix. Note that the dates are proposed with certain reservations (N. II, pp. xxxvii, n. a, and pp. li–lii; N. III, p. 575). The dates of writing of the *Spicilège* can be deduced approximately from the dates of the many press-cuttings which figure in the collection; nevertheless the chronological order is not strictly observed, *cf.* N. II, p. lxxi.

[53] *IIe Centenaire de l'Esprit des lois de Montesquieu, conférences organisées par la ville de Bordeaux*, Bordeaux, Delmas, 1949 [hereafter *IIe Centenaire*]; *La Pensée politique et constitutionnelle de Montesquieu, Bicentenaire de l'Esprit des lois*, Sirey, 1952 [hereafter *Bicentenaire*]; *Actes du congrès Montesquieu*, Bordeaux, Delmas, 1956 [hereafter *Congrès*].

research, has given us a definitive reassessment of the life and works of Montesquieu.[54]

A particular question that arises in connection with the interpretation of Montesquieu's works is that of his notebooks. One of the many endearing aspects of the *président* is that he never liked to abandon an idea once it had occurred to him: hence the importance he attached to his notebooks. He did not use *fiches* but made notes in various *recueils* entitled *Geographica, Politica, Juridica* (which are now lost, except for volume II of the *Geographica*), as well as in the *Spicilège* and the *Pensées*. He began the *Spicilège* in about 1718, and the *Pensées* in about 1720,[55] and added to both collections throughout most of his life. The *Pensées* in particular are of great intrinsic merit, showing Montesquieu to be among other things a *moraliste* of some calibre. In addition, both collections are a valuable aid to the interpretation of his character and works, since they are in part a record of his thoughts and reading. However, the fact that Montesquieu expressed a certain view in the *Spicilège* or in the *Pensées* should not necessarily be taken as evidence that he seriously held it. In some cases, it is true, the pieces are fragments which he had rejected from or might later incorporate into other works: the *Pensées* are, for example, the main source of our knowledge of the important *Traité des devoirs*, parts of which Montesquieu read to the Bordeaux Academy in 1725.[56] In other cases, however, it is possible that he was just playing with ideas, for he stated that

> Je me garderai bien de répondre de toutes les pensées qui sont ici. Je n'ai mis là la plupart que parce que je n'ai pas eu le temps de les réfléchir, et j'y penserai quand j'en ferai usage (*P.* 3, N. II, p. 1, Pl. I, p. 974).

Whether these lines were dictated by cautiousness or by modesty, it remains true that the unpublished works do not have quite the same

[54] See above, p. 10, n. 40. Shackleton's biography supersedes the two previous ones: P. Barrière, *Un Grand provincial, ... Montesquieu*, Bordeaux, Delmas, [1946], which is very readable, but incomplete; and L. Vian, *Histoire de Montesquieu: sa vie et ses œuvres d'après des documents nouveaux et inédits*, Didier, 1878, which is still useful, but contains many factual errors.

[55] *Cf.* N. II, pp. xlvi–xlvii and lxvii–lxxiii. Nos. 1–203 of the *Spicilège* were taken from a *recueil* by le Père P. N. Desmolets, librarian of the Paris Oratory and friend of M.. In the rest of the *Spicilège* M. made notes mostly on books and articles he had read; thus it differs from the *Pensées*, which is more a collection of personal reflections.

[56] Fragments of the *Traité des devoirs* are to be found in *Pp.* 220 and 1251–80, Bkn. 597 and 602–629, N. II, pp. 93–4 and 331–55, Pl. I, pp. 1126–7 and 1128–1150). A summary of the work was printed in the *Bibliothèque française* of 1726, and is reprinted in N. III, pp. 157–62, Pl. I, pp. 108–111.

status as the published ones, because they do not necessarily express an opinion that Montesquieu wished to be made public.

There is a question of authenticity that should be settled before any conclusions can be made on Montesquieu's attitude to natural law. It concerns the *Essai touchant les lois naturelles et la distinction du juste et de l'injuste*, sometimes attributed to the Montesquieu of the 1720's.[57] It is true that certain parallels of ideas can be found between the *Essai* and the *président*'s early works, but these parallels are largely commonplaces. In a recent article, Robert Shackleton has proved very convincingly that the factual evidence for attributing the *Essai* to Montesquieu is flimsy, that its style and intellectual level are inferior to that of his writings, and that in all probability it is the work of a disciple of Burlamaqui.[58] Hence, it will not be considered in the present study.

The *Pensées* and the *Spicilège* will help to establish Montesquieu's attitude to natural law, and will in particular help in the interpretation of the published works. But before embarking on this task, it is worth considering what external evidence there is that Montesquieu may have come into contact with the doctrines of natural law, especially during his formative years.

"Au sortir du collège", he said disarmingly, "on me mit dans les mains des livres de droit; j'en cherchai l'esprit, je travaillai, je ne faisais rien qui vaille". (Letter of 7th March 1749, N. III, p. 1200). These "livres de droit" which so displeased him (retrospectively at least) by their failure to deal with basic principles were in all probability textbooks of Roman law: the *Corpus*, together with the commentaries on it by scholars such as Theophilus (*Paraphrases*) and J. Godefroy (*Series digestorum et codicis*).[59] At university, he may well have had a surfeit of Roman law which, in spite of a growing emphasis on the teaching of French law, occupied most of the syllabus.[60] Proof of his labours

57 The *Essai* appears in N. III, pp. 179–99. Reasons for its attribution to M. are given in N. III, pp. 175–8; certain striking parallels between the *Essai* and various works by M., are made by P. Dimoff in 'La place dans l'œuvre de Montesquieu de l'*Essai touchant les lois naturelles*', *RHLF*, 1957, pp. 481–93.

58 'L'*Essai touchant les lois naturelles* est-il de Montesquieu?', in *Mélanges offerts à Jean Brethe de la Gressaye*, Bordeaux, Bière, [1967], pp. 763–775.

59 *Cf.* D'Aguesseau, *Instructions sur les études propres à former un magistrat* (1716), in *Œuvres choisies*, Didot, 1886, pp. 226–31. According to M.'s friend the abbé de Guasco, "Montesquieu était obligé par son père de passer toute la journée sur le *Code*" (cited by Vian, *op. cit.*, p. 21). It is unfortunate that M.'s work on *la manière d'apprendre ou d'étudier la jurisprudence* (see Shackleton, *M.*, p. 408), which might have told us more about his attitude both to Roman law and to natural law, is lost.

60 *Cf.* H. Barckhausen (ed.), *Statuts et règlements de l'ancienne université de Bordeaux* (*1441–1793*), Libourne, Bordeaux, G. Bouchon, 1886, pp. 86–7 and 89–90 (citing documents relating to the 1680's, but the situation does not appear to have been very different in the early 1700's,

in this field is provided by his *Collectio iuris*, which consists of detailed analyses of the *Digest* and other works from the *Corpus*.[61]

Is it legitimate to suppose, in view of Montesquieu's interest in the principles of law, that he was in particular dissatisfied with the sketchy and contradictory account of natural law given in the *Corpus*, and that he turned instead to the more systematic treatises of the School of Natural Law? Certainly, his professors would not have encouraged such an interest, for they scorned these foreign theorists.[62] Nevertheless, it is clear that from the late seventeenth century onwards, there was a growing interest in the writings of the School of Natural Law among a section of the educated public,[63] and an enlightened man such as D'Aguesseau did not hesitate to suggest to his son, who was embarking on his legal studies, that he should have a look at Grotius, in order to understand "les principes généraux des lois".[64] So it is at least possible that the young Montesquieu may have been tempted to open the works of these modern theorists of natural law. However, there is no concrete proof of such an acquaintance before the *Lettres persanes*.[65]

A seemingly promising source of external evidence is Montesquieu's library, which housed over 3000 volumes, including 349 works on Jurisprudence, and, in particular, many important treatises by Grotius, Hobbes and Pufendorf. However, it is not possible to determine with any precision the date at which he acquired these works,[66] and in any

cf. ibid., pp. 117–8). In Paris, too, Roman law dominated the syllabus, *cf.* C. Jourdain, *Histoire de l'Université de Paris au XVIIe et au XVIIIe siècle*, Paris, 1862–66, reprint, Brussels, 1966, p. 290 (citing documents relating to the 1700's). Apart from the introduction of a small amount of French law, it is doubtful whether the situation had altered much since the days of Corneille's Dorante, who complains of his having been obliged to study the *Corpus* and its numerous interpreters (*Le Menteur*, ll. 322–31, in *Œuvres de Corneille*, ed. Marty-Laveaux, Hachette, 1862, vol. IV, p. 158).

61 See Shackleton, *M.*, pp. 17–18.

62 *Cf.* R. Derathé, *Jean-Jacques Rousseau et la science politique de son temps*, Presses Universitaires de France, 1950, p. 29. Unlike Germany and Switzerland, France had no chairs of natural law (*ibid.*, p. 28).

63 Proof of the growing interest in natural law is provided by the number of editions of translations of Grotius, Pufendorf and Locke: see Derathé, *op. cit.*, pp. 424, 426–7, and 437. This trend may be seen as one sign among many of the growing dissatisfaction among intellectuals with the political philosophy of the French monarchy.

64 *Op. cit.*, p. 224; *cf.* Derathé, *op. cit.*, p. 66.

65 Even in the *Lettres persanes*, with its rather vague allusions to ideas also found in the works of Grotius, Hobbes and Locke, we do not have the impression that M. had studied the philosophy of natural law very recently or very deeply: perhaps he was relying on recollections of earlier reading? It is not until the time of the *Traité des devoirs* that we have textual proof of M.'s knowledge of Pufendorf.

66 The works of Grotius and Pufendorf on natural law were either inherited by M. or acquired before 1732 (*cf.* Desgraves, *op. cit.*, pp.xv–xvii and p. 241). M. acquired Aristotle's *Politics* in 1738 (*ibid.*, p. xix).

case, the fact that he owned a work does not prove when, or indeed whether he read it.[67]

The evidence provided by external sources concerning Montesquieu's knowledge of natural law is thus rather slender, and will not be further investigated in this study, which will rely instead on internal evidence drawn from Montesquieu's works, and on comparisons between his own attitude and that of previous moral and political theorists.

III. *The Problem of Montesquieu and Natural Law*

The question of Montesquieu's attitude to natural law is of the utmost importance. If, in the *Esprit des lois*, he broke with the tradition of natural law, studying instead the laws of different nations without any reference to morality, then his major work would seem to appeal only to those who take a scientific or sociological interest in mankind, to those who merely observe, sometimes laugh, but never judge (if such people exist). Montesquieu would likewise be a man who observed, laughed, but did not judge, and he would live up to his reputation of having been a cold, un-emotional man.

If on the other hand Montesquieu based his works on a belief in natural law, we should expect to find in them not only laughter, but also praise, blame, indignation – emotions that would link him with the ordinary reader and make him a more human figure.

Thus it is not only Montesquieu's philosophy that is in question but, in the last analysis, his character as well, and the permanent literary value of his works. Natural law is a touchstone of all these three aspects of the man.

It is not surprising, therefore, to find critics sharply divided on this central issue. Broadly speaking, we find four diverse points of view. Firstly, there are the moralists or traditionalists, who lament Montesquieu's abandonment of natural law. Then there are the progressives, who praise this same abandonment. These two kinds of critic are at least agreed on the evidence; it is difficult to reconcile them with the third kind of critics, the humanitarians, who admit that Montesquieu believed in natural law, and who usually praise him for it. The fourth group of critics, the logicians, hold that Montesquieu never made up his mind on the question, and see a contradiction between his method of explaining social and political phenomena and his belief in natural law.

[67] Hence we do not consider it helpful to note in each case whether or not M. owned a particular work. He had access to many libraries besides his own (*cf.* Shackleton, *M.*, pp. 55, 214, 230), and can have had little difficulty in obtaining any work he wanted.

It is instructive to trace the fortunes of these four points of view since the appearance of the *Esprit des lois*. In the eighteenth century, (leaving aside the too-frequently quoted and probably spurious letters purportedly written by Helvétius to Montesquieu and Saurin,[68] there are numerous critics who, like the abbé Fontaine de La Roche and the Sorbonne, took the first, moralistic and indignant point of view. In 1762, in his *Émile*, Rousseau petulantly reproached Montesquieu for having failed to discuss the general principles of political science;[69] in 1764, the historian Crevier was even more damning about the *Esprit des lois* where, he claimed, "le droit naturel est réduit presque à rien";[70] and towards the end of the century, the *philosophe* Condorcet renewed Rousseau's complaint.[71]

The eighteenth century did not have the advantage of an acquaintance with Marxism and positivism, so we do not find critics openly praising Montesquieu for abandoning natural law. In general, few people seem to have fully understood what the *président* was trying to do in the *Esprit des lois* (three exceptions being Boulenger de Rivery, François Risteau, and d'Alembert)[72] and often appraisals of the moral value of the work consisted of statements celebrating its contribution to the cause of humanity.

> Tout ce qui n'était pas jésuite ou janséniste, dévot ou bel esprit, le regarda comme le triomphe de l'humanité,

said the admittedly biassed L.A. de La Beaumelle, in 1751,[73] and in the same year Voltaire, though often ill-disposed towards Montesquieu, claimed that

> Le principal mérite de l'*Esprit des lois* est l'amour des lois qui règne dans cet ouvrage; et cet amour des lois est fondé sur l'amour du genre humain.[74]

[68] Printed in N. III, pp. 1102–5 and 1538–40. In his article on 'The Authenticity of the Letters on the *Esprit des lois* attributed to Helvétius', *Bulletin of the Institute of Historical Research*, 1951, pp. 19–43, R. Koebner claims that these letters were forged by Helvétius' editor, Lefebvre-La Roche. Koebner's case is fairly convincing, without being conclusive.

[69] *Émile, ou de l'education*, in *Œuvres complètes*, edited by B. Gagnebin and M. Raymond, Bibliothèque de la Pléiade, vol. IV, 1969, p. 836.

[70] J. B. L. Crevier, *Observations sur le livre de l'Esprit des lois*, Desaint et Saillant, 1764, p. 4.

[71] In A.-L.-C. Destutt de Tracy, *Commentaire sur l'Esprit des lois de Montesquieu, suivi d'observations inédites de Condorcet sur le vingt-neuvième livre du même ouvrage*, Desoer, 1819, p. 406.

[72] C. F. F. Boulenger de Rivery, *Apologie de l'Esprit des lois, ou réponses aux observations de M. de L. P.*, Amsterdam, 1751; [F. Risteau], *Réponse aux Observations sur l'Esprit des lois*, [Avignon?], 1751; d'Alembert, *Analyse de l'Esprit des lois* [1755], N. I, i, pp. xxxiv–lii.

[73] *Suite de la Défense de l'Esprit des lois* [1751], in Laboulaye ed. of M.'s works, vol. VI, p. 250. La Beaumelle was a friend of M.

[74] *Siècle de Louis XIV, Catalogue de la plupart des écrivains français qui ont paru dans le siècle de Louis XIV*, in *Œuvres complètes de Voltaire*, Garnier, 1877–85 [Moland edition], vol. XIV, p. 107.

In England, Lord Chesterfield, hearing of Montesquieu's death, praised him as "A friend to mankind" who "asserted their undoubted and inalienable rights".[75]

Some of these encomiums could perhaps be dismissed as flattery, but such motives cannot be attributed to the many nineteenth-century critics who praise Montesquieu's humanity or his belief in natural law. In 1858, the philosopher Adolphe Franck claimed that natural law is "le fond même" of the *Esprit des lois*,[76] and fourteen years later the ultra-conservative Ferdinand Béchard stated that Montesquieu had adhered to precisely the same immutable principles as Bossuet and Domat.[77] Béchard's hate of Rousseau is probably responsible for this remark. Two much more impartial nineteenth-century scholars, justly famous for their still widely-read interpretations of Montesquieu, Paul Janet of the Sorbonne and Albert Sorel of the École des sciences politiques, both wrote praising the services that the *président* had performed for humanity.[78]

The new nineteenth-century historians, such as Maine, saw in Montesquieu the destroyer of the anti-historical School of Natural Law,[79] while the positivist Auguste Comte, as early as the 1830's, and later his admirer, Franck Alengry, in 1900, keenly in search of precursors, regarded the *président* as a kindred spirit who, in his study of law, had made a complete break with the idealistic philosophers his predecessors and contemporaries.[80] In similar but more critical vein, the sociologist Émile Durkheim, in a work first published in 1892, while praising Montesquieu for having established the basis of a deterministic social science, reproached him with having introduced an element of contingency (namely the possibility of unnatural behavior on the part of individuals or society), that threatened to undermine that science.[81] This is one of the most famous and most explicit expressions of the

[75] Philip Dormer Stanhope, Earl of Chesterfield, *Miscellaneous Works*, Dilly, 1777, vol. I, p. 273.

[76] 'Publicistes du XVIIIe siècle: Montesquieu – *L'Esprit des lois*', *Revue contemporaine*, 1858, p. 55.

[77] 'La Monarchie de Montesquieu et la république de Jean-Jacques', *Correspondant*, 1872, p. 302.

[78] Paul Janet, *Histoire de la science politique dans ses rapports avec la morale* [1858, 1872], Alcan, 1887, vol. II, p. 379; Albert Sorel, *Montesquieu* [1887], Hachette, 1924, p. 108.

[79] *Op. cit.*, p. 97.

[80] A. Comte, *Cours de philosophie positive*, Schleicher, 1908, vol. IV, pp. 127–8; F. Alengry, 'Montesquieu' in *Essai historique et critique sur la sociologie chez Auguste Comte*, Alcan, 1900, pp. 389–403.

[81] É. Durkheim, *Quid Secundatus "politicæ scientiæ" instituendæ contulerit*, Thèse de Bordeaux, 1892, translated as 'Dans quelle mesure Montesquieu a-t-il contribué à constituer la science des sociétés', *Revue d'histoire politique et constitutionnelle*, 1937, p. 447 [hereafter *Thèse de Bordeaux*].

logician's point of view, mentioned at the beginning of this analysis.

On the whole, until quite recently, twentieth-century critics, and consequently twentieth-century readers, have tended to see Montesquieu through the eyes of the positivists, even when they do not accept the positivist philosophy: Léon Brunschvicg, in 1927, and Paul Hazard, in 1946, renewed Durkheim's complaint,[82] as did certain Anglo-Saxon critics of note, particularly George Sabine, who, in 1937, wittily remarked that Montesquieu was

> a moralist for whom the eternal verities had begun to wear thin but who lacked the constructive power to get on without them.[83]

One of the more recent expressions of this view is to be found in Sir Isaiah Berlin's lecture on Montesquieu.[84]

Probably the most positivistic of Montesquieu's twentieth-century interpreters, as well as the best-known, by virtue of his pithy style, was Joseph Dedieu. In 1909, while the religiously-minded Auguste Charaux was chanting the traditionalist lament that "la morale de Montesquieu est toute politique",[85] the abbé Dedieu was making the same point in enthusiastic tones, in his *Montesquieu et la tradition politique anglaise en France*, tones that were to become joyful in his *Montesquieu* of 1913, and triumphant in his more popular and in some respects less scholarly *Montesquieu l'homme et l'œuvre* of 1943.[86] A similar but more superficial approach is to be found in Charles Oudin's *Le Spinozisme de Montesquieu* (1911), a work whose rarity has given it a fame quite unjustified by its contents.[87] The positivist spirit also animates, to a greater or lesser extent, many of the perceptive and stimulating interpretations of Montesquieu written in the last thirty years: for example, those of F .T. H. Fletcher (1939), Jean Starobinski (1953), Paul Vernière (1954), Louis Althusser (1959), Robert Shackleton (1961), and, most recently, J. Robert Loy (1968).[88]

[82] L. Brunsvicg, *Le Progrès de la conscience dans la philosophie occidentale*, Alcan, 1927, vol. II, pp. 492–4; P. Hazard, *La Pensée européenne au XVIIIe siècle, de Montesquieu à Lessing*, Boivin, 1946, vol. II, p. 105.

[83] *A History of Political Theory*, Harrap, 1937, p. 558.

[84] 'Montesquieu', from the Proceedings of the British Academy, volume XLI, Oxford University Press, read October 19th, 1955, pp. 290–93.

[85] 'Montesquieu', in *Études franciscaines*, 1909, p. 615.

[86] *Montesquieu et la tradition politique anglaise en France*, Gabalda, 1909, p. 169; *Montesquieu*, Alcan, 1913, p. 184; *Montesquieu l'homme et l'œuvre*, Boivin, 1943, pp. 27–28 and 132–48.

[87] *Le Spinozisme de Montesquieu*, Pichon et Durant Auzias, 1911, p. 63, etc.

[88] F. T. H. Fletcher, *Montesquieu and English Politics (1750–1800)*, Arnold, 1939, p. 271; J. Starobinski, *Montesquieu par lui-même*, [1953], Seuil, 1961, pp. 86–7; P. Vernière, *Spinoza et la pensée française avant la Révolution*, Presses Universitaires de France, 1954, vol. II, pp. 456–7; L. Althusser, *Montesquieu, la politique et l'histoire* [1959], Presses Universitaires de France, 1964, pp. 8–21; Shackleton, *M.*, pp. 247–53; J. R. Loy, *op. cit.*, esp. p. 112.

However, alongside this positivistic approach to Montesquieu, there has arisen in the twentieth century a new trend, based on a more sympathetic outlook towards the philosophy of natural law: certain critics now refuse to accept the stock image of the author of the *Esprit des lois*, as a pragmatist who had little time for eternal truths; while not seeking to deny the importance of the empirical elements in his work, they try to relate him more closely to his precursors in the idealistic tradition. Gustave Lanson may be considered to have been at the start of this movement, when he claimed in 1916 that Montesquieu's method of studying civil law did not exclude a belief in idealism and progress,[89] and many latter-day liberals, such as Marcel Raymond, Bernard Grœthuysen and Pierre Barrière, see in Montesquieu a champion of their cause.[90]

Four of the most persuasive advocates of Montesquieu's belief in natural law are Raymond Aron, Lester Crocker, Jean Ehrard and Paul Meyer. In Aron's *Les Grandes doctrines de sociologie*, of 1960, we have a convincing assessment of the extent to which Montesquieu was in sympathy with the doctrine of natural law, but it is couched in rather technical terms, and deals with only a few aspects of the problem.[91] Crocker, in *Nature and Culture* (1963), while doing justice to the *président*'s attitude in fairly general terms, rashly suggests that his interest in natural law wanes after the first book of the *Esprit des lois*.[92] In his work on the concept of nature in the eighteenth century (1963), and more recently in his excellent *Politique de Montesquieu* (1965), Ehrard, one of the most penetrating modern interpreters of our author, corrects many of Dedieu's errors and places Montesquieu in the complex context of seventeenth- and eighteenth-century idealism.[93] Paul Meyer's study, 'Politics and Morals in the Thought of Montesquieu' (1967), lacks the perspective of Ehrard's work. Meyer argues persuasively that for Montesquieu, politics cannot be divorced from morals, but fails to

[89] 'Le Déterminisme historique et l'idéalisme social dans l'*Esprit des lois*' [1916], *Études d'histoire littéraire*, Champion, 1929, pp. 135–63.

[90] M. Raymond, 'L'Humanisme de Montesquieu', in his *Génies de France*, Neuchâtel, La Baconnière, 1942, pp. 124–49; B. Grœthuysen, *Montesquieu*, Geneva and Paris, Éditions des trois collines, 1947, pp. 45–72; P. Barrière, 'L'Humanisme de l'*Esprit des lois*', *IIe Centenaire*, pp. 31–64.

[91] *Les Grandes doctrines de sociologie historique*: *Montesquieu, Auguste Comte, Karl Marx, Alexis de Tocqueville, les sociologues et la révolution de 1848*, Les Cours de la Sorbonne, Centre de documentation universitaire, [1960], pp. 14–55.

[92] *Nature and Culture*: *Ethical Thought in the French Enlightenment*, Baltimore, Johns Hopkins Press, 1963, pp. 25–9.

[93] *L'Idée de nature*, vol. II, p. 718–36; *Politique de Montesquieu*, Colin, 1965, pp. 10–11, etc.; *cf.* also 'Les Études sur Montesquieu et l'*Esprit des lois*', *L'Information littéraire*, 1959, pp. 55–66, and the notes in Ehrard's edition of Dedieu's *Montesquieu l'homme et l'œuvre*.

prove his contention that such a belief is something new in modern political thought.[94]

These four scholars have reopened the problem but they have not solved it. In the present study we shall be in broad agreement with them, but we feel that they have not given a fully satisfactory answer to the accusation that there is a contradiction between Montesquieu's method and his belief in natural law, because they have not compared in detail his beliefs with those of the School of Natural Law and the Roman Catholic Church.

What is needed is a study of the similarities between Montesquieu's attitude to political science and that of his predecessors; a re-examination of the positivist view that natural law is an exclusively rationalistic doctrine; and a reassessment of the questions of the state of nature, the origin of society and the original contract; finally, though most critics have given Montesquieu the credit he deserves for his championship of enlightened causes, and though a few have studied the metaphysical implications of his conception of law, in neither case have his beliefs been sufficiently related to those of the philosophers of natural law. It is these aspects of the problem that will form the basis of the present study.

[94] 'Politics and Morals in the Thought of Montesquieu', in *Studies on Voltaire and the Eighteenth Century*, vol. LVI, pp. 845–91, esp. pp. 845, 850, 856–9, and 890–1. The same point may be made in respect of C. P. Courtney's valuable new study, 'Montesquieu', in *French Literature and its Background*, ed. J. Cruickshank, vol. III, *The Eighteenth Century*, O.U.P., 1968 pp. 30–44, esp. p. 38. Similarly, G. Benrekassa, in his *Montesquieu*, Presses Universitaires de France, 1968, pp. 30 and 64, shows convincingly, but in general terms only, that M. believed in natural rights; but he fails to link this belief with the tradition of natural law.

CHAPTER 2

THE ORIGINALITY OF MONTESQUIEU'S METHOD

1. *The Problem of Montesquieu's Method*

It is often thought that the *président*'s method of studying positive law precluded any reference to natural law. What was Montesquieu's method? Was it really different from that of the School of Natural Law?

In Book I, Chapter iii of the *Esprit des lois*, Montesquieu set out the aim he had in writing the work:

> La loi, en général, est la raison humaine, en tant qu'elle gouverne tous les peuples de la terre; et les lois politiques et civiles de chaque nation ne doivent être que les cas particuliers où s'applique cette raison humaine.
>
> Elles doivent être tellement propres au peuple pour lequel elles sont faites, que c'est un très grand hasard si celles d'une nation peuvent convenir à une autre.
>
> Il faut qu'elles se rapportent à la nature et au principe du gouvernement qui est établi, ou qu'on veut établir [...].
>
> Elles doivent être relatives au physique du pays; [...] au genre de vie des peuples [...]: elles doivent se rapporter au degré de liberté que la constitution peut souffrir, à la religion des habitants, à leurs inclinations, à leurs richesses, à leur nombre, à leur commerce, à leurs mœurs, à leurs manières: enfin elles ont des rapports entre elles; elles en ont avec leur origine, avec l'objet du législateur, avec l'ordre des choses sur lesquelles elles sont établies. C'est dans toutes ces vues qu'il faut les considérer.
>
> C'est ce que j'entreprends de faire dans cet ouvrage. J'examinerai tous ces rapports: ils forment tous ensemble ce que l'on appelle l'ESPRIT DES LOIS (N. I, i, pp. 8–9; Pl. II, pp. 237–8).

The phrase "ce que l'on appelle" is surely false modesty. The hostile abbé de La Porte, probably following Domat, thought that the *esprit* of laws was "l'intention qu'ont eue les législateurs qui les ont établies".[1]

[1] Joseph de La Porte, *Observations sur l'Esprit des lois, ou l'art de lire ce livre, de l'entendre et d'en juger*, Amsterdam, Mortier, 1751, pp. 10–11; *cf.* Domat, *op. cit.*, *Livre préliminaire*, i, 2, paragraph 1, vol. I, p. 6.

The meaning that Montesquieu gave to the term was far more complex since for him the *esprit* of a law is the sum of the relationships it has with "la nature des choses" of a given country, that is, with all the physical and moral factors found there.[2]

Montesquieu was proposing nothing less than a scientific analysis of the laws of mankind, and his project is easy enough to grasp in its outlines. The main difficulty arises when we try to see if he carried out his intention successfully in the rest of the work. Its plan has often been subject to attack, and this is not the place to renew the controversy about it,[3] though it is worth noting in passing that the form of Montesquieu's work bears a strong resemblance to that of the treatises of Grotius and Pufendorf: his book divisions correspond to their book or chapter divisions, and his multitudinous and oft-criticised chapter divisions, to their paragraph divisions. The most obvious difference is that his chapter headings are sometimes more witty, but less informative than theirs.

It is not so much the present order of the work that is important to this study, as the method by which Montesquieu proceeded in the collection and ordering of the innumerable laws and customs which form the raw material of the *Esprit des lois*. Did he conscientiously study all the facts first, and then induce his theories from them? In this case, he used the *a posteriori* method. Or did he rather use, or even distort the facts in order to back up a system he had already invented without them? In that case, he used the *a priori* method. It is impossible to give a clear-cut answer to these questions. They can only be answered indirectly, either by seeing what certain of Montesquieu's other works reveal about his method, or by comparing the information he may have had at his disposal with the use he made of it, or by examining what he said, in the *Esprit des lois* itself, about his method.

Following the first of these three indirect routes, some scholars have gone so far as to claim that, in the *Esprit des lois*, Montesquieu put into practice the experimental method he learnt in his scientific work for the Bordeaux Academy. Part of his duties as *directeur* of the Academy consisted in making and reading critical summaries (*résomptions*) of papers on scientific subjects prepared by various contributors. Until recently, these summaries were omitted from his works, and

[2] We use the word *moral* here in the French sense of *mental* or *intellectual*.

[3] Criticisms of the plan of the *Lois* are too numerous to mention; among the most remarkable defences of the plan are Barckhausen's (*Montesquieu, ses idées et ses œuvres*, pp. 253–66) and Oudin's (*De l'unité de l'Esprit des lois*, Rousseau, 1910 – a work greatly superior to his *Le Spinozisme de Montesqueiu*).

this may explain why scholars have tended, in the past, to exaggerate the scope of his scientific work.[4] However Montesquieu did also make certain observations and conduct certain experiments for himself, giving accounts of them to the Academy.

It is sometimes suggested, in particular, that Montesquieu's scientific method was Newtonian.[5] What evidence is there for this suggestion? Even though the Bordeaux Academy was predominantly Cartesian, it did nevertheless give prizes to certain dissertations containing Newtonian ideas.[6] In addition, two of Montesquieu's friends, the scientist Dortous de Mairan and the eccentric priest L.-B. Castel, were both interested in Newton's work; however, they both remained Cartesians in physics.[7] Apart from this external evidence, it is certain from internal evidence as well that Montesquieu knew of Newtonian physics (e.g. *P.* 1096, Bkn. 672, N. II, p. 298, Pl. I, p. 1171, and *P.* 1320, Bkn. 1356, N. II, pp. 398–9, Pl. I, p. 1324); nevertheless, like the Academy and his friends, he preferred that of Descartes.[8] For Montesquieu, Newton was "le successeur de Descartes" (N. III, p. 118, Pl. I, p. 43), but it is not clear in what sense the epithet is to be understood.

If Montesquieu knew of but did not accept Newton's physics, is it likely that he knew of and practised Newton's empirical scientific method? Perhaps, if we are to judge by a *Pensée* written between 1721 and 1731:

> Les observations sont l'histoire de la physique, et les systèmes en sont la fable (*P.* 163, Bkn. 681, N. II, p. 51, Pl. I, p. 1182).

This is, however, the only *Pensée* which reveals a possible influence of the Newtonian method on Montesquieu, and the other *Pensées* cited by Sergio Cotta as proof of that influence[9] do not in fact prove it. *Pensées* 775 (Bkn. 2105) and 1445 (Bkn. 2104), in which Montesquieu showed how Descartes' genius had enabled those who came after him to criticize his system intelligently, do not specify which aspects of

[4] *Cf.* N. I, pp. B–C.

[5] Three modern scholars holding this view are Seguin, 'Montesquieu' in É. Callot, *La Philosophie de la vie au XVIIIe siècle, étudiée chez Fontenelle, Montesquieu, Maupertuis, La Mettrie, Diderot, d'Holbach, Linné*, Rivière, 1965, pp. 74–6 and 90; S. Cotta, *Montesquieu e la scienza della società*, Turin, Ramella, 1953, p. 90; Starobinski, *op. cit.*, p. 18.

[6] Brunet, *op. cit.*, pp. 84, n. 2, and 89–90.

[7] *Ibid.*, pp. 104–7, 113–21, and 124–9.

[8] In particular, he accepted the Cartesian theory of vortices and rejected Newton's theory of gravitation: *P.* 206, Bkn. 1458, N. II, p. 79, Pl. I, p. 1345 (1721–31); *Spicilège* 565, N. II, p. 848, Pl. II, p. 1370 (1730–34); *P.* 1380, Bkn. 927, N. II, p. 408, Pl. I, p. 1252 (1734–45).

[9] *Loc. cit.*

Descartes' philosophy he found unsatisfactory (N. II, pp. 231 and 419, Pl. I, p. 1548). *Pensée* 799 (Bkn. 2093), to which Cotta also refers, contains a criticism not of hypotheses but of essences, in which neither Descartes nor Newton believed (N. II, p. 235, Pl. I, p. 1546).

Even if Montesquieu did believe in Newton's method, he does not seem to have put it into practice in his scientific work. The *Essai d'observations*, in which he gives an account of that work, is the touchstone in this question. In this *Essai*, read to the Academy in 1719 and 1721, he told of certain experiments he had conducted on ducks and a goose, and of certain observations he had made on various plants. In the case of the ducks, he was trying to see how long they would live under water. One lived longer than the other,

> parce que nous nous étions trompés, la première fois, dans la mesure du temps; ou peut-être bien ce canard a-t-il vécu plus que le premier parce qu'il était moins gras et qu'il n'avait point mangé (N. III, p. 113; Pl. I, p. 40 omits).

It is true that this rather naïve statement was later deleted by Montesquieu,[10], but it still reveals, followed as it is by several lines of undeleted conjecture based on this observation, two of the worst faults to be found in a scientist: inaccurate observation and precipitate conclusion. The second fault is also revealed by Montesquieu's observations on plants: here, it is evident that he started out with the conviction that certain plants are produced by spontaneous generation, and that he then tried to prove it by observation. But having put forward his theory, he then admitted that several years of experiment were necessary in order to "éclaircir cette matière" (N. III, p. 112, Pl. I, p. 39).

In adopting the theory of spontaneous generation, Montesquieu claimed he was a true Cartesian (N. III, p. 112, Pl. I, p. 39).[11] Moreover, his scientific method itself was Cartesian:

> [En vain nous abandonnerions-nous à nos raisonnements, si nous ne les confirmons par des expériences];[12] ce n'est point dans les méditations d'un cabinet qu'il faut chercher les preuves, mais dans le sein de la nature même (*ibid.*).

[10] See N. III, p. 113.

[11] See also *P.* 76, Bkn. 690, N. II, pp. 23–4, Pl. I, pp. 1187–8; *cf.* C. Beyer, 'Montesquieu et l'esprit cartésien', *Congrès*, pp. 161–2.

[12] The sentence in square brackets was later deleted by M. and is not printed in Pl. I, p. 39.

At a superficial glance this statement looks "progressive" and empirical, but it in fact reveals that his idea of experimentation was Cartesian. The use of the words "confirmons" and "preuves" shows us that he was reasoning *a priori*, like Descartes, who did not use experiment as a means of inducing his natural laws, but only of confirming their truth.[13] Thus if Montesquieu believed that observation and experiment are important, it is not because he is an empiricist, in the modern sense of the term.

Advocates of Montesquieu's empiricism are often prepared to admit that in his work for the Bordeaux Academy, he reasoned *a priori*, but, so anxious are they to see him in a positivistic light that they forget about the limitations of his scientific method when they come to discuss its influence on his later work. The most flagrant example of this peculiar logic is to be found in the very works through which so many readers are introduced to Montesquieu, namely Dedieu's *Montesquieu* and his *Montesquieu l'homme et l'œuvre*. In the first book, Dedieu admits that in his scientific work, Montesquieu

> s'annonce comme un esprit éminemment spéculatif, que les expériences positives retiennent sans doute, mais pas assez longuement pour qu'il s'abstienne de toute conclusion précipitée, ni assez servilement pour qu'il persiste à demeurer sur le seul terrain des faits.[14]

So far, so good, but on the very next page Dedieu contradicts himself by saying that "la science a conduit Montesquieu [...] à ne donner sa confiance qu'aux faits", and later he claims that in his scientific work the *président* acquired "la discipline scientifique".[15] It would seem that the only proof Dedieu has of these last assertions is itself an *a priori* one: he sees Montesquieu as a positivist, *ergo* Montesquieu must have practised the scientific method, both in his early career, and in many parts of the *Esprit des lois* where, so Dedieu tells us, the author, "abandonnant le terrain des spéculations [...] va droit sur le terrain des faits".[16]

[13] *Cf.* Descartes, *Discours*, VI, p. 63 and *Principes*, II, xxxvii, xxxix and xlii, pp. 84, 86, 87–8, also Blake, Ducasse and Madden, *op. cit.*, pp. 75–103; for a more favourable account of Descartes as an experimenter, see G. Milhaud, *Descartes savant*, Alcan, 1921, pp. 191–212, but even Milhaud admits (pp. 197, 204) that Descartes was only a good experimenter when he forgot his *a priori* theories. For two specialist accounts of M.'s Cartesianism in the sciences, see D. André, 'Sur les écrits scientifiques de Montesquieu', *Correspondant*, 1880, pp. 1054–81 and J. Jaffray, 'La Carrière scientifique de Montesquieu', *La Nature*, 1928, pp. 465–7.

[14] *Montesquieu*, p. 9.

[15] *Ibid.*, pp. 10 and 68.

[16] *Ibid.*, p. 187.

In his later book, Dedieu brushes aside all reservations, giving a completely false picture of Montesquieu's scientific work and its influence on his later thought. Talking mainly of the *Essai d'observations*, and ignoring its patent *a priorism*, Dedieu proclaims

> Tout cela est révélateur d'un esprit positif, acquis aux nouvelles méthodes expérimentales, et qui sait que la science, avant d'être une magnifique synthèse, est d'abord une patiente analyse. Montesquieu s'est formé à cette rude et bienfaisante école de l'analyse scientifique. Il lui en restera, toute sa vie, une empreinte ineffaçable.[17]

Without any evidence, Dedieu has seen in Montesquieu a practitioner of the science of a later age.[18]

It is clear that all too often, Montesquieu's work is called scientific, without its being explained which kind of scientific method he followed. If it was the Cartesian deductive method, then it cannot rightly be called scientific.[19] Thus remarks such as Janet's, that Montesquieu is

> le premier qui ait appliqué l'esprit scientifique, l'esprit moderne aux faits politiques et sociaux. Il est au moins le Descartes, s'il n'est pas le Newton de la politique,[20]

tell us little about Montesquieu's method. Janet wishes to convey the impression that it is essentially different from that of his predecessors, but unless he can prove that it is Newtonian, that is, strictly empirical, he has not shown that Montesquieu's method is original. The same confusion is to be found in many other interpreters of Montesquieu, such as Barckhausen and George Havens.[21]

We now turn to the second way of discovering Montesquieu's method, by a comparison of the evidence Montesquieu had at his disposal and the use he made of it. Obviously, a complete examination of this question is impossible: no one scholar has the necessary knowledge to pronounce on every aspect of Montesquieu's erudition. We shall limit ourselves to a few significant examples.

Dedieu, followed by many other scholars, two of the most recent being Étiemble and Loy,[22] tries to prove that Montesquieu's method

[17] *Montesquieu l'homme et l'œuvre*, p. 28.

[18] *Cf.* n. 1 to p. 29 of the Ehrard edition of *Montesquieu l'homme et l'œuvre*.

[19] Even though Oudin, *Le Spinozisme de Montesquieu*, p. 116, claims that Descartes put forward "les principes de la vraie méthode scientifique".

[20] *Histoire de la science politique*, vol. II, p. 399.

[21] Barckhausen, *Montesquieu, ses idées et ses œuvres*, p. 15; G. R. Havens, *From Reaction to Revolution. The Age of Ideas in Eighteenth-Century France*, New York, Holt, 1955, pp. 101–2.

[22] Étiemble, 'Montesquieu', in *Encyclopédie de la Pléiade*, vol. III, Gallimard, 1958, pp. 707–8; Loy, *op. cit.*, p. 92–3.

in the *Esprit des lois* was empirical. While admitting that Montesquieu frequently used deductive methods, he nevertheless claims that the work is based on the distinction between physical and moral causes which, in its turn, is based on *l'expérience*.[23]

Dedieu would seem to be bent on proving a case contradicted by the majority of the evidence. It is of course possible that Montesquieu's theory of climate and its influence was discovered empirically, but when one reads Books XIV–XVIII, one has the impression of a mind working deductively from the principles stated in Book XIV, Chapter ii. In order to maintain his theory of climate, Montesquieu was frequently obliged to distort the facts: despotisms, he claimed, are found in hot countries (*Lois*, V, xv, N. I, i, p. 85, Pl. II, p. 297), but how did Russia, which was a despotism, fit into this scheme of things? Suicide, so he claimed, is, in England, entirely a result of the climate: the tenacity with which he defended this dramatic over-simplification indicates his *a priorism*. A similar over-simplification is found in his discussion of polygamy, which he again tried to explain by climatic influences. These famous examples of Montesquieu's rationalism are not mentioned in order to discredit him, but merely in order to show that he was not, as the positivists would have us believe, a marvel of impartiality, a kind of calculating machine: if he had been, who would read his works nowadays?

Montesquieu's rationalism also emerges from Books I–XIII. Here, one has the impression that, though there is indeed a large amount of observation in them, they are essentially the result of a process of deduction from the definition of the three types of government, and the "nature" and "principe" of each.[24] Above all, though, we feel that Montesquieu is not being impartial in these books. Though his picture of the democracies and aristocracies of Antiquity is based on careful documentation, it is difficult to say the same of his picture of contemporary institutions. In particular, his famous description of the English Constitution in Book XI, Chapter vi, is not simply the result of his observations when in England; it is also a vision of the home of liberty idealized for political motives, in order to impress upon the French the possibility of a monarchy limited by laws.

23 *Montesquieu*, pp. 80–92.
24 *Cf.* Berlin, *Montesquieu*, p. 277.

Montesquieu used the hypothetical style, describing the constitution as it ought to work, not as it did work.[25]

Furthermore, his picture of despotic governments, designed to warn the French of the dangers that threatened them, is almost entirely imaginary.[26] One of the most convincing accounts of this point is in the work of Muriel Dodds on *Les récits de voyages, sources de l'Esprit des lois de Montesquieu*. She shows, *pièces en main*, how in the VIIIth Book of the *Esprit des lois*, Montesquieu deliberately selected evidence to suit his case. There were two kinds of account available to him for his chapter on "l'empire de la Chine" (*Lois*, VIII, xxi, N. I, i, pp. 168–71; Pl. II, pp. 365–8): those of the missionaries, who, partly because they knew the people well, and partly because of the *querelle des rites*, had formed a favourable impression of China; and those of the merchants, who had not. Montesquieu wanted to see China as a despotism, so that it would fit in with his theory of the relationship between the size and climate of a country, and the nature of its government. In the accounts of China given by the missionaries, he did not find the picture of a despotic country:

> Il ne peut concilier ces faits avec les principes qu'il a posés; il ne peut faire entrer la Chine dans le cadre étroit de sa définition du despotisme. Au lieu d'élargir le cadre, [...] il repousse ces témoignages, et il va chercher des examples qui lui conviennent chez des voyageurs tels que Anson et Lange, bien que ceux-ci connaissent très mal la Chine.[27]

From such evidence, Miss Dodds is led on to make general statements about Montesquieu's method. In the early books of the *Esprit des lois* he is "purement cartésien": "Il ne cherche les faits, que pour prouver un principe qu'il a déjà posé"; she sees the concept of the "esprit général" (*Lois*, XIX, iv, N. I, i, p. 412, Pl. II, p. 558) as "un écart passager" in the direction of empiricism, and concludes that Montesquieu "reste essentiellement jusqu'au bout, fidèle à la méthode cartésienne".[28] Further precise evidence of Montesquieu's manner of

[25] The following scholars, the first three of whom have a specialized knowledge of constitutional law, claim that M.'s picture of the English Constitution is distorted: E. Eichthal, *Souveraineté du peuple et gouvernement*, Alcan, 1895, pp. 93, 123–4, 126–39; O. W. Holmes, *Collected Legal Papers*, Constable, 1920, p. 263; B. Mirkine-Guetzévitch, 'De l'*Esprit des lois* à la démocratie moderne', *Bicentenaire*, p. 14; Ehrard, *Politique de Montesquieu*, p. 127. For a contrary view, also by an expert, see C. Eisemann, 'L'*Esprit des lois* et la séparation des pouvoirs', *Mélanges R. Carré de Malberg*, Sirey, 1933, p. 184, n. 1; *cf.* also Loy, *op. cit.*, pp. 110–11.

[26] Among innumerable critics holding this view, see especially P. Vernière, 'Montesquieu et le monde musulman', *Congrès*, pp. 200–1.

[27] *Op. cit.*, Champion, 1929, p. 153.

[28] *Ibid.*, pp. 153–6.

using his sources is to be found in F. Weil's comparison of his notebook, *Les Geographica*, with the *Esprit des lois*: she finds in particular that he sometimes altered quotations when transferring them to his main work, and that he tended to generalize from single examples.[29]

These two well-substantiated accounts of Montesquieu's method confirm the theory put forward some seventy years ago by Gustave Lanson, who stated that in the *Esprit des lois*

> Montesquieu a tout simplement suivi la méthode analytique et mathématique de Descartes.[30]

Lanson continues by showing that the work has three main parts: Books I–XIII deal with "les choses en soi"; Books XIV–XXVI, with the *rapports* that arise from "[les] choses dans l'espace"; and Books XXVII–XXXI, with those arising from "[les] choses dans le temps". In the first part, Montesquieu "part des notions simples et premières", the prior existence of justice and reason; then he examined man before society began, then in society in general, then in particular societies – that is, he examined man and society deductively. Similarly, Lanson sees the second part as deduced from the *rapports* between climate and various other factors, and the third part as an historical illustration, based on the principles he had previously posited, of the rules he had put forward. Lanson adds that Montesquieu made much use of *l'expérience* in order to prove and illustrate what he already believed, but that he did not use it in order to induce his theories. Hence, Lanson is able to conclude that Montesquieu followed in political science exactly the same method as Descartes followed in physics.[31]

In later years, Lanson changed his position. Pointing to Montesquieu's great use of historical documentation in the *Esprit des lois*, he claimed that its *a priorism* was due merely to the way in which the ideas were expressed, not to the way in which they were discovered,[32] a point also made more recently by G. Davy.[33] There is no easy way of proving or disproving this ingenious suggestion, except in the way that M. Dodds and F. Weil have done. As it now appears to the reader,

[29] 'Le Manuscrit des *Geographica* et l'*Esprit des lois*', *RHLF*, 1952, pp. 456–9.

[30] 'L'Influence de la philosophie cartésienne sur la littérature française' [1896], *Études d'histoire littéraire*, Champion, 1929, p. 84.

[31] 'L'Influence de la philosophie cartésienne', pp. 85–9.

[32] Lanson made this point in 'Le Rôle de l'expérience dans la formation de la philosophie du XVIIIe siècle en France', *Revue du mois*, 1910, p. 6. He restated it in a note to his 'Le Déterminisme historique et l'idéalisme social dans l'*Esprit des lois*', p. 135.

[33] 'Montesquieu et la science politique' *IIe Centenaire*, p. 154.

the *Esprit des lois* is a work of rationalism, in which an astonishingly wide erudition is put at the service of certain social and political theories.

Finally, in this section, we turn to the third way of discovering Montesquieu's method, namely an examination of what he said about it. In the Preface to the *Esprit des lois*, he made two statements which seem to imply that he was following the empirical method. Firstly:

> Je n'ai point tiré mes principes de mes préjugés, mais de la nature des choses (N. I, i, p. lx, Pl. II, p. 229).

But this is probably not so much a general indication of method, as a precaution against censorship. The other statement is more significant:

> J'ai d'abord examiné les hommes; et j'ai cru que, dans cette infinie diversité de lois et de moeurs, ils n'étaient pas uniquement conduits par leurs fantaisies (N. I, i, p. lix, Pl. II, p. 229).

This looks like a statement of the empirical method, but is it? It might equally well indicate that when Montesquieu examined the world of men, he already had the conviction that they were not "conduits par leurs fantaisies". If Montesquieu was a positivist, he was one who had the *a priori* conviction that reality can be expressed in mathematical terms. As he said in Book I, Chapter i:

> Il y a [...] une raison primitive; et les lois sont les rapports qui se trouvent entre elle et les différents êtres, et les rapports de ces divers êtres entre eux (N. I, i, p. 2, Pl. II, p. 232).

Thus he was a positivist in the sense that he was not a sceptic with regard to the rationality of human affairs, as Montaigne and Pascal had been.[34] But he was not a true positivist, not only in that he had a political axe to grind, but also in that he appears to have started out with the conviction that all facts are explainable.

The paragraph beginning "J'ai d'abord examiné les hommes" is followed by the famous remark:

> J'ai posé les principes; et j'ai vu les cas particuliers s'y plier comme d'eux-mêmes, les histoires de toutes les nations n'en être que les suites, et chaque loi particulière liée avec une autre loi, ou dépendre d'une autre plus générale (N. I, i, p. lix, Pl. II, p. 229).

[34] Montaigne, *Essais*, II, xii, Les Belles Lettres, vol. III, 1947, pp. 365–74; Pascal, *Pensées*, V, 294, in *Œuvres de Blaise Pascal*, Hachette, 1908–21, vol. XIII, pp. 214–22.

In spite of the rationalism implicit in these lines, those who believe Montesquieu's method to be empirical will continue to argue, on the strength of the two paragraphs taken together, that his intended method was: examination – induction – verification.[35] Even if this were so, even if it were possible to ignore the latent rationalism of the first of the two paragraphs, we would still argue that the first stage of this scientific process was not thorough enough to be truly empirical, and that the second stage, the induction, often became deduction; that Montesquieu was following, whether he knew it or not, an *a priori* method.

Now the philosophy of natural law is also, in part at least, based on *a priori* methods. This method finds its classic expression in St. Thomas:

> from the precepts of the natural law, as from general and indemonstrable principles, [...] the human reason needs to proceed to the more particular determination of certain matters (*S.t.*, II, i, Q. 91, Art. 3, vol. VIII, p. 13).

Within the School of Natural Law, perhaps the best examples of the use of deductive methods are to be found in Pufendorf. Starting, in Book I of *Le Droit de la nature et des gens*, with a discussion of morality in general and with a definition of law, he then went on, in Book II, to deduce natural law from human nature and from man in the state of nature; in the remaining books, he deduced natural and civil laws from the nature of society and of man in society. The order is not quite the same in the *Devoirs de l'homme et du citoyen*, but the method is. In fact, all the members of the School of Natural Law – Grotius, Pufendorf, Burlamaqui – as well as Hobbes, Locke and Domat, follow a similar deductive procedure. Robert Shackleton is the only scholar so far to have pointed with any precision to the similarity of their method to that of Montesquieu.[36] But Shackleton does not go far enough, and we intend to show in the remainder of this section, that Montesquieu's very conception of social and political science was the outcome of that of the School of Natural Law.

If both Montesquieu and the School of Natural Law employed deductive methods, what then is the difference between them? In a passage that is justly famous, though not for the elegance of its style, Auguste Comte said that the *président*'s superiority over the other

[35] *Cf.* Davy, 'Montesquien et la science politique', pp. 153–4.
[36] 'Montesquieu in 1948', *French Studies*, 1949, pp. 309–12; *M.*, p. 260.

political philosophers of his age lay in the "tendance prépondérante", revealed in the *Esprit des lois*, to

concevoir désormais les phénomènes politiques comme aussi nécessairement assujettis à d'invariables lois naturelles que tous les autres phénomènes quelconques. [...] A une époque où les plus éminents esprits, essentiellement préoccupés de vaines utopies métaphysiques, croyaient encore à la puissance absolue et indéfinie des législateurs [...], combien ne fallait-il pas être en avant de son siècle pour oser concevoir [...] les divers phénomènes politiques comme toujours réglés, au contraire, par des lois pleinement naturelles.[37]

Comte thus holds that Montesquieu was the only philosopher who regarded social and political phenomena as capable of being formulated in scientific, as opposed to moralistic terms. He is contrasting Montesquieu with the *philosophes*, but not with the School of Natural Law, which he conveniently ignores. However, his disciple Durkheim was not content to ignore them. Being apparently unfamiliar with the philosophy of natural law, he resorts to vague generalisations and claims that before Montesquieu, the philosophers who believed in natural law derived this law from a "principe unique", that is, from human nature, since for them,

Seule [...] la nature de l'homme considéré seul paraît à ce point définie et stable, qu'elle peut fournir au droit un fondement solide.[38]

Durkheim thus imagines that natural law is based only on the concept of man in the state of nature; Oudin makes a similar claim.[39]

There are in fact two kinds of natural law. Burlamaqui made the point most clearly, when he distinguished between *primary* and *secondary* natural law. The primary natural law is that which "découle immédiatement de la constitution primitive de l'homme [...] indépendamment d'aucun fait humain", whereas the secondary natural law "suppose quelque fait ou quelque établissement humain; comme l'état civil, la propriété des biens" (*Principes du droit naturel*, II, iv, 24, p. 203). This distinction is made, either implicitly or explicitly, by all philosophers of natural law, and it is quite wrong to imagine that natural law is only derived from man in the state of nature. Durkheim has forgotten the secondary natural law, based on the concept of man in society, and roughly equivalent to what we term civil law.

37 *Cours de philosophie positive*, vol. IV, pp. 127–8.
38 *Thèse de Bordeaux*, p. 425; *cf.* p. 452.
39 *Le Spinozisme de Montesquieu*, p. 63.

Not only had the School of Natural Law made this distinction, they had also envisaged the possibility of putting both the primary and the secondary natural law into scientific terms. Grotius, it is true, had said that

> les lois naturelles étant toujours les mêmes, peuvent aisément être ramenées aux règles de l'art: mais celles qui doivent leur origine à quelque établissement humain étant différentes selon les lieux, et changeant souvent dans un même endroit, ne sont pas susceptibles de système méthodique (*Dg.*, *Disc. prél.*, xxxi, vol. I, p. 21).

In fact, however, Grotius's conception of natural law, based partly at least on universal consent meant that he regarded many civil laws as being natural laws, and as capable of being examined methodically.[40]

As the seventeenth century progressed in the field of science, moral philosophers became more and more convinced of the scientific nature of their subject. Pufendorf claimed that whereas it is difficult to formulate the art of politics,

> La morale, au contraire [. . .] est appuyée sur des fondements inébranlables, d'où l'on peut tirer de véritables démonstrations, capables de produire une science solide (*Dn.*, I, ii, 4, vol. I, pp. 24–5).

It is on such scientific demonstrations that he believed the substance of his book to be based. Similarly Locke held that "les véritables mesures du juste et de l'injuste" could be deduced from certain self-evident propositions "par des conséquences nécessaires, et aussi incontestables que celles qu'on emploie dans les mathématiques",[41] and he employed this kind of deduction (though not with all the scientific accuracy one might desire) in his second *Treatise on Government*, which is concerned both with primary and with secondary natural law. Finally, Barbeyrac was convinced of "la possibilité qu'il y a de réduire la science des mœurs à un système aussi bien lié, que

[40] In the *Disc. prél.*, xli, vol. I, p. 24, Grotius claimed that universal consent is an indication only of the law of nations, not of the law of nature; but in the body of the work, I, i, 12, vol. I, pp. 53–4, he said that natural law itself can be derived *a posteriori* from universal consent; he used this *a posteriori* method particularly in the case of slavery and of international relations (see below, Ch. 6, II and IV).

[41] Locke's *Essay on Human Understanding*, cited in Pierre Coste's famous translation, *Essai philosophique concernant l'entendement humain*, Amsterdam, Schelte, 1700, IV, iii, 18, p. 698. It was through this translation that many eighteenth-century *philosophes* became acquainted with Locke; *cf.* J. Hampton, 'Les traductions françaises de Locke au XVIIIe siècle', *Revue de littérature comparée*, 1955, pp. 240–51. M. owned Coste's translation (D. 1489). Like Locke, Cumberland believed that morality can be formulated scientifically, *Traité philosophique des lois naturelles*, i, 7, p. 47.

ceux de géométrie, par exemple, ou de mécanique" (*Dn.*, *Préface*, sec. ii, vol. I, p. xix).

Hence it can be seen how false is the following statement that Durkheim makes about the "successeurs" of Aristotle:

> Quant aux mœurs, à la religion, au commerce, à la famille ... c'étaient pour eux choses si fortuites et si changeantes que personne ne devait raisonablement entreprendre de les ramener à des genres et à des espèces.[42]

Durkheim does not tell us who are these "successeurs", so presumably he means to include all the philosophers between Aristotle and Montesquieu. His remark is untrue both in respect of such philosophers as Cicero, who formulated men's duties in his *De officiis*, of St. Thomas, who did the same thing from a Christian point of view, and of the School of Natural Law.

It is futile to try to disguise, as the positivists and their followers do, Montesquieu's debt to the philosophers of natural law for his general conception of social and political science.[43] In *Pensée* 1537 (Bkn. omits), Montesquieu spoke of his predecessors in eulogistic terms:

> Je rends grâce à Messieurs Grotius et Pufendorf d'avoir si bien exécuté ce qu'une partie de cet ouvrage demandait de moi, avec cette hauteur de génie, à laquelle je n'aurais pu atteindre (N. II, p. 443; *cf. P.* 1863 (Bkn. 191), N. II, p. 556, Pl. II, p. 1038).

It is unfortunate that in this tribute, which seems to have been intended for the Preface to the *Esprit des lois*, Montesquieu did not tell us which part of the work he was talking about. The passage has in fact two possible interpretations: either Montesquieu was admitting his debt to Grotius and Pufendorf in certain parts of the work; or he was referring the reader to them for matters that he had not treated in detail because they had already done it. In either case, Montesquieu clearly considered that he owed much to them, even though he had gone much further than they had done.

For, if it is futile to disguise the influence of the philosophers of natural law on Montesquieu's method, it is equally futile to disguise the fact that he surpassed them. The real difference between them is not that he jettisoned their concept of natural law, but that he went much further than they had done in his scientific demonstration of

[42] *Thèse de Bordeaux*, p.415; C.-J. Beyer, in 'Le Problème du déterminisme social dans l'*Esprit des lois*', *Romanic Review*, 1948, pp. 103–4, exaggerates M.'s originality in the same way as Durkheim.

[43] *Cf.* Courtney, 'Montesquieu', p. 36.

social and political science – indeed, their efforts are often lamentable compared with his. Montesquieu was in a large degree original in that he set out to classify civil and political law in its relation to the "nature des choses" of each different country. In this sense, he had a scientific outlook, that is, he had an intense desire to explain in detail the seeming irrationality of the world of man. What the positivists do not admit is that the School of Natural Law had prepared the way for this kind of explanation, with their belief that moral and social phenomena can be classified. It is true that they often did not succeed in putting this belief into practice, but then, according to Comte, neither did Montesquieu.[44]

We have shown that the positivistic interpreters of Montesquieu err in thinking that his method was *a posteriori* and essentially different from that of the School of Natural Law. But we have not yet disposed of all the misinterpretations of Montesquieu fostered by an unhistorically-minded group of scholars. Many of them assume, for example, not only that his method was original, but also that it was actually incompatible with a belief in the *a priori* natural law.

So anxious are some of them to make us accept this assumption, that they distort Montesquieu's meaning. Thus the positivist Alengry, and even the more impartial historian of philosophy Émile Bréhier, think that the mathematical analogy used by Montesquieu in Book I, Chapter i of his main work, is meant to prove the necessity of the various general laws he was to discover governing human institutions.[45] Such a sense was perhaps implied by Montesquieu, but it was not his main intention in using the analogy. His main intention was to prove the prior existence of natural law.

II. The Prior Existence of Natural Law

As was shown in our historical survey of natural law, many famous philosophers have believed that the law of nature existed before there were any human laws, to which it is consequently superior. One of the most eloquent expressions of this idea is in Cicero's *De republica*:

> True law is right reason in agreement with nature; it is of universal application, unchanging and everlasting; [...]. We cannot be freed from its obligations by senate or people [...]. And there will not be different laws at Rome and at Athens, or different laws now and in the future, but

[44] *Cours de philosophie positive*, vol. IV, p. 129.
[45] Alengry, *op. cit.*, p. 392; Bréhier, *op. cit.*, vol. II, p. 374.

one eternal and unchangeable law will be valid for all nations and all times.[46]

More modern philosophers of natural law fervently accepted this idea, though they often lacked Cicero's eloquence in expressing it. Pufendorf, Malebranche, and the English divine Samuel Clarke,[47] saw in it a means of denying Hobbes's assertion that justice has no absolute existence and is the same as human law (*P.R.*, xiv, 10, pp. 190–1; *Leviathan*, II, xxvi, pp. 253–4).

Montesquieu was just as concerned as the philosophers of natural law to refute Hobbes. His antipathy towards the English political theorist dates from as early as the *Lettres persanes*. This work is often thought of as revealing a profound moral scepticism, but Usbek, the elder of the two Persian visitors to France, nevertheless affirmed that

> la justice est éternelle, et ne dépend point des conventions humaines. Et, quand elle en dépendrait, ce serait une vérité terrible, qu'il faudrait se dérober à soi-même (*L.p.* LXXXIII, N. I, iii, p. 170, Pl. I, p. 256).[48]

Montesquieu made a similar but even stronger affirmation in his *Traité des devoirs* of 1725 (N. III, p. 160, Pl. I, p. 109).

When they are viewed together with these earlier statements, instead of being lifted out of their historical context to support more modern ideas, Montesquieu's words at the opening of the *Esprit des lois* take on once more their proper meaning, appearing as an acknowledgement of the prior existence of natural law:

> Les êtres particuliers intelligents peuvent avoir des lois qu'ils ont faites: mais ils en ont aussi qu'ils n'ont pas faites. Avant qu'il y eût des êtres intelligents, ils étaient possibles; ils avaient donc des rapports possibles, et par conséquent des lois possibles. Avant qu'il y eût des lois faites, il y avait des rapports de justice possibles. Dire qu'il n'y a rien de juste ni d'injuste que ce qu'ordonnent ou défendent les lois positives, c'est dire qu'avant qu'on eût tracé de cercle, tous les rayons n'étaient pas égaux.

[46] *De republica*, III, xxii, 33; in the Loeb edition, *De republica, De legibus*, p. 211.

[47] *Dn.*, VIII, i, 5, vol. II, p. 358; Malebranche, *Entretiens sur la métaphysique et sur la religion* [1688], VIII, xiv, in *Œuvres complètes*, Vrin, 1958–68, vol. XII, 1965, p. 192; Samuel Clarke, *A Discourse Concerning the Being and Attributes of God* [1704–5] [hereafter *Discourse*], in *Works*, Knapton, 1738, vol. II, p. 624–6.

[48] Apart possibly from the slight doubt revealed in the last sentence, there is no evidence to support R. Caillois' view that for M. justice is merely a convention ('Montesquieu et l'athéisme contemporain', *Congrès*, p. 335).

Il faut donc avouer des rapports d'équité antérieurs à la loi positive qui les établit (N. I, i, pp. 2–3; Pl. II, p. 233).

Though Montesquieu does not here use the word *natural law*, reserving this term for the more physical laws of Chapter ii, it is clear, from the four examples he gives, that these "rapports d'équité" are the traditional *a priori* natural law: the first is that it is right to obey the laws of society; the second, to be grateful for benefits received; the third, to respect the Creator as a superior being; and the fourth, that if an intelligent being harms another intelligent being, he deserves to receive the same harm himself; "et ainsi du reste" (N. I, i, p. 3, Pl. II, p. 233). These four laws are basically two. The duty to be grateful for benefits received is the counterpart of being punished for evil actions; together the two laws form a version of the age-old maxim of natural law, *do as you would be done by*, to which Montesquieu specifically referred, in Book X, as "la loi de la lumière naturelle" (N. I, i, p. 184; Pl. II, p. 378). The precept of *do as you would be done by* is regulated in society by civil laws, which should thus be obeyed. So Chapter i postulates the two basic duties of natural law: duty to others, duty to God.[49]

According to certain critics, this is almost the only reference Montesquieu made to natural law in the whole of the *Esprit des lois*. In the first place, there are the indignant moralists: for them, the promise of Book I, Chapter i, is not fulfilled in the rest of the work. In the words of the famous translator of Aristotle, Barthélemy Saint-Hilaire:

Le monument a été commencé sous de magnifiques auspices; mais ces splendides avenues ne mènent point à un temple.[50]

In the second place, there are the positivists and their followers among literary critics. They claim that even though Chapter i may contain "quelques résidus métaphysiques",[51] the rest of the work shows that Montesquieu aimed to establish certain scientific laws governing social and political phenomena, with no reference to moral or natural laws, without perpetuating what Althusser scornfully calls the "travers idéal" of "la tradition la plus fade"[52] – that is, of the tradition of natural law.

[49] *Cf.* Aron, *Les grandes doctrines*, p. 46.

[50] *Politique d'Aristote*, Dumont, 1848, *Préface*, p. lxxxviii.

[51] *Cf.* P. Martino, 'De Quelques résidus métaphysiques dans l'*Esprit des lois*', *Revue d'histoire de la philosophie et d'histoire de la civilisation*, 1946, p. 241.

[52] *Op. cit.*, pp. 44 and 33–4.

In the first part of this chapter, we showed the falsity of the assertion that Montesquieu's method in theory excludes natural law. In the next chapters, we turn to a re-examination of the claims just mentioned, namely that there is in practice little or no allusion to natural law in the body of the *Esprit des lois*, and that in any case, the doctrine of natural law is concerned only with metaphysical subtleties, and with judging positive law from the standpoint of an uncompromising idealism. Before these contentions can be examined, however, it must first be decided how far Montesquieu set out, in the *Esprit des lois*, with the intention of incorporating the principles of natural law into his study of civil law.

III. Civil Law and Natural Law in the "Esprit des lois"

In his main work, Montesquieu does not appear to have relied on the original contract as a means of establishing the rights of ruled and ruler, even though there is more than a passing reference to the contract at the beginning of the work.[53] He was therefore, it would seem, unable to say, as the School of Natural Law had said, that a man is obliged to obey the laws of his country because there is an implicit or explicit agreement between himself and his ruler, by which he agrees to obey any just command of the latter.

However, the contract was not the only way in which the School of Natural Law established the obligation of the ruled to obey their rulers. This obligation was also derived from the belief that without society and laws, anarchy would develop. Hobbes, Pufendorf and Gravina all held that human nature being what it is, men without society would live in a state of fear and violence, and that to prevent this happening, the laws of society must be obeyed (*P.R.*, vi, 4, p. 75; *Dn.*, VII, i, 7, vol. II, pp. 219–20; *Origines iuris civilis*, II, xvii–xviii, pp. 256–8).

Montesquieu accepted this argument, and since it is a commonplace of natural law theory, Oudin is wrong to claim that it proves he was following Spinoza.[54] The *président* expressed this commonplace in *Pensée* 883 (Bkn. 1848), written between 1734 and 1738, which echoes part of *Pensée* 174 (Bkn. 1935) (1721–31):

> L'autorité des princes et magistrats n'est pas seulement fondée sur le droit civil, elle l'est encore sur le droit naturel: car, comme l'anarchie est contraire au droit naturel, le genre humain ne pouvant subsister par elle, il

[53] See below, Ch. 4, IV.
[54] *Le Spinozisme de Montesquieu*, pp. 69–70.

faut bien que l'autorité des magistrats, qui est opposée à l'anarchie, y soit conforme (N. II, p. 255; Pl. I, p. 1441).

In *Pensée* 883 there is therefore the germ of the idea in Book I, Chapter iii of the *Esprit des lois*, that the only way to prevent the state of war that accompanies the establishment of societies is to institute positive laws (N. I, i, p. 7; Pl. II, p. 236). Such, no doubt, is also the reasoning behind paragraph 9 of Chapter i of the same Book, where the first natural law is said to be that "supposé qu'il y eût des sociétés d'hommes, il serait juste de se conformer à leurs lois" (N. I, i, p. 3; Pl. II, p. 233).

Thus Montesquieu, although he does not seem to have used the original contract, seems to have followed one tradition of natural law regarding the obligation of civil law. However, there is an important difference between his arguments and those of the School of Natural Law. When Pufendorf stated that natural law enjoins obedience to the civil law, he immediately qualified this by adding that such obedience is required only so long as the law is just (*Dv.*, II, xii, 8, p. 337).

Montesquieu, it appears, made no such statement in the *Esprit des lois*, even though he had done so in his earlier works, showing that subjects have the right to rebel against their rulers in certain cases,[55] and stating categorically in a *Pensée* that could have been written any time between 1721 and 1738, that:

> Une chose n'est pas juste parce qu'elle est loi; mais elle doit être loi parce qu'elle est juste (*P.* 460, Bkn. 1906, N. II, p. 167, Pl. I, p. 1458).

The absence, in the *Esprit des lois*, of any such statement might lead the reader to suppose that, like Alexander Pope, Montesquieu in his later life believed that whatever is, is right,[56] and various remarks in the work seem to support this view.

Firstly there is the famous statement in the Preface, "Je n'écris point pour censurer ce qui est établi dans quelque pays que ce soit" (N. I, i, p. lx, Pl. II, p. 230). This phrase, however, proves nothing beyond Montesquieu's cautiousness – it is a "ruse philosphique",[57] and is quite untrue: not that he took pleasure in a purely destructive kind of analysis, but he did make many criticisms of various laws and governments.

In any case, Montesquieu did not say in the Preface that all citizens

[55] See below, Ch. 4, IV.
[56] *An Essay on Man* [1733–4], I, x, l.294, Methuen, 1950, p. 51.
[57] *Cf.* E. Bersot, 'Montesquieu', in *Études sur le XVIIIe, siècle*, Durand, 1855, vol. II, p. 317.

must obey the laws of their country, but simply that he wished they had better reasons for so doing:

> Si je pouvais faire en sorte que tout le monde eût de nouvelles raisons pour aimer ses devoirs, son prince, sa patrie, ses lois; [...] je me croirais le plus heureux des mortels (N. I, i, p. lxi, Pl. II, p. 230).

It is true that these "nouvelles raisons" are partly a realization by the people of the purpose of and reason for each particular law that may seem irksome. But these "nouvelles raisons" are also a more enlightened attitude on the part of legislators:[58]

> Si je pouvais faire en sorte que ceux qui commandent augmentassent leurs connaissances sur ce qu'ils doivent prescrire, et que ceux qui obéissent trouvassent un nouveau plaisir à obéir, je me croirais le plus heureux des mortels (N. I, i, p. lxi, Pl. II, p. 230).

In these lines, Montesquieu showed that he was not simply concerned with justifying the *status quo*, but that he was also concerned with the promulgation of better laws, even if "dans un temps de lumière, on tremble encore lorsqu'on fait les plus grands biens" (N. I, i, p. lxi, Pl. II, p. 230). The Preface indicates that many laws could be improved, but that it is unwise to be too hasty with reforms, which should be based on a true knowledge of the facts of each situation: it was the aim of the *Esprit des lois* to supply these facts.

In claiming that the lines "Je n'écris point pour censurer" show a purely positivistic outlook, Durkheim has failed to examine the *président*'s words in their context.[59]

Secondly, two statements made by Montesquieu in the body of the work would again seem to indicate that he believed that whatever is, is right. The Faculty of Theology thought that in his account of education in monarchies (*Lois*, IV, ii), he had placed too much emphasis on the political "principe" of honour, and not enough on moral virtue.[60] In order to placate the Faculty, Montesquieu added a footnote to the effect that "On dit ici ce qui est, et non pas ce qui doit être".[61] Alengry, and more recently the sociologist Georges Gurvitch, seize hold

58 *Cf.* Lanson, 'Le Déterminisme historique', pp. 138–9.

59 *Thèse de Bordeaux*, pp. 420–1.

60 1752: 12th Proposition: see Beyer, 'Montesquieu et la censure religieuse', pp. 107–8, and p. 108, n. 1.

61 N. I, i, p. 43; Pl. II, p. 265; *cf.* Brethe de la Gressaye, *Lois*, vol. I, p. 259, n. 9, to p. 77, and M.'s *Réponses et explications*. N. III, p. 662, Pl. II, p. 1183.

of this remark, and claim that it is true of Montesquieu's whole attitude.[62]

They have evidently not noticed that in this very Chapter ii of Book IV Montesquieu, discussing the effects of honour in monarchies, praised the action of Crillon, who refused to assassinate the duc de Guise when ordered to do so by Henri III, and that of the vicomte D'Orte, who refused to obey an order to massacre the Huguenots (N. I, i, pp. 42–3, Pl. II, p. 264). In praising these acts, Montesquieu showed that he did not believe in unconditional obedience to one's sovereign, and that the "principe" of honour is a moral as well as a political concept.[63]

The second statement, also seized on by Durkheim, Alengry and Gurvitch,[64] is found in Book XVI, Chapter iv, in Montesquieu's discussion of polygamy:

> Dans tout ceci, je ne justifie pas les usages; mais j'en rends les raisons (N. I, i, p. 353, Pl. II, p. 511),

a remark he had already taken the precaution of including in the first edition of the work.[65] But it is not true that these words are a fair account of his method, since he in fact criticized polygamy.[66]

A third place where Montesquieu is sometimes said to have approved what is, instead of showing what should be, is in his definition of liberty. Here it is the idealists who complain, not the positivists who exult. Janet for example criticizes the *président* for deriving "le droit de la loi au lieu de faire dériver la loi du droit", because in Book XI, Chapter iii, he had defined liberty as "le droit de faire tout ce que les lois permettent" (N. I, i, p. 206, Pl. II, p. 395); for it might seem that according to this definition the citizens could still be called *free*, even if some of them had to obey unjust or anti-social laws.[67]

In fact Janet has isolated this sentence from its context, thus distorting its meaning. A few lines previously, Montesquieu had said that liberty

[62] Alengry, *op. cit.*, pp. 390–1; G. Gurvitch, 'La Sociologie juridique de Montesquieu', *Revue de métaphysique et de morale*, 1939, p. 623.

[63] *Cf.* Barrière, 'L'Humanisme de l'Esprit des lois', p. 49, and Meyer, 'Politics and Morals . .', pp. 871–2.

[64] Durkheim, *Thèse de Bordeaux*, p. 420, n. 2; Alengry, *loc. cit.*; Gurvitch, *loc. cit.*

[65] Brethe de la Gressaye, *Lois*, vol. II, pp. 427–8, n. 20, to p. 247.

[66] See below, pp. 112–5.

[67] Janet, *Histoire de la science politique*, vol. II, p. 366; *cf.* P. Archambault, *Montesquieu, choix de textes et introduction*, Michaud, 1883, p. 42; J. Charmont, *La Renaissance du droit naturel*, Chauny et Quinsac, 1927, p. 39.

ne peut consister qu'à pouvoir faire ce que l'on doit vouloir, et à n'être point contraint de faire ce que l'on ne doit pas vouloir (N. I, i, p. 205, Pl. II, p. 395).

By using the words "doit" and "ne doit pas" Montesquieu introduced a normative principle, and there is no reason to suppose that he was talking only of the obligation of the civil law, and not of the natural law as well.[68] In any case, in Book XI he was discussing liberty "dans son rapport avec la constitution", he was fighting arbitrariness in government; but in the next Book, where he was dealing with liberty "dans son rapport avec le citoyen", it can be seen that he also believed in the conventional natural right of freedom, as protected by a fair system of criminal law. His conception of liberty is twofold – political liberty ensured by constitutional checks, personal liberty ensured by just laws.[69]

We have seen that in his study of civil law, Montesquieu was not impartial and did not advocate total obedience to government. If we now return to the opening book of the *Esprit des lois*, we find further confirmation of this view, since he there stated that the civil law should be a practical expression of the natural law:

Fait pour vivre dans la société, [l'homme] y pouvait oublier les autres; les législateurs l'ont rendu à ses devoirs par les lois politiques et civiles (*Lois*, I, i, N. I, i, p. 4, Pl. II, p. 234).

The general purpose of the civil law is thus to enforce the natural law of sociability, which Montesquieu mentioned in Chapter ii.

That the civil law should express the natural law is further shown by the definition of law given in Chapter iii:

La loi, en général, est la raison humaine, en tant qu'elle gouverne tous les peuples de la terre; et les lois politiques et civiles de chaque nation ne doivent être que les cas particuliers où s'applique cette raison humaine (N. I, i, p. 8, Pl. II, p. 237).

As Camille Jullian showed many years ago, this definition is similar to those given in Antiquity by Plato and Cicero.[70] Cicero, expressing the doctrine of the Stoics, identified the universal and unwritten law with right reason and with the mind of God.[71] In the *Pensées*, Mon-

[68] *Cf.* Franck, *op. cit.*, p. 73; É. Faguet, *La Politique comparée de Montesquieu, Rousseau et Voltaire*, Lecène et Oudin, 1902, pp. 14–15; Dedieu, *Montesquieu*, p. 156.

[69] *Cf.* V. Delbos, *La Philosophie française*, Plon, 1921, pp. 183–4, and Ehrard, *Politique de Montesquieu*, p. 124.

[70] *Montesquieu, livre premier de l'Esprit des lois, accompagné d'un commentaire*, Hachette, 1897, p. 25.

[71] *Cf. De legibus*, II, iv, 10; in the Loeb edition, *De republica, De legibus*, pp. 382–3.

tesquieu quoted one of Cicero's definitions of law:

Lex est ratio summi Jovis (*P.* 1519, Bkn. 109, N. II, p. 435, Pl. I, p. 1002),

as a motto for the *Esprit des lois*. Another *Pensée* provides an illuminating commentary on Book I, iii:

C'est une pensée admirable de Platon [...], que les lois sont faites pour annoncer les ordres de la raison à ceux qui ne peuvent la recevoir immédiatement d'elle (*P.* 1859, Bkn. 208, N. II, p. 555, Pl. II, p. 1042).

Clearly, in these passages, Montesquieu accepted that civil law is a practical expression of natural law.

It could be argued that these *Pensées* are irrelevant to the *Esprit des lois* (even though they were probably written soon after its publication); it could further be argued that since in his definition of law in Book I, iii, Montesquieu did not say "la raison de Dieu" as Cicero had done, but "la raison humaine", he really meant that civil and political laws are not the expression of an absolute standard of reason, but simply of the nature of things, which happens to be rational.[72] It is quite true that the definition has a connection with the paragraphs that follow, where the relationship between positive law and *la nature des choses* is discussed and where consequently the descriptive aspect of law predominates. But it also has a connection with Chapter i, where the normative aspect of law is emphasized, in the passage dealing with "les rapports d'équité antérieurs à la loi positive qui les établit". The deleted manuscript version of the definition, "La raison humaine donne des lois politiques et civiles à tous les peuples de la terre",[73] which stresses the active side of the legislator's task, makes even more obvious the normative aspect of Montesquieu's conception of law, which exists alongside the descriptive aspect.[74]

The idea that morals can be formulated mathematically is one that can only occur in an age such as the seventeenth century, when confidence in science had not given way to disillusionment about the value of its achievements. By his ambitious plan of explaining the whole world in rational terms, Descartes helped to foster this con-

[72] *Cf. Montesquieu e la scienza della società*, p. 372.

[73] See Barckhausen, *Montesquieu, l'Esprit des lois*, p. 23; not given in Nagel, Pléiade or Brethe de la Gressaye editions.

[74] Among the many critics who accept this interpretation of *Lois*, I, iii, see: Janet, *Histoire de la science politique*, vol. II, p. 330; Barckhausen, *Montesquieu, ses idées et ses œuvres*, p. 46; Brethe de la Gressaye, 'La Philosophie du droit de Montesquieu', *Archives de philosophie du droit*, Sirey, 1962, p. 208; Ehrard, 'Les Études sur Montesquieu', p. 66.

fidence, which lasted during the eighteenth and even into the nineteenth century. To say that Montesquieu was an optimist may be going too far, but the *Esprit des lois* is the work of a philosopher who, like Descartes, believed in the ability of reason to explain the world of man. It is the work of a rationalist who tried to deduce positive law mathematically from a few basic concepts.

The School of Natural Law were also rationalists, in that they tried to deduce natural and positive law scientifically, again from a few basic concepts, principally the nature of man and of society. These concepts were fewer than those which interested Montesquieu, since the School of Natural Law were not so concerned with the relation between laws and such factors as the character and history of each people, the constitution and climate of their country. Because he studied in detail the influence of these factors, Montesquieu can justly be called more scientific than his predecessors. But this does not mean that his proposed method of studying positive law excludes their two basic normative concepts, the nature of man and the nature of society.

Both Montesquieu and the School of Natural Law were rationalists, but they were not exclusively rationalists. The majority of critics claim that Montesquieu's attitude both to natural and to positive law was, in practice, more empirical than that of the School of Natural Law. In the next four chapters, it will be shown whether such claims are based on a real understanding of natural law.

CHAPTER 3

MONTESQUIEU AND EMPIRICISM IN NATURAL LAW

It is often suggested that Montesquieu's attitude to natural law was more empirical than that of the School of Natural Law in that it was more firmly based on physical realities and concrete facts and less on metaphysical ideas. This claim merits careful consideration, not only because it has a bearing on his whole conception of natural morality, but also because we find it expressed by some of his most shrewd interpreters.

Thus Brethe de la Gressaye, talking of Book XXVI of the *Esprit des lois*, says:

> Les exemples choisis par Montesquieu révèlent sa conception – un peu étroite – du Droit naturel. Pour lui, les principes de Droit naturel découlent de réflexes élémentaires [...]. Ce qui est de Droit naturel est instinctif, procédant de la biologie humaine ou d'une psychologie primitive .[1]

It is strange that Brethe de la Gressaye does not make the same point in his analysis of Book I, ii, where the physical nature of Montesquieu's conception of natural law is apparently more obvious. Shackleton, on the other hand, though he is talking of the *président*'s attitude as a whole, is probably thinking in particular of Book I, ii, when he states that

> The natural law system which reigned scarcely challenged was based on rational and *a priori* abstractions. Montesquieu sought instead to link it with natural science.[2]

How far is this contention correct?

[1] *Lois*, vol. III, p. 287; *cf.* also Oudin, *Le Spinozisme de Montesquieu*, p. 63; Cotta, *Montesquieu e la scienza della società*, pp. 356–61; Vernière, *Spinoza et la pensée française*, vol. II, pp. 456–7.
[2] *M.*, p. 252.

I. Physical and Moral Concepts in Natural Law

The laws of nature, as they are set out in Book I, ii, of the *Esprit des lois,* are five in number:

> Cette loi qui, en imprimant dans nous-mêmes l'idée d'un créateur, nous porte vers lui, est la première des *lois naturelles*, par son importance, et non pas dans l'ordre de ces lois. L'homme, dans l'état de nature, aurait plutôt la faculté de connaître, qu'il n'aurait des connaissances. [...]
>
> Dans cet état, chacun se sent inférieur; à peine chacun se sent-il égal. On ne chercherait donc point à s'attaquer, et la paix serait la première loi naturelle.
>
> Le désir que Hobbes donne d'abord aux hommes de se subjuger les uns les autres, n'est pas raisonnable. L'idée de l'empire et de la domination est si composée, et dépend de tant d'autres idées, que ce ne serait pas celle qu'il aurait d'abord.
>
> [...]
>
> Au sentiment de sa faiblesse, l'homme joindrait le sentiment de ses besoins. Ainsi une autre loi naturelle serait celle qui lui inspirerait de chercher à se nourrir.
>
> J'ai dit que la crainte porterait les hommes à se fuir: mais les marques d'une crainte réciproque les engageraient bientôt à s'approcher. D'ailleurs, ils y seraient portés par le plaisir qu'un animal sent à l'approche d'un animal de son espèce. De plus, ce charme que les deux sexes s'inspirent par leur différence, augmenterait ce plaisir; et la prière naturelle qu'ils se font toujours l'un à l'autre, serait une troisième loi.
>
> Outre le sentiment que les hommes ont d'abord, ils parviennent encore à avoir des connaissances; ainsi ils ont un second lien que les autres animaux n'ont pas. Ils ont donc un nouveau motif de s'unir; et le désir de vivre en société est une quatrième loi naturelle (N. I, i, pp. 5–6, Pl. II, pp. 235–6).

This passage apparently has a commonsensical, down-to-earth approach to the question. Montesquieu's natural laws look empirical, in that they are based on man's physical and instinctive characteristics. They are simply the expression of what Montesquieu thought man would do in a state of nature, and they are not, so it seems, what natural laws in the state of nature had been for Pufendorf or Locke, that is, a set of rules which man discovers by his reason and tries to observe. They are descriptive rather than normative.[3]

However, two features of the passage undermine its superficially empirical appearance. Firstly, there is the normative vocabulary in which some of the laws are phrased: man *would receive* ("celles qu'il recevrait", *Lois*, I, ii, paragraph 1) certain natural laws in the state of nature; the first natural law *imprints* ("en imprimant") a notion of the Creator in his mind; the second secular natural law *would inspire*

[3] See Shackleton's helpful analysis, *M.*, p. 251.

("celle qui lui inspirerait") natural man to feed himself. Either these laws are badly expressed, which is unlikely, or else they are intentionally presented as the commands of God or nature, obeyed, albeit unconsciously, by primitive man.

Secondly, there is the fact that the whole passage is a piece of conjecture. Montesquieu may have used the hypothetical style because he did not believe in the historical existence of the state of nature;[4] nevertheless it makes the passage look remarkably like a piece of *a priori* reasoning, like a deduction from a hypothetical concept, namely *man before society began*. This impression is confirmed when we realize that Montesquieu has made various gratuitous assumptions. The fact that primitive man would feed himself and would mate, is indisputable, and hence scientific. On the other hand the first and fourth secular natural laws, of peace and of the desire to live in society, are not so obviously scientific, not so clearly induced from man's physical or instinctive nature. The law of peace is purely polemic, being directed against Hobbes; and the law of sociability, true as it may be of man in society, is not necessarily true of "un homme avant l'établissement des sociétés" (*Lois*, I, ii, Paragraph 1). Further, the basic assumption that primitive man would have no complex ideas is open to question. When Rousseau makes the same assumption, in his *Discours sur l'inégalité*, (which was published seven years after the *Esprit des lois*), he is generally accused of being unscientific.[5] Montesquieu seems to escape an equally well-deserved accusation. Where, if he is being truly scientific, is his evidence based on observation, statistics or experiment? True, he refers once to the example of certain savages, in order to prove natural man's timidity (*Lois*, I, ii, paragraph 2). But savages are already in society and prove nothing about the state of nature.[6]

On the surface, then, Montesquieu's conception of natural law as revealed in Book I, ii of the *Esprit des lois*, is different from that of the School of Natural Law. When we delve more deeply, we realize that the difference is not so great, and that both were making deductions from an *a priori* concept. On the other hand, if Montesquieu's conjectures are presented in a factual manner, so are Pufendorf's, for even he tried to present the peace of the state of nature as a fact

[4] *Cf.* Alengry, *op. cit.*, pp. 393–4.

[5] *Discours sur l'origine et les fondements de l'inégalité parmi les hommes* [1755], in *The Political Writings of Jean-Jacques Rousseau*, edited by C. E. Vaughan, Cambridge University Press, 1915, vol. I, pp. 148–52.

[6] *Cf.* Ehrard, *L'Idée de nature*, vol. II, pp. 472–3.

resulting from man's physical and moral condition (*Dn.*, II, ii, 7–9, vol. I, pp. 162–6); similarly, Hobbes had tried to present the state of war in the state of nature as a fact resulting from that condition (*P.R.*, i, 4–12, pp. 7–11). Indeed, Hobbes's picture of the state of nature (from which Pufendorf borrowed several elements[7]) is frighteningly realistic, and far more credible than Montesquieu's.

What of the other references to natural law in the *Esprit des lois*? Do they present the same mixture of gratuitous assumptions and physical facts found in Book I, ii ?

Montesquieu was particularly interested in self-defence, that most basic of natural rights. In Book I, ii, he had said that natural man would think above all of "la conservation de son être" (paragraph 2). In the state of nature, this self-preservation would not, apparently, conflict with the self-preservation of others. In society such conflicts do arise, and here a man has the right to defend himself against others, because, as Montesquieu put it in Book X of the *Esprit des lois*,

> Dans le cas de la défense naturelle, j'ai droit de tuer; parce que ma vie est à moi, comme la vie de celui qui m'attaque est à lui (*Lois*, X, ii, N. I, i, p. 182, Pl. II, p. 377).

What in the state of nature was merely an instinct, becomes a right once society is established.

Now there is nothing unusual in Montesquieu's having based this right on man's physical nature. Pufendorf, though an *a priorist*, derived the right of self-defence both from a rational principle, "la raison même", and from an instinctive one, "l'amour-propre" (*Dn.*, II, v, 1, vol. I, p. 253). Grotius had gone even further, since in deriving this right from "la droite raison et [...] la sociabilité" and from "les premières impressions de la nature", he made liberal use of examples taken from animal behaviour (*Dg.*, I, ii, 1, vol. I, pp. 68–9).

A woman's defence of her honour is another related question where Montesquieu's arguments are apparently influenced by physical considerations. In Book XII, xiv, entitled 'Violation de la pudeur, dans la punition des crimes' – the chapter which shocked Albert Sorel so much[8] – Montesquieu said that it is unnatural and unwise to break the universally-observed "règles de pudeur", in the punishment of crimes (N. I, i, pp. 267–8, Pl. II, pp. 444–5). In Book XXVI, iii, he

[7] In particular, he emphasized the dangers and uncertainties of the state of nature, as Hobbes had done: *Dn.*, II, ii, 12, p. 168, and *Dv.*, II, i, 9, pp. 253–4.

[8] *Op. cit.*, p. 114.

extended this argument to cover not only physical, but also moral violation of *la pudeur*. He strongly criticized two laws designed to prevent sexual licence, abortion and infanticide: the first law, made in Henry VIII's reign, obliged a girl to reveal if she were no longer a virgin, the second, made by Henri II, condemned to death any unmarried girl whose child died, if she had not previously revealed her pregnancy. He said that the first law "violait la défense de la pudeur naturelle" because

> il est aussi déraisonnable d'exiger d'une fille qu'elle fasse cette déclaration, que de demander d'un homme qu'il ne cherche pas à défendre sa vie (N. I, ii, pp. 128–9, Pl. II, pp. 752–3);

he condemned the second law in similar though slightly milder terms. When he said "il est [...] déraisonnable", he meant that it is *wrong* or *unnatural*: the reference to a man defending his life is merely a striking analogy, and it does not alter the fact that Montesquieu was referring primarily not to a physical principle, but to an *a priori* one, based on the right of self-defence.[9]

Domat had specifically approved Henri II's law,[10] and the Sorbonne was to condemn Montesquieu for criticizing it.[11] The *président*'s attitude was, by present-day standards, more humane than that of the Church, but was it more humane than that of the School of Natural Law? Yes, according to W. Stark, a recent interpreter of Montesquieu: he says that the *président*, in the discussion of Henri II's law, is original in that he is not talking so much of human rights as of human dignity, and in that his approach is unlegalistic.[12] Though he did not specifically discuss this law, Pufendorf showed himself to be more humane than the Church on the related question of lies made in self-defence. Such lies were condemned by Catholic dogma, where crime is seen from God's point of view (*S.t.*, II, ii, Q. 69, Art. 1, vol. X, p. 256), but the German thought they were justified from a temporal point of view. He proved his argument by referring to man's instinctive nature:

> Personne n'étant [...] tenu de s'exposer soi-même à la peine, et l'homme ne pouvant naturellement que la regarder avec une extrême horreur, surtout si elle va jusqu'à priver de la vie, ou à faire souffrir quelque mal

[9] M. had first criticized this law in the *L.p.*: Letter CXX, N. I, iii, pp. 239–40, Pl. I, pp. 309–10.

[10] *Op. cit.*, Part I, III, vi, vol. I, p. 242.

[11] 1752: 16th Proposition: see Beyer, 'Montesquieu et la censure religieuse', p. 127, n. 1.

[12] W. Stark, *Montesquieu, Pioneer of the Sociology of Knowledge*, Routledge and Kegan Paul, 1960, p. 196.

fort sensible: pourquoi ne pourrait-on pas chercher toutes sortes de voies pour l'éviter [. . .]? (*Dn.*, IV, i, 20, vol. I, p. 451).[13]

Montesquieu had equally revealed his humaneness when he said that in Japan

On punit de mort les mensonges qui se font devant les magistrats; chose contraire à la défense naturelle (*Lois*, VI, xiii, N. I, i, p. 115, Pl. II, p. 322).

The School of Natural Law were by no means always as humane in their approach as Montesquieu. This is shown by the other two examples in Book XXVI of laws which violate the natural right of self-defence. In the first case he criticized a law suggested by Plato, whereby a slave who murdered a freeman was to be treated not simply as a murderer, but as a parricide. Clearly, his reasoning is based on the *a priori* concept of equality before the law. In the second case he criticized a law by which a man could be condemned "sans que les témoins lui eussent été confrontés" – again an implicit reference to a natural right (N. I, ii, p. 128, Pl. II, p. 752).

Montesquieu's reasons for criticizing such laws are made even clearer in the manuscript version of Book XXV, xii. This chapter, which in the printed text is a plea that "Il faut éviter les lois pénales en fait de religion" (N. I, ii, p. 119, Pl. II, p. 745), was originally a more strongly-worded attack on the Inquisition and similar institutions. He exclaimed that

Il est étonnant que l'on ait si souvent violé les lois naturelles dans les lois pénales que l'on a faites contre la religion,

and he went on to instance Charlemagne's Remerc where heretics were tried according to

des formes de procéder qu'aucun coupable ne mérite, parce qu'il est homme avant d'être coupable.[14]

According to Montesquieu, then, the natural right of self-defence entitles every accused man to defend himself in a court of law, whether civil or religious, and we can assume that these passages were deleted from the final version not because the *président* no longer believed in natural rights, but because he had an eye on the censor.

The difference between Montesquieu and the School of Natural Law,

[13] In this passage, Pufendorf was talking mainly of crimes where the offender has already offered restitution for the damage done, but he seems to go on to apply the principle to all crimes, as he does in *Dn.*, VIII, iii, 4, vol. II, p. 376.

[14] Brethe de la Gressaye, *Lois*, vol. III, p. 438, n. 36, to p. 278.

as shown by his treatment of the laws just mentioned, is not that his approach was more "physical" than theirs, but on the contrary that it was more humanitarian. Neither Grotius nor Pufendorf allowed that the rights of slaves are the same as those of freemen.[15] Pufendorf implied that if the accused had the right to see and contradict witnesses, it would lead to "une infinité de parjures" (*Dn.*, V, xiii, 9, vol. II, p. 148). Brethe de la Gressaye's claim that for Montesquieu "les principes de Droit naturel découlent de réflexes élémentaires"[16] is misleading. For Montesquieu, the *principles* of natural law are based on certain *a priori* concepts, particularly the right of self-defence and of equality before the law. These principles are in turn related to certain instinctive reflexes, but so they were for Grotius and Pufendorf. There was no difference of principle between Montesquieu and the School of Natural Law: to claim otherwise is to misunderstand the doctrine of natural law.

It is Montesquieu's humanitarianism that is shown when he rejected cruelty and injustice in the name of natural law. What precisely did the concept of *humanité* mean to him?[17] Two passages help to provide the answer. In the *Considérations*, abandoning for a moment the impartial historical approach, he commented on the attitude of the Romans towards their slaves and children:

> Les Romains, accoutumés à se jouer de la nature humaine, dans la personne de leurs enfants et de leurs esclaves, ne pouvaient guère connaître cette vertu que nous appelons humanité (Ch. xv, N. I, iii, p. 451, Pl. II, p. 148).

In *Pensée* 2194 (Bkn. 171), probably written after 1749, he gave some examples of this inhumanity; among other things, the Romans deprived their slaves

> de tous les sentiments naturels les plus chers: [...] de la vertu de leurs femmes, de la chasteté de leurs filles, de la propriété de leurs enfants.
>
> Pourquoi dégrader une partie de la nature humaine? (N. II, p. 659, Pl. II, p. 220).

"Humanité" is thus for Montesquieu a concept based both on emotion and on reason. It is firstly a *sentiment naturel*, which the Romans apparently did not have, and which causes men to love and care for those in their charge. It is secondly a rational principle, "cette vertu", which dictates that it is right to have this affection.

[15] See below, Ch. 6, II.
[16] *Lois*, vol. III, p. 287.
[17] *Cf.* P. Vernière, 'L'Idée d'humanité au XVIIIe siècle', *Studium Generale*, 1962, pp. 171–9.

A glance at the work of Domat, who incidentally made the same strictures on the Romans' treatment of their slaves,[18] shows that Montesquieu's dual conception of "humanité" was quite orthodox. For Domat, "le sentiment de l'humanité" is basically an instinct which inspires movements of pity and charity; when it is combined with "la vue de la raison" it produces the virtue of equity, which is the very basis of natural law.[19] For both Domat and Montesquieu "humanité" is a rational principle based on an instinct.

Another field where it is suggested that Montesquieu's approach is more empirical than his predecessors', is that of sexual relations. In a later Chapter we shall see the connection that this topic had, in Montesquieu's eyes, with positive law. Here we are concerned with its relation to natural law.

To treat the philosophers of natural law simply as *a priorists* is to ignore, in particular, the large part that instinct and practical considerations play in their discussion of sex. Pufendorf, although he disliked basing natural law on instinct, did precisely that when he argued against those who think that marriage is not a natural law. "A quoi bon", they claim "ordonner ce qu'un instinct naturel nous inspire déjà d'une manière assez forte [...]?" He replied that

> bien loin qu'il s'ensuive de là que le droit naturel ne prescrit point de pareilles choses, il faut en inférer au contraire, que la nature veut qu'on s'en acquitte fort exactement, puisque se défiant [...] des impressions que la raison toute seule pourrait faire, pour nous porter à la pratique de ces devoirs, d'où dépend directement [...] la conservation du genre humain, elle a appelé au secours un instinct si puissant, qu'il est bien difficile d'y résister (*Dn.*, VI, i, 3, vol. II, pp. 150–1).

Marriage, like self-defence, is an instinct which is reinforced by a moral natural law, founded on the preservation of society.[20]

Montesquieu's reasoning is very similar. In Book I, ii, of the *Esprit des lois*, he said that the sexual instinct, the "prière naturelle" as he coyly called it, is one of the four basic natural laws of man (N. I, i, p. 6, Pl. II, p. 236). He returned to the subject in Book XXIII, x, when, talking of marriage, he claimed that "La nature y porte assez" (N. I, ii, p. 49, Pl. II, p. 688), and in a later chapter he argued that legislators should do all they can to encourage marriage, if Europe is not soon to become depopulated (Ch. xxvi, N. I, ii, pp. 75–6, Pl. II, p. 710). For

[18] *Op. cit.*, *Traité des lois*, i, 1, vol. I, p. i.
[19] *Ibid.*, *Le Droit public*, Preface, vol. II, p. [viii].
[20] *Dn.*, VI, i, 2–5, vol. II, pp. 150–3; *cf.* Gravina, *Origines iuris civilis*, II, iv, p. 238.

both Pufendorf and Montesquieu, the physical natural law of reproduction becomes the moral duty of marriage, aimed at continuing the human race.

If, in the eyes of the philosophers of natural law, the aim of marriage is essentially practical, there is very little to prevent its being only a temporary affair, lasting only while the children need protection. In Book XXIII, ii, Montesquieu said:

> L'obligation naturelle qu'a le père de nourrir ses enfants, a fait établir le mariage, qui déclare celui qui doit remplir cette obligation [...].
>
> Cette obligation, chez les animaux, est telle que la mère peut ordinairement y suffire. Elle a beaucoup plus d'étendue chez les hommes (N. I, ii, p. 43, Pl. II, p. 683).

This statement annoyed the abbé de La Roche, who claimed that "Un chrétien rapporterait l'institution du mariage à Dieu même, qui donna une compagne à Adam" (*Examen critique*, p. 128). This is just what Domat, whom Fontaine de La Roche admired so much, had done.[21]

But these Jansenists were extremists: the Sorbonne did not censure Montesquieu on this point; most philosophers who believe in natural law have held views similar to those of the *président*. In particular he seems to have been closely following St. Thomas, who derived marriage precisely from the fact that children need to be brought up by both parents, and not simply by the mother, as happens in some species of animals (St. Thomas's biology is more accurate than that of Montesquieu). The Angelic Doctor was not even certain that by natural law, marriage need be lifelong: he simply said rather vaguely that in the interests of the children, a man should live with one woman "a long time, or even for a whole lifetime" (*S.t.*, II, ii, Q. 154, A. 2, vol. XIII, p. 134).[22] This puts us in mind of the suggestion Locke was to make many centuries later:

> the father, who is bound to take care for those he hath begot, is under an obligation to continue in conjugal society with the same woman longer than other creatures (*T.T.*, II, vii, 80, p. 338),

with its implication that the duration of marriage depends entirely on the needs of the children.

Of course, there is a difference of emphasis between Montesquieu

[21] *Op. cit.*, *Traité des lois*, iii, 1–2, vol. I, p. iv.

[22] In the Latin: "non per modicum tempus, sed diu: vel etiam per totam vitam" (*S. Thomæ Aquinatis Summa totius theologiæ*, Antwerp, Ex officina Christophori Plantini, 1585, Secunda secundæ, p. 303).

and the School of Natural Law on the one hand, and St. Thomas on the other, since the theologian did not limit himself, as they did, to a secular view of marriage,[23] but showed its religious aspects too. Nevertheless, Oudin is mistaken when he says that in Montesquieu's time, jurists regarded the institution "uniquement comme un sacrement et négligeaient son rôle social".[24] There seems to be no commonplace of natural law, whether secular or religious, the invention of which some critic would not like to attribute to Montesquieu.

If Montesquieu was following the tradition of natural law in his attitude to marriage, what was his view of the related question of paternal power? In the seventeenth century, some theorists had claimed that since paternal power is absolute, political power should be so to: this point will be examined in detail later; all that need be said at this stage is that Montesquieu, who disliked political absolutism, was led to refute paternal absolutism.

He touched on the question of paternal power briefly in *Lettre persane* CXXIX, where he called it "la plus sacrée de toutes les magistratures" (N. I, iii, p. 258, Pl. I, p. 323); and in *Pensée* 174 (Bkn. 1935), where he said it was in accordance with natural law (N. II, p. 57, Pl. I, p. 1467); but his discussion is most comprehensive in the *Traité des devoirs*. Here he showed, just as Pufendorf had done (*Dn.*, VI, ii, 6, vol. II, pp. 191–2), that paternal power can never be absolute since the father's aim is not to dominate his children, but to ensure their wellbeing (*P.* 1267, Bkn. 616, N. II, p. 345, Pl. I, p. 1141). This is a moral argument based on a physical fact, here a particular emotion. St. Thomas had also limited paternal power by reference to physical drives (*S.t.*, II, ii, Q. 104, A. 5, vol. XII, pp. 36–7).

The second way in which Montesquieu, in the *Traité des devoirs*, proved that paternal power is not absolute, was by showing that it varies according to the respective ages of father and children:

> L'autorité paternelle se borne toute seule, parce qu'à mesure que les enfants sortent de la jeunesse, les pères entrent dans la vieillesse, et que la force des enfants augmente à mesure que le père s'affaiblit (*P.* 1267, Bkn. 616, N. II, p. 345, Pl. I, p. 1141).

It is quite true, as Cotta states, that Montesquieu here placed on paternal power "una limitazione naturale, fisiologica";[25] but this in

[23] Though Pufendorf did mention that marriage had been instituted by God, it was only in passing (*Dn.*, VI, i, 2, vol.II p. 150).
[24] *Le Spinozisme de Montesquieu*, pp. 36–7.
[25] *Montesquieu e la scienza della società*, p. 192.

no way proves, as Cotta thinks, that the *président* had a more realistic or "physical" attitude to the question than did the School of Natural Law. The very similar limitation of paternal power alleged by Grotius, Pufendorf and Locke, namely that parents' rights diminish as their children become stronger and more responsible,[26] is based on physical and psychological facts, just as Montesquieu's limitation was. Indeed, their argument is more sound than Montesquieu's, since it is truer that children become more capable of looking after themselves as they grow up, than it is that their strength increases exactly as their parents' strength decreases, in a kind of mathematical proportion, as Montesquieu seems to have thought.

Next in this series of topics concerned with sexual relations comes the question of perversions. Montesquieu, like his predecessors, seems to have enjoyed treating certain aspects of this question quite fully.

There is however no prurience in his discussion of child marriages. In Book XXVI, iii of the *Esprit des lois* he criticized a law which allowed a seven year old girl to choose a husband:

> Cette loi était révoltante de deux manières: elle n'avait aucun égard au temps de la maturité que la nature a donné à l'esprit, ni au temps de la maturité qu'elle a donné aux corps (N. I, ii, p. 129, Pl. II, p. 753).

Clearly, he based his objection on the obvious mental, emotional and physical grounds. But these criteria are precisely those referred to by the *Summa theologica* (III, *Supplement*, Q. 58, A. 5, vol. XIX, pp. 263–4), and by Pufendorf:

> selon le droit naturel, il faut que ceux, qui veulent se marier ensemble, aient [...] les qualités nécessaires, tant physiques que morales. Par qualités physiques, j'entends une constitution propre au principal but du mariage, qui est la propagation de l'espèce (*Dn.*, VI, i, 25, vol. II, p. 176).

The only important difference between Montesquieu and Pufendorf on this question is that the German philosopher's language is less emotional.

In his long and complicated discussion of incest, on the other hand, Montesquieu showed little indignation, probably because, like Grotius and Pufendorf before him (*Dg.*, II, v, 12, vol. I, pp. 290–1; *Dn.*, VI, i, 28, vol. II, p. 178), he found it difficult to tell why or in what cases incest is forbidden by natural law. Neither the Bible (Leviticus, XVIII, 6–18) nor the *Corpus* (*Digest*, XXIII, ii, pp. 295–9; *Institutes*, I, x, p. 4)

[26] *Dg.*, II, v, 2–6, vol. I, pp. 279–81; Pufendorf, *Dn.*, VI, ii, 7–12, vol. II, pp. 192–9; *T.T.*, II, vi, 58–65, pp. 324–9.

were of much help, since they merely said which were the prohibited degrees, without giving any specific reasons. St. Thomas and the author of the *Supplement* to the *Summa theologica*, however, had provided those reasons. Did Montesquieu follow the theologians or the jurists?

The arguments against incest fall into two categories, physical and moral. The physical objection put forward by the *Supplement* was that the offspring of incestuous marriages are unhealthy (Q. 54, A. 3, vol. XIX, p. 203); both Grotius and Pufendorf scorned this *a posteriori* argument (*Dg.*, II, v, 12, vol. I, p. 292; *Dn.*, VI, i, 32, vol. II, p. 182). Montesquieu however accepted a version of it, since he claimed that such marriages are unlikely to produce any children at all (*Lois*, XXVI, xiv, N. I, ii, pp. 142–3, Pl. II, p. 764).

Before it is said that this proves that his approach was more empirical than theirs, it should be noted that they did tentatively accept a second physical argument, also used by St. Thomas (*S.t.*, II, ii, Q. 154, A. 9, rep. obj. 3, vol. XIII, p. 155), based on the instinctive repugnance of man or animals to incest. Grotius wondered if

> il n'y aurait pas dans toutes les personnes dont les sentiments n'ont pas été corrompus par une mauvaise éducation, je ne sais quelle aversion naturelle d'un commerce charnel avec ceux de qui on a reçu la vie, ou à qui on l'a donnée, puisqu'on voit même des bêtes qui témoignent naturellement une pareille aversion (*Dg.*, II, v, 12, vol. I, p. 292).

Such *a posteriorism*, stemming from a lack of confidence in reason, is perhaps not surprising in Grotius. But it is surprising to find similar arguments in Pufendorf, who has the reputation of being exclusively *a priori* in his reasoning. He claimed, though in rather hesitant terms, that the sense of shame that men feel in respect of the organs of generation is the origin of the interdiction of incest (*Dn.*, VI, i, 30, vol. II, p. 181): he was inferring the existence of a moral natural law from the existence of a certain emotion; he was therefore reasoning *a posteriori*, just as Montesquieu was to do when he argued that incest would be incompatible with the natural desire parents have to ensure their children's *pudeur* (*Lois*, XXVI, xiv, N. I, ii, p. 143, Pl. II, p. 764).

There is a second, moral reason why incest is condemned by natural law. The *Supplement* to the *Summa theologica* had expressed it very clearly:

> it is out of order that a daughter be mated to her father [...] since in all things she ought to be subject to her father [...]. Hence by natural law a father and mother are debarred from marrying their children; and the mother still more than the father, since it is more derogatory to the reverence due to the parents if the son marry his mother than if the father marry his

daughter; since the wife should be to a certain extent subject to her husband (*S.t.*, III, *Supplement*, Q. 54, A. 3, vol. XIX, p .204).[27]

This principle had not been accepted by the sceptical Pufendorf (*Dn.*, VI, i, 32, vol. II, p. 182), but Gravina, like a good Catholic, did accept it (*Origines iuris civilis*, III, lxxxviii, p. 681), as did Montesquieu:

> Le mariage du fils avec la mère confond l'état des choses: le fils doit un respect sans bornes à sa mère, la femme doit un respect sans bornes à son mari; le mariage d'une mère avec son fils renverserait, dans l'un et dans l'autre, leur état naturel.
>
> [. . .]
>
> Le mariage entre le père et la fille répugne à la nature, comme le précédent; mais il répugne moins (*Lois*, XXVI, xiv, N. I, ii, pp. 142–3, Pl. II, pp. 763–4).

We note, in confirmation of the orthodoxy of Montesquieu's views, that the Sorbonne did not censure them.[28]

Cotta is surely wrong to affirm that Montesquieu's discussion of incest has a "carattere fisico realistico" not to be found in the arguments of the School of Natural Law.[29] All the philosophers of natural law, in their treatment of the question, examined both physical and moral arguments. Indeed, the School of Natural Law preferred the physical arguments to the moral ones. The main difference between the *président* and the jurists is that he had more confidence in the validity of both kinds of arguments than they had: clearly their empiricism (or scepticism) was less helpful to him than Catholic dogmatism, in his quest to explain everything. It must be emphasized, finally, that all these arguments against incest are pure conjectures, plausible of course, but quite unverifiable: Book XXVI, xiv of the *Esprit des lois* proves Montesquieu's rationalism rather than his empiricism.

Lastly, among the perversions, there are the questions of onanism, homosexuality and sodomy. According to Montesquieu, "le péché d'Onan et celui des villes qui périrent par les flammes" are simply "contraires au droit naturel" (*P.* 205, Bkn. 1928, N. II, p. 75, Pl. I, p. 1463). In particular, "le crime contre nature" is condemned by "la religion, la morale et la politique" (*Lois*, XII, vi, N. I, i, p. 258, Pl. II, p. 437). This is all he tells us on the subject. Presumably he accepted the eminently "physical" arguments of the Catholic Church,

[27] The same reasoning is found in *S.t.*, II, ii, Q. 154, A. 9, vol. XIII, pp. 153–4.

[28] We are here considering only the *Lois*; in *P.* 205 (Bkn. 1928), N. II, pp. 74–7, Pl. I, pp. 1463–5, M. did not consider incest to be unnatural, but he did refer to the principle of respect.

[29] *Montesquieu e la scienza della società*, p. 368.

which condemned these practices both because they are not found in the animals – at least, so St. Thomas tells us (*S.t.*, II, i, Q. 94, A. 3, rep. obj. 2, vol. VIII, p. 46)– and because they involve a "venereal act from which generation cannot follow" (*S.t.*, II, ii, Q. 154, A. 1, vol. XIII, p. 132). Montesquieu is relatively original in that, although he did not justify sexual perversion, as many writers in the eighteenth century did,[30] he did advocate, in rather veiled terms, that it should not be punished too severely, thus incurring the violent wrath of the reactionary Crevier, who exclaimed that "la qualité du crime ne connaît point de supplice trop rigoureux".[31]

Montesquieu's confidence in what he called "la nature" – in this case, heterosexual love – is revealed in the poetic ending to Book XII, vi, the chapter on homosexuality:

Que l'on ne prépare point ce crime; qu'on le proscrive par une police exacte, comme toutes les violations des mœurs; et l'on verra soudain la nature, ou défendre ses droits, ou les reprendre. Douce, aimable, charmante, elle a répandu les plaisirs d'une main libérale; et, en nous comblant de délices, elle nous prépare, par des enfants qui nous font, pour ainsi dire, renaître, à des satisfactions plus grandes que ces délices mêmes (N. I, i, p. 259, Pl. II, pp. 437–8).

Clearly Montesquieu was by temperament incapable of understanding the predicament of those whom Rousseau calls the "chevaliers de la manchette",[32] though his sense of humanity made him deplore the harsh way in which their conduct was punished by society.

II. The Example of the Animals

In all these questions related to self-defence and marriage, it has been shown that the philosophers of natural law were just as "physical" or empirical in their approach as Montesquieu was, and conversely that the *président* was as rationalistic as they were. Natural law, in the moral sense, is, in the last analysis, an *a priori* concept, but it is not exclusively *a priori*. Grotius and Pufendorf were not, as certain scholars make out, unaware of the facts of life, and nor was St. Thomas: they all used those facts as a basis for their normative natural laws, just as Montesquieu was to do.

Shackleton rightly draws attention to the similarity between Montes-

[30] *Cf.* Crocker, *Nature and Culture*, pp. 360–1.
[31] *Observations sur le livre de l'Esprit des lois*, p. 214.
[32] *Les Confessions*, II, in *Œuvres complètes*, edited by B. Gagnebin and M. Raymond, Bibliothèque de la Pléiade, vol. I, 1962, p. 69.

quieu's version of natural law and that of Cumberland:[33] the English philosopher had shown that "toute la philosophie morale, et toute la science des lois naturelles" could originate from "des observations physiques", both of natural phenomena, and of what we should now term psychology (*Traité philosophique des lois naturelles*, i, 3, pp. 41–2). But Cumberland merely provided the clearest expression of the empiricism already essential to the philosophy of natural law; he put this empiricism into the fashionable scientific language of his day, but he did not invent it. Furthermore, in spite of what his words, just quoted, may convey to twentieth-century readers, he did not believe, any more than did Montesquieu, that these "observations" were the only element needed to form natural laws. The other element was reason or judgment:

> la raison pourquoi j'ai dit, que les lois naturelles ne sont propres qu'à l'homme, c'est que ce sont certaines propositions touchant les effets qui dépendent des actions comme de leurs causes, ou certains jugements de notre entendement [...]. Mais je ne vois rien, d'où il paraisse que les bêtes forment des propositions, surtout des propositions de cette nature (*ibid.*, v, 2, p. 212).

Cumberland thus accepted the conventional idea of a normative natural law.

Similarly, when Gravina, whom Shackleton cites as a precursor of Montesquieu,[34] distinguished between two kinds of natural law, one of the reason, one of the body (*Origines iuris civilis*, II, ii–iv, pp. 234–9), he was doing no more than repeating, in "interesting terms",[35] it is true, the doctrine of the Stoics and of Christianity, that the first law should prevail over the second if they are not in harmony.[36]

Gravina, then, only accepted with reservations the idea of a natural law common to man and the animals; the same is true of St. Thomas;[37] Grotius and Pufendorf claimed to reject the idea completely (*Dg.*, I, i, 11, vol. I, pp. 52–3; *Dn.*, II, iii, 2–3, vol. I, pp. 169–73). The Roman jurist Ulpian, on the other hand, had affirmed that

> Ius naturale est, quod natura omnia animalia docuit: nam ius istud non humani generis proprium, sed omnium animalium, quæ in terra, quæ in

[33] *M.*, p. 253.
[34] *Ibid.*, pp. 255–6.
[35] *Ibid.*, p. 256.
[36] *De finibus bonorum et malorum*, III, v–vii; in the Loeb edition, pp. 232–45; St. Paul, *Epistle to the Romans*, VII, 22–3.
[37] In *S.t.*, II, i, Q. 94, A. 2, vol. VIII, p. 44, he accepts that one kind of natural law is common to man and the animals, but he gives priority to the natural law of reason, found in man alone (*cf.* also *S.t.*, II, i, Q. I, A. 1, vol. VI, p. 2).

mari nascuntur, avium quoque commune est. Hinc descendit maris atque feminæ conjunctio, quam nos matrimonium appellamus, hinc liberorum procreatio, hinc educatio (*Digest*, I, i, 1, p. 1).

Ulpian was apparently denying that the term natural law can be applied to any moral concept. What was Montesquieu's attitude to this question, and what bearing does it have on his empiricism?

Both in the *Traité des devoirs* and in the *Esprit des lois*, Montesquieu did in fact induce natural law from the behaviour of the animals. In *Pensée* 1266 (Bkn. 615), a fragment of the *Traité*, he used the example of the animals to prove against Hobbes that the state of nature is not a state of war. Firstly, he claimed, all animals like to associate with members of their own species; secondly, animals do not usually fight with members of their own species: therefore "Hobbes veut faire faire aux hommes, ce que les lions ne font pas eux-mêmes" (N. II, pp. 344–5, Pl. I, pp. 1139–40).

In the final version of the *Esprit des lois* Montesquieu did not use the second of these two arguments, in order to establish that the state of nature would be peaceful, though he did use the first argument in order to show that man is sociable (*Lois*, I, ii, paragraph 7, N. I, i, p. 6, Pl. II, p. 236). However, in a fragment which he at one time intended to appear in Book I, ii, he said:

Les animaux (et c'est surtout chez eux qu'il faut aller chercher le droit naturel) ne font pas la guerre à ceux de leur espèce parce que, se sentant égaux, ils n'ont point le désir de s'attaquer. La paix est donc la première loi naturelle (N. III, p. 579, Pl. II, p. 996).

This passage, clearly directed against Hobbes,[38] is both a statement of and an application of the method by which natural law is induced from the behaviour of the animals. Scholars' reactions to it have varied widely. Barckhausen calls it "une théorie bien singulière", and approves its deletion by Montesquieu from the printed version.[39] Shackleton, on the other hand, sees it as further proof of Montesquieu's empiricism, and, taking a more historical attitude than Barckhausen, suggests that it is reminscent of Ulpian and Gravina.[40]

One could equally well say, though, that it is reminiscent of St. Thomas. Both these scholars seem perhaps to have missed the point:

[38] Hobbes tried to prove that the equality of primitive man, or rather, the ability of even the weakest to kill the strongest, made the state of nature into a state of war (*P.R.*, i, 3, pp. 6–7).

[39] *Montesquieu, l'Esprit des lois*, p. 23.

[40] *M.*, p. 258, n. 1.

in all probability, Montesquieu took the idea from Hobbes himself. Since the Englishman had used an animal analogy to prove his conception of human nature – the famous "homo homini lupus"[41] – and had talked about man in the state of nature as if he were merely an animal,[42] Montesquieu must have felt obliged to refute Hobbes by using the latter's own method. This is something that the School of Natural Law had not done.

Grotius was nearing the end of his life when he came to know Hobbes's theories. Consequently, his denial of them is not fully developed, and did not contain any animal analogies.[43] However, in spite of what he had said at the beginning of *De iure belli ac pacis*, he was by no means averse to using animal analogies when they happened to suit his purpose, for example in his discussion of incest, as has just been seen, or in his discussion of war (*Dg.*, I, ii, 1, vol. I, p. 68).

With Pufendorf the case is rather different, since he kept to his principles and refrained from using animal analogies: in his refutation of the Hobbesian state of nature, he did not once refer to animal behaviour (*Dn.*, II, ii, 6–10, vol. I, pp. 161–6). He did mention the "inclination dominante de tous les animaux, qui les porte invinciblement à chercher toutes les voies imaginables de se conserver" as the basis of his first right of nature (*Dn.*, II, ii, 3, vol. I, pp. 153–4). But at no time did he suggest that natural law, as distinct from natural right, should be looked for in the animals, rather than in man.

Montesquieu's position is thus fairly close to that of Grotius, and rather different to that of Pufendorf. It has been suggested by Shackleton that in making use of the example of the animals, Montesquieu was "adapting, extending and rejuvenating, within the limits of Cartesian science, the notion of Ulpian".[44] The first way of examining this claim is to see how far Cartesian philosophy may be said to favour natural law derived from animal behaviour. According to Descartes animals are mere machines, and so is man's body:[45] man is distinguished from

[41] Plautus' maxim is quoted by Hobbes in the *Dedicatory Epistle* to *De cive*, *P.R.*, p. ii; he limits its application to times of war, but for him the state of nature was a state of war.

[42] Hobbes's conception of natural man, both in *De cive* and in *Leviathan*, is of a creature ruled only by violent instincts; *cf.* in particular *Leviathan*, I, xiii, p. 113, where the life of man in the state of nature is described as "solitary, poor, nasty, brutish, and short".

[43] On the 11th April 1643, two years before his death, Grotius wrote to his brother:

> Librum *De cive* vidi, placent quæ pro regibus dicit. Fundamenta tamen quibus suas sententias superstruit, probare non possum. Putat inter homines omnes a natura esse bellum et alia quædam habet nostris non congruentia (*Epistolæ quotquot reperiri potuerunt*, Amsterdam, Blaeu, 1687, pp. 951–2).

[44] *M.*, p. 259.

[45] *Discours de la méthode*, V, pp. 45–6; *Traité de l'homme*, p. 120; *cf.* F. Bouillier, *Histoire de*

the animals only by the possession of reason (*Discours de la méthode*, I, p. 2). In one sense, therefore, it can be said that Cartesianism favours a natural law common to man's body and the animals, a purely physical natural law.

On the other hand, in denying that animals have any kind of reason, and in claiming in opposition to Montaigne, that even the cleverest of their actions are mechanistic, Descartes drew a sharp dividing line between man and the animals:[46] to believe that the animals have a soul is to support atheism (*Discours de la méthode*, V, p. 59). So it can be said that Cartesianism also favours the *a priori* view of natural law, in which the actions of man, being rational, cannot be compared with those of the animals. This was, as has been seen, Cumberland's view of natural law, and he was, by his method, a Cartesian.[47]

It is difficult to say that any one conception of natural law is inherently Cartesian: in the eighteenth century, however, the trend, as Aram Vartanian has shown,[48] was towards the first conception, where man's actions are seen as mechanistic. Now although Montesquieu has frequently been accused of being a determinist,[49] mainly because of his theory of climate, it is significant that he specifically rejected the idea that man is merely an animal or a machine. In the *Traité des devoirs*, arguing against what he saw as Spinoza's doctrine, he showed his distaste for a philosophy where "dans l'universalité de la substance, ont été, ont passé sans distinction le lion et l'insecte, Charlemagne et Chilpéric" (*P.* 1266, Bkn. 615, N. II, pp. 342–3, Pl. I, p. 1138). In Book I, i, of the *Esprit des lois* he claimed that God's existence is proved by man's intelligence, and he carefully distinguished between man and the animals. Montesquieu's use of the example of the animals in Book

la philosophie cartésienne, Delagrave, 1868, vol. I, pp. 150 and 163–6.

46 *Cf.* Bouillier, *op. cit.*, vol. I, pp. 148–9.

47 At least, he claimed to be following the *a priori* method, in his attempt to deduce natural law from the principle of benevolence (*Traité philosophique des lois naturelles*, *Disc. prél.*, iv, pp. 6–7 and i, 7, pp. 46–7).

48 *Diderot and Descartes, A Study of Scientific Naturalism in the Enlightenment*, Princeton University Press, 1953: see especially pp. 203–88.

49 Some recent exponents of M.'s determinism are: Henry Vyverberg, *Historical Pessimism in the French Enlightenment*, Harvard University Press, 1958, pp. 158–9; L. G. Crocker, *An Age of Crisis, Man and World in Eighteenth-Century French Thought*, The Johns Hopkins Press, 1959, p. 75. Convincing denials of this interpretation have been made by: C. E. Vaughan, *Studies in the History of Political Philosophy Before and After Rousseau*, Manchester University Press, 1925, vol. I, p. 271; G. Davy, 'Sur la méthode de Montesquieu', *Revue de métaphysique et de morale*, 1939, pp. 575–82; Sir Isaiah Berlin, 'Montesquieu', pp. 286–7; Roger Mercier, 'La Notion de loi morale chez Montesquieu', Proceedings of the Sixth Triennial Congress of the International Federation for Modern Languages and Literatures, Oxford, Blackwell, 1955, pp. 191–2; Aron, *op. cit.*, p. 36.

I, ii does not indicate a Cartesian or post-Cartesian influence: it is not scientific but polemic.

The second way of examining Shackleton's claim is by looking closely at the text of Book I, ii. The style of this Chapter, unlike that of Chapter i, is not flavoured with Cartesian terms, but rather with terms borrowed from the philosophy of natural law. True, the term "lois de la nature" could be Cartesian (*cf. Principes*, II, xxxvii, p. 84), but Montesquieu uses the traditional "loi naturelle" more often in this Chapter.[50] As for expressions such as "la constitution de notre être", "avant l'établissement des sociétés", "état de nature", "la conservation de son être", "égal", "la paix", etc., these are all reminiscent of the writings of the School of Natural Law, not of the writings of the Cartesians.

In Book I, ii, Montesquieu had three aims, similar to those of the School of Natural Law: to refute Hobbes, to introduce the idea of self-preservation which recurs so frequently in the rest of the work, and to provide a basis for the establishment of society. Thus in spite of its superficial empiricism, in spite of the example of the animals, introduced in order to refute Hobbes, this Chapter is not inspired by Cartesian science, but, like Book XII and Book XXVI, by the philosophy of natural law.

This is not to say, however, that Montesquieu's attitude to natural law was exclusively *a priori*. It has been shown that the concept of natural law, for both the Church and the School of Natural Law, was not incompatible with an empirical approach to certain human problems, an approach also found in Montesquieu, though to a lesser extent than is sometimes imagined.

One of the reasons why it is sometimes felt that natural law is a predominantly rationalistic philosophy is because it has been associated with the concepts of the state of nature and of the original contract. In the next chapter, Montesquieu's attitude to these and related concepts will be examined, in order to see if it reveals any departure from a belief in natural law.

50 Crocker, *Nature and Culture*, pp. 28–9, seems to overlook this fact.

CHAPTER 4

THE STATE OF NATURE AND THE ORIGIN OF SOCIETY

Until fairly recently the eighteenth century was generally regarded as over-confident with respect to human nature. Though there is undoubtedly an optimistic strain in the thought of the Enlightenment,[1] it was usually based on humanity at some future date, not in the present.[2] The *philosophes* were, it is now seen, quite realistic in their assessment of the possibilities of human nature.[3] Montesquieu in particular has benefitted from this reappraisal. Sainte-Beuve's claim that "Montesquieu accorde trop non seulement en dehors, mais en secret et dans sa propre pensée, au décorum de la nature humaine",[4] is now seen to be exaggerated. The story of the Troglodytes shows that man is good or evil more by choice than by nature; in the *Esprit des lois*, though Montesquieu's natural man was good by nature, this goodness ends as soon as society is established, when "l'état de guerre commence" (*Lois*, I, iii, N. I, i, p. 7, Pl. II, p. 236), and when men shamelessly try to dominate each other.[5]

All the same it is impossible to accept Crevier's suggestion that Montesquieu had an 'Idée basse de l'humanité' and that he was in secret agreement with Hobbes.[6] It was one of the *président*'s deepest ambitions to refute the English philosopher's idea that justice is the will of the strongest and that self-preservation is ultimately incompatible

[1] *Cf.* Lanson, 'Formation et développement de l'esprit philosophique du XVIIIe siècle', *Revue hebdomadaire des cours et conférences*, 1908–10, vol. XVII, ii, 1909, pp. 657–66, 713–20, 796–804, 843–57; Roger Mercier, *La Réhabilitation de la nature humaine* (*1700–1750*), Villemonble, La Balance, 1960.

[2] See Vyverberg, *op. cit.*, Chs. 9 and 10.

[3] *Ibid.*, Chs. 11 and 18–22; also Crocker, *An Age of Crisis*, Chs. 7–12, and pp. 454–5.

[4] *Causeries du lundi*, Garnier, 3rd. ed., [*s.d.*], vol. VII, p. 68.

[5] Eg.: "tout homme qui a du pouvoir est porté à en abuser", *Lois*, XI, iv, N. I, i, p. 206, Pl. II, p. 395.

[6] *Observations sur le livre de l'Esprit des lois*, p. 156.

with the well-being and even the existence of others. To argue against Hobbes involved making certain assumptions about the nature of man, and these assumptions Montesquieu presented, just as the School of Natural Law had done, in two ways: either by discussing human nature and its laws in general terms, or by projecting it into a state of nature where it could be studied without the various changes that society may have brought about. These two methods are found both in the *Lettres persanes* and in the *Traité des devoirs*, which is inspired throughout by the philosophy of natural law, and before examining Montesquieu's attitude to the state of nature, it is instructive to see how he dealt with the more general question of human nature in its relation with morality.

In the famous *Lettre persane* LXXXIII, having shown that justice is "un rapport de convenance, qui se trouve réellement entre deux choses", and hence that it does not depend on convention, Usbek continued by asserting that men's interests often lead them to ignore these "rapports", but that "nul n'est mauvais gratuitement". Drawing a picture of mankind resembling that of Hobbes, he nevertheless introduced a more optimistic element:

> Nous sommes entourés d'hommes plus forts que nous; ils peuvent nous nuire de mille manières différentes; les trois quarts du temps, ils peuvent le faire impunément: Quel repos pour nous, de savoir qu'il y a, dans le cœur de tous ces hommes, un principe intérieur qui combat en notre faveur, et qui nous met à couvert de leurs entreprises? (N. I, iii, pp. 169–70, Pl. I, pp. 256–7).

Whether it is innate or acquired, this "principe" indicates a fundamentally anti-Hobbesian attitude to the question of human nature.[7]

The same attitude is revealed in the *Traité des devoirs*, where Montesquieu again hoped that men have "un principe intérieur" to prevent them from behaving anti-socially (*P.* 1266, Bkn. 615, N. II, p. 344, Pl. I, p. 1139). His statement that

[7] Certain critics see in this passage an indication that M. believed in innate ideas (for example Caillois, Pl. I, p. 1666). The logic of Letter LXXXIII leaves much to be desired, since this "principe intérieur" is not hinted at in the previous paragraphs, where Usbek had shown only that men are not gratuitously evil. It is doubtful whether M. was seriously referring to an innate idea, in view of his attitude elsewhere. *P.* 1187 (Bkn. 2064), written in the years 1734–8, is a summary of the sensualist theory of perception, and in *Lois*, I, ii, M. seems to have denied the existence of innate ideas, when he stated that "L'homme, dans l'état de nature, aurait plutôt la faculté de connaître, qu'il n'aurait des connaissances" (N. I, i, p. 5, Pl. II, p. 235). But even if M. did not believe in innate ideas, this does not prove that he did not believe in natural law; although St. Thomas saw a necessary connection between the two (*S.t.*, II, i, Q.63, A. 1, vol. VII, p. 157), philosophers in the late 17th and early 18th centuries did not: Locke denied the existence of innate ideas but still believed in natural law, and Barbeyrac was at pains to show that Locke's refutation of the former in no way damaged the latter (*Dn.*, Preface, iv, vol. I, pp. xxxi–xxxiv).

Les actions humaines sont le sujet des devoirs. C'est la raison qui en est le principe, et qui nous rend propres à nous en acquitter. Ce serait abaisser cette raison que de dire qu'elle ne nous a été donnée que pour la conservation de notre être (*P.* 220, Bkn. 597, N. II, p. 93, Pl. I, p. 1126),

is very similar to the arguments of the School of Natural Law. Pufendorf, refuting Hobbes's conception of human nature, had said:

il ne s'agit point ici de l'état d'un animal qui ne se conduise que par un mouvement aveugle [...]; mais d'un animal dont la partie principale [...], c'est la raison (*Dn.*, II, ii, 9, vol. I, p. 165).

It has already been shown by Shackleton that not only the concept but the very structure of the *Traité des devoirs* is closely based on the work of certain philosophers of natural law.[8] What has not been done is to show in detail how Montesquieu's opposition to Hobbes, and in particular his examination of the question of self-preservation, led him, both in the *Traité* and in his other works, to explore the notion of the state of nature and of the origin of society.

I. Montesquieu and the State of Nature

The particular theory of the state of nature that originated in the Middle Ages under the influence of travellers' accounts of primitive peoples in America appears to bear only a superficial resemblance to the myth so prevalent in Antiquity of a Golden Age when peace and justice reigned.[9] When it was discussed by members of the School of Natural Law, the state of nature was not generally characterized by nostalgia for a carefree primitive existence: Hobbes had temporarily destroyed such feelings. For Hobbes and for the School of Natural Law, the state of nature was a semi-scientific concept, though such a term may seem surprising to those who regard it simply as an unhistorical phantasy, and refuse to see that it has an important place in the history of ideas. In using the state of nature, the aim of such philosophers as Hobbes, Pufendorf and Locke, was not to write history but to examine human nature, in order to give a realistic foundation to certain moral

[8] See 'La Genèse de l'*Esprit des lois*', *RHLF*, 1952, p. 435, and *M.*, pp. 71–3, where Shackleton demonstrates the close affinities between the plan of the *Traité* and the work of Pufendorf and Clarke. The other source of the *Traité* is Stoic philosophy: *cf.* Barrière, *Un Grand provincial*, pp. 252–3, and a letter written by M. in 1750, N. III, pp. 1327–8.

[9] *Cf.* Esmein, *op. cit.*, vol. I, p. 279, also J. Bryce, *Studies in History and Jurisprudence*, Oxford University Press, 1901, vol. II, p. 598, and W. A. Robson, *Civilisation and the Growth of Law*, Macmillan, 1935, pp. 258–9. The essential work on the Golden Age and the state of nature is: A. O. Lovejoy, G. Chinard, G. Boas, and R. S. Crane, *A Documentary History of Primitivism and Related Ideas*, vol. I, by Lovejoy and Boas, *Primitivism and Related Ideas in Antiquity*, Baltimore, Johns Hopkins Press, 1935.

and political theories. What they all wanted to know was whether human nature (or man in the state of nature) is or should be essentially altruistic or selfish.

Hobbes had no doubt about the answer. He believed that a man's natural right, in the state of nature, is to preserve his own life by any means, and specifically by those which appear to him to be the most expedient. Since men in the state of nature are all equal, in that they can all kill each other either by force or stealth, since they have a "mutual will of hurting" each other, since they are vain, and since, finally, they all desire things which are in short supply, it follows that

> the natural state of men, before they entered into society, was a mere war, and that not simply, but a war of all men against all men.[10]

Reason may dictate to natural man that 'The right of all to all is unprofitable', but any individual attempts to establish peace are vitiated by the fact that no agreements can be enforced in the state of nature. Hobbes's conclusion is that only government of an absolute kind is capable of preserving peace and of ending the anarchy of the state of nature.[11]

It may have been the political consequences of Hobbes's theory that Montesquieu disliked most, but there can be no doubt that he was also appalled by the Englishman's premise that human nature is essentially amoral. The story of the Troglodytes, as told by Usbek, was one of his first contributions to the controversy.[12] Hobbes's very method perhaps suggested to Montesquieu that in his refutation he should look at men in a primitive state, but his own inclination also led him the same way:

> Ce qui me charme dans les premiers temps, c'est une certaine simplicité de mœurs, une naïveté de la nature, que je ne trouve que là, et qui n'est plus à présent dans le monde [...] chez aucun peuple policé.
>
> J'aime à voir dans l'homme lui-même des vertus qu'une certaine éducation ou religion n'ont point inspirées; des vices que la mollesse et le luxe n'ont point faits (*P.* 1607, Bkn. 589, N. II, p. 460, Pl. I, p. 1081).

[10] This account of Hobbes's state of nature is based on *De cive*, which was one of his best-known works. M. possessed it both in Latin (D. 1473) and in Sorbière's famous translation (D. 2394). See *P.R.*, i, 3–12, pp. 6–11. Spinoza's conception of man's natural right was very similar to that of Hobbes: see the *Tractatus theologico-politicus*, xvi, pp. 880–1.

[11] *P.R.*, i, 11, p. 11; ii, 11, p. 21; vi, 4–20, pp. 75–92.

[12] See A. Crisafulli, 'Montesquieu's Story of the Troglodytes: its Background, Meaning, and Significance', *Publications of the Modern Language Association of America*, 1943, pp. 372–92, (also 'Parallels to Ideas in the *Lettres persanes*', in *ibid.*, 1937, pp. 773–77); P. Dimoff, 'Cicéron, Hobbes et Montesquieu', *Annales universitatis savariensis*, 1952, pp. 19–47.

To go back in time in order to discover more about human nature was no new exercise, and in doing so, Montesquieu was led to draw on certain literary and philosophical traditions. The sobriety, virtue and simplicity of the virtuous Troglodytes remind us of the inhabitants of Salente in Fénelon's *Télémaque*.[13] The story would also appear to owe something to the travel literature of the seventeenth and eighteenth centuries, as Crisafulli has suggested,[14] but above all it recalls the work of various writers in Antiquity, a fact that has not received so much critical recognition.[15] The wicked Troglodytes resemble the men of Hesiod's Age of Iron, when might, not right ruled the earth.[16] The moral behind the story of the Troglodytes is not dissimilar to that of the myth of Protagoras, as told by Plato: primitive men lived in societies but, as they did not practise justice, they dispersed or perished; then Zeus, fearing that the human race would die out, gave men law and justice.[17] Again, the virtuous Troglodytes are like the primitive pastoral people whom Plato described in Book III of the *Laws*: descended from a few shepherds who had survived a flood, they lived in peace, since food was abundant; they practised justice, but had no need of written laws since they lived under a patriarchal régime.[18]

The story of the Troglodytes also bears a resemblance to the Epicurean accounts of primitive man: the absence of justice, of law, and of concern for the common good characterized, according to Lucretius, the existence of the first men; later, he continued, men agreed to practise justice, and appointed kings, but, as happened in the case of the Troglodytes, the kings were slain through greed and ambition; finally magistrates were appointed in order to secure peace.[19] Since the theory that justice is based on a convention, put forward in Plato's *Republic* by Glaucon,[20] and accepted by the Epicureans, was similar to that later adopted by Hobbes, it is not surprising that the story of

[13] *Télémaque*, x and xvii, in *Œuvres de Fénelon*, Didot, 1857, vol. III, pp. 71–7 and 130–2; *cf.* A. Cherel, 'Fénelon et Montesquieu' in *Fénelon au XVIIIe siècle en France (1715–1820), son prestige, son influence*, Hachette, 1917, pp. 322–6, and 'Le Président de Montesquieu' in *De Télémaque à Candide*, Del Duca, 1958, pp. 263–95.

[14] 'Montesquieu's Story of the Troglodytes', p. 377.

[15] Apart from Crisafulli, 'Montesquieu's Story of the Troglodytes', pp. 375–6, and Dimoff, 'Cicéron, Hobbes et Montesquieu', *loc. cit.*

[16] *Works and Days*, ll. 174–201; in the Loeb edition, *The Homeric Hymns and Homerica*, pp. 14–17.

[17] *Protagoras*, 322 a-d; in the Loeb edition, *Laches, Protagoras, Meno, Euthydemus*, pp. 133–5. On M. and Plato, see J. Flach, 'Platon et Montesquieu, théoriciens politiques', *Revue politique et littéraire (Revue bleue)*, 1909, pp. 3–7 and 36–42.

[18] III, 677a–680b, vol. I, pp. 167–77.

[19] *De rerum natura*, V, ll. 925–1160; in the Loeb edition, pp. 406–23.

[20] II, 358e–359a; in the Loeb edition, vol. I, pp. 113–115.

the Troglodytes, written primarily against Hobbes, should remind us of these accounts of the origins of mankind.

Destutt de Tracy once commented that Montesquieu "a souvent le tort, comme Tacite, de beaucoup trop respecter les peuples barbares et leurs institutions".[21] It is certainly true that Montesquieu admired Tacitus,[22] and he may have remembered the *Germania* when writing about the virtuous Troglodytes, who are like the tribe that the Latin author described in Book XXXV: just, peaceful and without ambition, they never start a war; but when it comes to defending themselves against aggressors, they are hardy warriors.[23] The virtuous Troglodytes, peaceful as they were, had to undertake a war in self-defence, and were very successful in repulsing their enemies (*L.p.* XIII, N. I, iii, pp. 34–5, Pl. I, pp. 151–2).

Even if it is generally true that the seventeenth- and eighteenth-century conception of the state of nature has little in common with such stories and myths from Antiquity, in the story of the Troglodytes, at least, Montesquieu has blended both modern and ancient conceptions. From the point of view of the School of Natural Law, the Troglodytes are partly in a state of nature. Though the wicked Troglodytes are in a sense a nation, in that they live together in a certain territory, they cannot be said to form a society, since they kill their leaders and obey no-one. Sergio Cotta, who holds that they are not in a state of nature, makes it appear that they *have* a despotic ruler;[24] in fact, in the main part of the story, they are without a ruler: "Tous les particuliers", we are told early in the story, "convinrent qu'ils n'obéiraient plus à personne" (*L.p.* XI, N. I, iii, p. 27, Pl. I, p. 146). The act of agreement usually associated with the beginning of society, here marks its end, and the wicked Troglodytes no longer have any corporate existence, as the rest of the story shows. They are in a Hobbesian state of nature. According to Hobbes, the state of nature never existed in its full form "over all the world"; nevertheless,

> it may be perceived what manner of life there would be, were there no common power to fear, by the manner of life, which men that have formerly lived under a peaceful government, use to degenerate into, in a civil war (*Leviathan*, I, xiii, pp. 114–5).

[21] *Commentaire sur l'Esprit des lois*, p.77.

[22] For M.'s references to Tacitus, see Weil, 'Les lectures de Montesquieu', p. 512.

[23] In the Loeb edition *Dialogus, Agricola, Germania*, pp. 312–3.

[24] *Montesquieu e la scienza della società*, p. 147:" I Trogloditi [. . .] non vivono allo stato di natura, sono un populo già costituo in ordine consorzio, non solo, ma hanno un re [. . .]"; *cf.* G. Chinard, 'Montesquieu's Historical Pessimism', *Studies in the History of Culture*, Menasha, Banta, 1942, p. 164.

These words, written by Hobbes as an ironic comment on England in the 1640's, neatly sum up the condition of the Troglodytes, and it could well be that Montesquieu was thinking of this very passage when he wrote the story.

The virtuous Troglodytes are not, in the same way, in a state of nature.[25] It is true that they have no written law, and no rulers, since they live under a patriarchal régime, but they do form a community and are intensely aware of their corporate existence: "Le peuple troglodyte se regardait comme une seule famille" (*L.p.* XII, N. I, iii, p. 33, Pl. I, p. 150). Though Pufendorf admitted the existence of families in the state of nature, he held that each family would be separate from the others (*Dv.*, II, i, 6, p. 250). The virtuous Troglodytes are thus only in a state of nature in that they are ruled by *mœurs* not by laws.

Montesquieu set about refuting Hobbes's idea of the state of nature by showing what an unhappy kind of existence it would lead to. The wicked Troglodytes behave with complete selfishness, having agreed that "chacun veillerait uniquement à ses intérêts, sans consulter ceux des autres" (*L.p.* XI, N. I, iii, p. 27, Pl. I, p. 146). Usbek gives examples of this selfish conduct. Each Troglodyte refuses to grow more grain than appears necessary for himself; in consequence he does not grow even enough to tide himself over a lean year, and as the others do not care to help him, he starves. There are no laws, and no-one is willing to act as an arbitrator in disputes; pacts that are made do not last, and end in violence; cunning meets cunning in commercial dealings. Finally, the Troglodytes will not pay the doctor who cured them of the plague, so when the epidemic returns, he refuses to treat them, and they perish (*L.p.* XI, N. I, iii, pp. 27–30, Pl. I, pp. 146–8). The moral of each of Usbek's examples is that these selfish acts result not in a gain but a loss. He is demonstrating that Hobbes's notion of self-preservation, the liberty that each man has to act entirely as he pleases, does not in fact procure self-preservation, but self-destruction.[26]

Hobbes himself was of course aware of the unsatisfactoriness of the

[25] But *cf.* Crisafulli, 'Montesquieu's Story of the Troglodytes', p. 390.

[26] According to Dimoff, 'Cicéron, Hobbes et Montesquieu', pp. 29–32, each of the incidents recounted by Usbek was written with a particular part of Hobbes's doctrine in mind. Thus the story of the famine shows that Hobbes's conception of liberty (*Leviathan*, I, xiv, pp. 116–8) will not do; the story of the man who refuses to be an arbitrator refutes Hobbes's idea that arbitrators might be appointed in the state of nature (*ibid.*, I, xv, p. 143); the story of the two men who unite to dispossess a third of his land, and then quarrel, shows the fragility of Hobbes's pact (*ibid.*, I, xiv, pp. 124–5). Cotta, *Montesquieu e la scienza della società*, p. 147, claims that such a refutation was unnecessary, since Hobbes himself knew the fragility of all these laws of nature. Even so, Dimoff's argument is convincing.

rights and laws of the state of nature,[27] and it is not so much the premises of Hobbes and Montesquieu that differ, as their conclusions. Hobbes's answer to the unsatisfactoriness was the establishment of absolute government. Montesquieu's answer is more optimistic: absolute government is of no use in keeping the wicked in check, for they will simply kill their rulers, as the Troglodytes did. The only answer is that men must learn to practise justice, if they are to live in any kind of society, even if, as the later letters show, a society based only on *mœurs* will eventually degenerate.[28]

The virtuous Troglodytes in fact exemplify the conventional, dull doctrine of enlightened self-preservation as put forward by the School of Natural Law in opposition to Hobbes. *Do as you would be done by* is the basic rule of that doctrine. The virtuous Troglodytes taught their children

> que l'intérêt des particuliers se trouve toujours dans l'intérêt commun; que vouloir s'en séparer, c'est vouloir se perdre; que la vertu n'est point une chose qui doive nous coûter; [...] et que la justice pour autrui est une charité pour nous (*L.p.* XII, N. I, iii, p. 31, Pl. I, p. 149).

Behind these phrases we find the same allusions to self-interest and utility that we find in Pufendorf:

> Le but de la sociabilité est [...] que par un commerce de secours et de services chacun puisse mieux pourvoir à ses propres intérêts (*Dn.*, II, iii, 18, vol. I, p. 201).

Indeed, the story of the Troglodytes, or at least its moral, might be summed up in the words of the German philosopher:

> une licence sans bornes ne pouvant jamais passer dans l'esprit d'une personne raisonnable pour un moyen propre à nous conserver longtemps, on ne saurait absolument supposer que la nature l'ait accordée à qui que ce soit (*Dn.*, II, ii, 3, vol. I, p. 154).

Montesquieu's obvious superiority over a writer such as Pufendorf is that by drawing on a classical tradition, and on his own talent as a storyteller and a moralist, he illustrated this dull theory in a fable that can be read and enjoyed for its own sake, without any knowledge of Hobbes or the state of nature. But it can also be appreciated on a more historical level, by those who wish to see its background. It is at once universal in its appeal and relevant to the times in which it was written

[27] *P.R.*, i, 11–13, pp. 11–13, and v, 1–9, pp. 63–9.

[28] *L.p.* XIV, N. I, iii, pp. 35–6, Pl. I, pp. 152–3; and the unpublished continuation of the story, *P.* 1616, Bkn. 120, N. II, pp. 463–5, Pl. I, pp. 377–9.

– it is a work of art, where Pufendorf produced only words and ideas.

In his later contributions to the self-preservation controversy, Montesquieu abandoned the allegory and concentrated on logic and analogy, but he still referred to the state of nature. In the *Traité des devoirs* he argued against Hobbes's conception of that state by saying that "il est faux que la défense entraîne nécessairement la nécessité d'attaquer" (*P.* 1266, Bkn. 615, N. II, p. 344, Pl. II, p. 1139). Logical as this statement is, it does not answer the English philosopher, who had not claimed that man in the state of nature was obliged to attack others in order to defend himself, only that it would be difficult to stop him if he wished to do so. In addition, Hobbes had denied that the state of war is always a state of open hostility: it is simply a state of mistrust, where there is an ever-present possibility of violence, just as, to use his quaint analogy, the nature of foul weather is not just a shower of rain, but a general disposition to rain, continuing for some days (*Leviathan*, I, xiii, p. 113). In refuting Hobbes, Montesquieu had slightly distorted his doctrines.

His misunderstanding is probably a result of his having taken Hobbes too literally. For Hobbes, the *state of nature* simply meant human nature if it is not held in check by laws. In his refutation of Hobbes in the *Esprit des lois*, Montesquieu did not so much talk about human nature in general, as about primitive man, which is not really what the Englishman had in mind, even though he had suggested that savages are partly in a state of nature (*Leviathan*, I, xiii, p. 114). The *président* showed that Hobbes's idea of the state of nature is too rationalistic, because it attributes to men certain abstract ideas, such as that of domination, which they would not have had in a state of nature. Hobbes might have answered that men do not always fight in order to dominate each other; that they sometimes fight merely because it is in their nature to do so, because they have 'the will of mischieving each other' (*P.R.*, i, 4, p. 7); and that Montesquieu is equally guilty of being rationalistic, in that he ignores man's aggressive instincts.

This rationalism is also revealed in Montesquieu's criticism of a famous passage in the *Leviathan* where Hobbes had proved that men in the state of nature would be at war by arguing that even in society they distrust each other, as is shown by the fact that they carry arms and lock their houses (*Leviathan*, I, xiii, p. 114; also *P.R.*, Preface, p. xv). Montesquieu claimed that it is wrong to make inferences about the state of nature, from man's behaviour in society. He does not seem to have realized this is exactly what he himself was doing in his first natural law, of peace.[29]

Another rather unsatisfactory feature of Montesquieu's account of the state of nature is that he failed to discuss the important question of competition. True, in the *Lettres persanes*, Usbek had shown that the virtuous Troglodytes, working for the common good, did not have to compete for food since "la terre semblait produire d'elle-même, cultivée par ces vertueuses mains" (*L.p.* XII, N. I, iii, p. 31, Pl. I, p. 149). But the virtuous Troglodytes are not in a state of nature, and in any case, they are too good to be true. Again, in *Pensée* 1747 (Bkn. 366), Montesquieu stated hopefully that

> Les bêtes, qui ont toutes des intérêts séparés, s'entre-nuisent toujours. Les hommes seuls, faits pour vivre en société, ne perdent rien de ce qu'ils partagent (N. II, p. 523, Pl. II, p. 1094).

This vague statement does not start to answer the question of how far self-preservation can be reconciled with social behaviour.

As we have seen, Montesquieu criticized Hobbes's notion that men in the state of nature would wish to dominate each other. But according to Hobbes, the wish for domination was only one among many causes of the state of war. Another important cause was competition (*P.R.*, i, 6, p. 8). Pufendorf, arguing against Hobbes on this point, claimed that men in the state of nature would be too far apart to be able to harm others or their property (*Dn.*, II, ii, 8, vol. I, p. 163). Similarly, Rousseau was later to show that the earth in primitive times was very fertile, and that primitive man had very few wants; that for various reasons there would be little sexual competition; and finally that there were so few men, that they would rarely meet (*Discours sur l'inégalité*, I, pp. 143, 148, 165, 199, and 203). Montesquieu did not discuss any of these solutions. One is tempted to think that his account of the state of nature would have been not more orthodox, perhaps, but more realistic and convincing, had he made mention of the fall of man. In this particular instance, Sainte-Beuve's criticism of Montesquieu's optimism is justified.

For the realists Hobbes and Spinoza, man's natural right in the state of nature is to perform any act leading to self-preservation. Montesquieu did not discuss this conception, but his attitude can be inferred from Book I, ii of the *Esprit des lois*. According to Shackleton, he aban-

29 *Cf.* Ehrard, *L'Idée de nature*, vol. II, pp. 472–3.

doned the identification of *ius naturale* and *lex naturalis* that had been made by Grotius.[30] The natural laws of Book I, ii are supposedly primitive man's impulses. It has just been seen that Montesquieu was apparently not aware of the possibility of conflict between what man in the state of nature requires (i.e. *ius*) and what he owes to others (i.e. *lex*).[31] Thus, far from abandoning the identification of *ius* and *lex* Montesquieu retained it. The difference between Montesquieu and Grotius on this point is that Grotius claimed to identify *ius* and *lex* under the heading of reason, whereas Montesquieu wished to identify them under the heading of instinct. So had Spinoza, but his rights and laws were entirely selfish, whereas Montesquieu's were not.[32]

The *président* was very proud of his attempts at counteracting the poison of Hobbes and Spinoza. This pride can be seen both in the *Défense de l'Esprit des lois* (N. I, ii, pp. 436–7, Pl. II, pp. 1122–3), and in a letter he wrote in 1750:

> Tout le monde convient en Angleterre que personne n'a plus ni mieux combattu Hobbes que moi et Spinoza aussi (N. III, p. 1328).

Certainly, Montesquieu's opposition to these two philosophers was consistent: the "plus" is perhaps justified. But the "mieux"? It is true that in his refutation of them in the *Esprit des lois*, Montesquieu seemed to be innovating (or rather returning to an older tradition) in that he fought Hobbes with his own weapons, namely instinct and animal analogy. But it cannot be said that his refutation is very satisfactory. By using animal analogy, he sidestepped the real issue of how far, within the limits of human nature, self-preservation is compatible with altruism. Pufendorf, with all his dullness and narrowness, realized that the only way to fight Hobbes's arguments was on moral grounds, not on "scientific" ones. Book I, ii of the *Esprit des lois* is not a significant contribution to the history of ideas, whereas the story of the Troglodytes, which deals with the same problem precisely from a moral point of view, is a contribution to literature.

[30] 'Montesquieu in 1948', pp. 312–3; *cf.* Grotius, *Dg.*, I, i, 9, vol. I, pp. 46–7.

[31] For the meaning of these terms, and for a view opposed to that of Grotius and Montesquieu, *cf.* Hobbes:

> The names *lex* and *ius*, that is to say, law and right, are often confounded, and yet scarce are there any two words of more contrary signification. For right is that liberty which law leaveth us, and laws those restraints by which we agree mutually to abridge one another's liberty (*Tripos*: *De corpore politico*, II, x, 5, p. 222).

[32] *Cf. Tractatus theologico-politicus*, xvi, pp. 880–1, and in particular the phrase "droit ou loi d'institution naturelle", in the Latin: "ius et institutum naturæ" (*Benedicti de Spinoza opera*, The Hague, Nijhoff, 1895, vol. II, p. 121).

In order to refute Hobbes, Montesquieu was compelled to make use of the concept of the state of nature. The positivists and their followers, in an attempt to justify what they would otherwise be forced to regard as a surrender to idealism and woolly thinking, claim that the *président* had a completely new approach to the concept of the state of nature and to the problem of the origin of society.

II. The Origin of Society

Only in fairly recent times has it become fashionable to hold that society never had a beginning. In Antiquity philosophers had no qualms about discussing the question. There are two points of view, one based on instinct, the other on utility. In the *Republic* of Plato, Socrates says that society was started because "we do not severally suffice for our own needs".[33] This idea is similar to that of the Sophists[34] and the Epicureans.[35] Aristotle, on the other hand, held that society started with the family or household; several households grouped together form a village; finally, a union of several villages produces a city state, which can thus be said to exist "by nature".[36] Though both instinct and utility played a part in forming society, instinct was more important than utility:

> man is by nature a political animal; and so even when men have no need of assistance from each other they none the less desire to live together. At the same time they are also brought together by common interest, so far as each achieves a share of the good life.[37]

The Stoics, like the Peripatetics, emphasized that society originated with the family, and they linked such an origin with the doctrine of the universal brotherhood of mankind.[38] The issue became more complex in the seventeenth and eighteenth centuries with the growth of the theory of the original contract, and it was probably in reaction against contractualists – Grotius, Pufendorf, Hobbes and Locke in particular – that Montesquieu wrote *Lettre persane* XCIV.

In this letter, Usbek appears to cut through all the speculation about the origin of society with the knife of common sense:

> Je n'ai jamais ouï parler du droit public, qu'on n'ait commencé par rechercher soigneusement quelle est l'origine des sociétés; ce qui me paraît

[33] *Republic*, II, xi, 369b, vol. I, p. 149.
[34] *Cf. ibid.*, II, ii, 358e–359a, vol. II, pp. 113–115.
[35] *Cf.* Lucretius, *De rerum natura*, V, ll. 1019–29, p. 413.
[36] *Politics*, I, i, 6–9; in the Loeb edition, pp. 7–9.
[37] *Politics*, III, iv, 2–3, p. 201.
[38] *Cf. De finibus*, II, xiv, p. 133 and III, xix, p. 281–3.

ridicule. Si les hommes n'en formaient point, s'ils se quittaient et se fuyaient les uns les autres, il faudrait en demander la raison [...]: mais ils naissent tous liés les uns aux autres; un fils est né auprès de son père, et il s'y tient: voilà la société, et la cause de la société (N. I, iii, p. 187, Pl. I, p. 269).

As Crisafulli has pointed out, there is a very similar scornful passage in the Earl of Shaftesbury's *Essay on the Freedom of Wit and Humour*:[39]

> How the wit of man should so puzzle this cause, as to make civil government and society appear a kind of invention, and creature of art, I know not.[40]

But Shaftesbury, like Usbek, was merely repeating in witty fashion the Peripatetic or Stoic theory that the family is the first social group and the basis of larger communities.[41] The scorn of both the Englishman and the Persian can be attributed to a lack of understanding of the political science of their day. One might even tentatively suggest that these two conservative-minded philosophers liked to ridicule everything connected with a theory that threatened their beliefs – though it will be seen that Montesquieu himself was not opposed to the social contract.

Letter XCIV is based on an equivocation with the word *société*. It is true that certain theorists used the state of nature and the social contract to show the *political* foundations of a good *civil* society, but they did not necessarily use them to show how or why men are united in groups rather than living separately. Like Usbek, many commentators fail to make this all-important distinction between informal society and political society, and consequently manage to make certain theorists look very silly.[42]

It is necessary to make this distinction in the case of Grotius, for example. Though he believed in the contractual origin of certain societies (*Dg.*, I, iii, 13–17, vol. I, pp. 141–51), he nevertheless admitted, just as Aristotle had done, that "une [des] choses propres à l'homme, est le désir de la société" (*Dg.*, *Disc. prél.*, vi, vol. I, pp. 4–5), that man has "un désir exquis de société" (*ibid.*, vii, p. 7), and that "la nature humaine [...] nous porterait à rechercher le commerce de nos semblables, quand même nous n'aurions besoin de rien" (*ibid.*, xvii, p. 12). If the distinction between political society and informal

39 'Parallels to Ideas in the *Lettres persanes*', pp. 775–6.

40 In *Characteristicks of Men, Manners, Opinions, Times* [1711], 1727, vol. I, p. 111.

41 *Ibid.*, p. 110: by growing family links, "a clan or tribe is gradually formed; a public is recognized".

42 Eg. Althusser, *op. cit.*, pp. 15–16.

society is borne in mind, then there is no contradiction in Grotius's thought.

In the case of Hobbes and Pufendorf, Usbek's criticism is more justified. For Hobbes, society is definitely formed by art, not by nature, since he did not believe that man is naturally sociable (*P.R.*, i, 2, pp. 2–6). The same is true of Pufendorf, who denied that family relationships are sufficient to explain the origin of society, even of informal society (*Dn.*, VII, i, 4–5, vol. II, pp. 215–8). But he did admit that the family existed in the state of nature, for that state can be defined as the time when

> une personne étant unie avec quelques autres par une société particulière, n'a rien de commun avec tout le reste des hommes que la qualité de créature humaine [...]. C'est sur ce pied-là que vivaient autrefois les familles séparées et indépendantes les unes des autres (*Dv.*, II, i, 6, p. 250).

Pufendorf seems to have been caught in a dilemma: on both logical and religious grounds, he had to admit that the family had existed almost from the time the human race began; yet in order to give the contract some semblance of reality, and perhaps because of the influence of Hobbes, he minimized the importance of the family in the state of nature.

No such contradiction is to be found in Locke. Marriage is natural for, in the state of nature, "The first society was between man and wife", but this society nevertheless "came short of political society" (*T.T.*, II, vii, 77, p. 337), which was not formed until men agreed to surrender their natural liberty into the hands of the community (*ibid.*, 87, pp. 341–2). A similar view is to be found in Gravina – for him also informal society started with the family, but political society was begun because it was feared that anarchy would result if men were left to their own devices (*Origines iuris civilis*, II, x, pp. 245–6 and II, xvii, p. 256).

Thus in Letter XCIV, Usbek misunderstood, or pretended to misunderstand, the nature and purpose of the theory of the contract: Grotius, Locke and Gravina, at least, admitted the same instinctive origin of society that the Persian believed in.

One has the impression, from reading certain scholars, that Letter XCIV is the only place in Montesquieu's works where he discussed the origin of society. Vaughan, for instance, in his discussion of Montesquieu's conception of society in the *Esprit des lois*, does not mention Book I, Chapters ii and iii; instead, he quotes from Letter

XCIV.[43] This peculiar attitude to chronology is all the more inexcusable in view of the fact that the letter does not even give a complete picture of Montesquieu's outlook in the 1720's. Admittedly, Letter CIV, where societies both formal and informal are said to have originated at once from family feelings ("l'amour") and from utility ("les bienfaits"), is rather obscure, and recounts a second-hand opinion (N. I, iii, pp. 206–7, Pl. I, p. 284). But the account of the origin of society in the story of the Troglodytes has neither of these disadvantages.

When the wicked Troglodytes, who had been in a Hobbesian state of nature, perished "par leur méchanceté même", there remained only two families, who practised justice. All the virtuous Troglodytes seem to have descended from these two families, and their society may therefore be said to have begun with the family (*L.p.* XII, N. I, iii, pp. 30–1, Pl. I, pp. 148–9). However, Usbek then goes on to show the origin of a formally constituted society. It was decided to choose a king because, as Usbek puts it, "le peuple grossissait tous les jours"; it is clear from the king's reproaches that the Troglodytes were tiring of their virtue, which involved too much personal effort (*L.p.* XIV, N. I, iii, pp. 35–6, Pl. I, pp. 152–3). Thus, in the story of the Troglodytes, Montesquieu shows that communities start with the family but that political societies start for reasons of utility.

If it is difficult to reconcile Letter XCIV with the story of the Troglodytes, it is also difficult to reconcile it with the *Traité des devoirs*, written only a few years later. The instinctive origin of society was there emphasized by Montesquieu:

> Le premier et le seul ne craint personne. Cet homme seul, qui trouverait une femme seule aussi, ne lui ferait point la guerre. Tous les autres naîtraient dans une famille, et bientôt dans une société (*P.* 1266, Bkn. 615, N. II, p. 344, Pl. I, p. 1139).

But this "société" is not the same as civil society, since the latter had to be constituted by a formal agreement:

> Les familles se sont divisées; les pères étant morts ont laissé les collatéraux indépendants. Il a fallu s'unir par des conventions et faire, par le moyen des lois civiles, ce que le droit naturel avait fait d'abord (*P.* 1267, Bkn. 616, N. II, p. 346, Pl. I, p. 1141).

It is quite clear from this passage that Montesquieu was well aware that political society did not originate with the family. Similarly,

43 *Studies in the History of Political Philosophy*, vol. I, pp. 258–9.

Pufendorf had argued that to imagine that society is entirely the result of instinct is as sensible as saying that a ship is "fait par une suite naturelle de choses" because wood comes from trees (*Dn.*, VII, i, 5, vol. II, p. 217).

In the *Esprit des lois,* Montesquieu's analysis of the causes of society is by no means as clear as in the *Traité.* Instinctive causes predominate, but they are a result of similarity of situation or of species, rather than of family feelings: men in the state of nature would be frightened of each other, but "les marques d'une crainte réciproque les engageraient bientôt à s'approcher"; secondly, they would be encouraged in this sociable behaviour by "le plaisir qu'un animal sent à l'approche d'un animal de son espèce" (*Lois*, I, ii, N. I, i, p. 6, Pl. II, p. 236). Montesquieu had already used this argument in the *Traité* (*P.* 1266, Bkn. 615, N. II, p. 344, Pl. I, pp. 1139–40). Thirdly, sexual attraction would give added stimulus to the sociability already caused by the fact of belonging to the same species (N. I, i, p. 6, Pl. II, p. 236); this is the nearest Montesquieu came, in the *Esprit des lois,* to saying that society originated with the family.

The fourth secular natural law, which specifically relates to the origin of society, is said to be based on "le sentiment" – presumably the three instincts just mentioned – and on "des connaissances" which men gradually acquire (N. I, i, p. 6, Pl. II, p. 236). Montesquieu did not explain what he meant by "des connaissances". Did he mean that men are able to tell that the state of nature does not offer all that they need? Or was he thinking of the building up of knowledge in the minds of successive generations, gradually forming a culture and hence a society?[44] In either case, these "connaissances" are a rational cause, "que les autres animaux n'ont pas", and they reveal a further implicit denial of Usbek's oversimplified view. It is clear from this Chapter of the *Esprit des lois* that Montesquieu did not envisage even informal society as starting purely with the family, or purely by instinct. And as for formal society, this was started some time later for practical reasons, when both political and civil laws were *established* in order to bring to an end the state of war resulting from the beginning of informal society.[45] Usbek on the other hand seems naïvely to have imagined that families always live in harmony and that civil law is unnecessary.

[44] *Cf. P.* 1379, Bkn. 1754, N. II, p. 408, Pl. I, p. 1419; see also Pascal's famous development on a similar theme in the *Préface sur le Traité du vide, Œuvres,* vol. II, pp. 129–45.

[45] *Lois,* I, iii, paragraphs 1–3, N. I, i, p. 7, Pl. II, p. 236: "Ces deux sortes d'états de guerre [i.e. civil and international] font établir les lois parmi les hommes".

In view of the fact that *Lettre persane* XCIV expresses a view that is contradicted by the *Traité des devoirs* and the *Esprit des lois*, it is particularly unhelpful to imply, as Vaughan and certain other scholars do, that it sums up his attitude, and that Usbek is here Montesquieu's spokesman.[46] It is a brillant but shallow *boutade*, more worthy of the immature Rica than of Usbek. It is impossible to agree with Dedieu when he states that "Sur l'origine des sociétés [...]" Montesquieu "avait poursuivi de brillantes et personnelles enquêtes";[47] or with Cotta, who says that "Montesquieu ne s'est jamais proposé le problème de l'origine de la société",[48] and that because the *président* sought in *Lettre persane* XCIV a psychological or organic solution to the problem, he differs from Aristotle or the School of Natural Law;[49] similarly, Althusser is wrong to suggest that Letter XCIV and Book I, ii, in their treatment of the problem, show that Montesquieu is an "adversaire de la théorie du droit naturel".[50] In none of Montesquieu's works is there a new conception of the origin of society.

To believe that formal, and even informal society had a beginning is not necessarily the same thing as believing that man's pre-social condition is exactly represented by the hypothesis of the state of nature as it was seen in the seventeenth and eighteenth centuries. What was Montesquieu's attitude to that hypothesis?

III. The Historicity of the State of Nature

Once it is admitted that successive degrees of civilization may have been accompanied by certain changes in man's character, then it is legitimate to speculate on what that character might have been at an earlier stage of civilization. The difficulty, of course, is to distinguish between what in man's character is primitive, and what has been acquired later. Nowadays, we try to solve this problem with the help of anthropology and archeology. In the seventeenth and eighteenth centuries, these sciences were in their infancy, and philosophers often referred instead to a more or less imaginary a-social or pre-social state, in their search for human nature: this "state of nature" was not therefore solely

[46] *Cf.* also Barckhausen, *Montesquieu, ses idées et ses œuvres*, p. 27; *Lettres persanes*, ed. A. Adam, Droz, 1954, p. 238. Ehrard, *L'Idée de nature*, vol. II, p. 472, is the only scholar to have previously drawn attention to the naïveté of Usbek's theory; but he does not compare Letter XCIV with Montesquieu's other writings.

[47] *Montesquieu*, p. 119; *cf.* Oudin, *Le Spinozisme de Montesquieu*, pp. 61 and 155.

[48] 'Montesquieu, la séparation des pouvoirs et la constitution fédérale des États-Unis', *Revue internationale d'histoire politique et constitutionnelle*, 1951, p. 239.

[49] *Montesquieu e la scienza della società*, pp. 163–5.

[50] *Op. cit.*, p. 20.

a political hypothesis, since it had these philosophical uses too. Experiments designed to distinguish nature from habit had been suggested by many philosophers,[51] but the eighteenth century saw a remarkable growth of interest in the question,[52] which had important religious and moral implications. Bayle, at the beginning of the century, put the problem most clearly:

ceux qui philosophent exactement m'avoueront, que pour être bien assuré qu'une telle et telle chose nous sont inspirées par la nature, il faudrait savoir que de jeunes gens les connaissent, sans le secours d'aucune instruction. Je ne crois pas qu'on ait des expériences de ce qui se passe dans l'esprit d'un homme, à qui l'on n'ait rien appris. Si l'on avait fait élever un certain nombre d'enfants par des personnes, qui se fussent contentées de les nourrir, sans leur enseigner aucune chose, nous verrions de quoi la nature toute seule est capable, mais nous ne connaissons que des gens que l'on a sifflés dès le berceau, et à qui l'on a fait accroire tout ce que l'on a voulu.[53]

Bayle seems to have been rather pleased that the experiment has not been and is not likely to be undertaken. Montesquieu, however, who proposed a similar experiment, appears to have envisaged it as a practical proposition, without stopping to consider the cruelty it might involve, or to wonder whose children should be chosen for it:

Un prince pourrait faire une belle expérience. Nourrir trois ou quatre enfants comme des bêtes, avec des chèvres ou des nourrices sourdes et muettes. Ils se feraient une langue. Examiner cette langue. Voir la nature en elle-même, et dégagée des préjugés de l'éducation (*P.* 158, Bkn. 775, N. II, p. 50, Pl. I, p. 1213).

From such a statement one might infer that Montesquieu was dissatisfied with the hypothesis of the state of nature as it had been used by his predecessors. However, this inference would not be justified.

Albert Sorel supposes the contents of Book I, ii of the *Esprit des lois* to be an original but misguided phantasy: "Faute de notions précises, [Montesquieu] s'abandonne à son imagination", he claims, and he talks amusingly of the *président*'s "sauvages timides, faibles et amoureux".[54] This piece of Voltairean satire does not tell us why Montes-

[51] *Cf.* Herodotus, *Histories*, II, ii; in the Loeb edition, vol. I, pp. 274–7; Montaigne, *Essais*, II, xii, vol. III, p. 181; Pufendorf, *Dn.*, II, i, 8, vol. I, p. 148.

[52] *Cf.* Mercier, *op. cit.*, pp. 399–402; G. L. Van Roosbroeck, *Persian Letters Before Montesquieu*, New York, Institute of French Studies, 1932, pp. 25–30; La Mettrie, *L'Homme machine. A Study in the Origins of an Idea*, Critical Edition by A. Vartanian, Princeton University Press, 1960, pp. 221–4; also Buffon, *Œuvres philosophiques*, in the *Corpus général des philosophes français*, vol. XLI, i, 1954, p. 374.

[53] *Réponses aux questions d'un provincial* [1704–7], II, cv, *Œuvres diverses*, The Hague, Husson, etc., 1727–31, 4 vols., vol. III, ii, p. 713.

[54] *Op. cit.*, p. 71.

quieu should have described the state of nature, or what precedents he had for so doing. The main precedent was provided by Hobbes.

Those who would like Montesquieu simply to have said that the state of nature is a fiction, do not seem to have realized that this would have been no answer at all to Hobbes. By using the conditional tense in Book I, ii, he did indeed imply that it was a fiction; but Hobbes had done the same. "It may peradventure be thought", he said, that

> there was never such a time, nor condition of war as this; and I believe it was never generally so, over all the world.

He went on to show that the state of nature had only ever existed partially, for example in civil war, among savages with "no government at all" living in a "brutish manner", and finally between different nations (*Leviathan,* I, xiii, pp. 114–5). Therefore, it would be no answer to Hobbes's contention that human nature is basically evil, and that it must be held in check by an authoritarian régime, to say that the state of nature, which illustrates that evil to the fullest extent, never existed, since Hobbes also thought it never existed.

Thus Hobbes never proposed the state of nature as a factual explanation of the origin of society, but only as a hypothesis, in which we may

> consider men as if but even now sprung out of the earth, and suddenly, like mushrooms, come to full maturity, without all kind of engagement to each other.[55]

In refuting Hobbes, Pufendorf recognized the hypothetical nature of his conception of the state of nature (*Dn.*, II, ii, 7, vol. I, p. 162). In his own opinion too, that state never existed except

> en partie et avec quelque tempérament, savoir, lorsque chacun s'étant joint avec d'autres pour former une société civile ou quelque chose d'équivalent, a conservé sa liberté naturelle par rapport à tout le reste des hommes (*Dn.*, II, ii, 4, vol. I, p. 158).

He did not accept that men ever lived solitarily. The state of nature in its polemic form, where men were supposed to live alone, is a hypothesis, since it is defined as the state

[55] *P.R.*, viii, 1, p. 109. In the *Traité des devoirs*, M. urged against Hobbes that

> il ne faut pas, comme il fait, supposer les hommes comme tombés du ciel ou sortis tout armés de la terre, à peu près comme les soldats de Cadmus, pour s'entre-détruire: ce n'est point là l'état des hommes (*P.* 1266, Bkn. 615, N. II, p. 344, Pl. I, p. 1139).

In these lines, M. was not arguing against the idea of imagining men in a solitary state, since he went on to do exactly the same thing himself. He was simply arguing that such men would not be warlike.

où l'on conçoit que chacun se trouve par la naissance, en faisant abstraction de toutes les inventions et de tous les établissements ou purement humains, ou inspirés à l'homme par la Divinité (*Dn.*, II, ii, 1, vol. I, p. 149).

The use of the concept of the state of nature for polemic purposes is by no means incompatible with a belief that no such state ever existed. Shaftesbury himself, though like Montesquieu in *Lettre persane* XCIV he laughed at the state of nature, nevertheless referred "in the fashionable language of our modern philosophy", both to the state of nature and to the original contract, in order to refute Hobbes[56] – a fact that seems to have been overlooked.[57] Rousseau's reproach to the School of Natural Law:

Il n'est pas même venu dans l'esprit de la plupart des nôtres de douter que l'état de nature eût existé (*Discours sur l'inégalité*, p. 141),

is unjustified in the case of Hobbes, Pufendorf and Shaftesbury.

The concept of the state of nature is open to two kinds of objection, anthropological and religious. Pufendorf and Hobbes tried to overcome the first objection by claiming that the idea of man's pre-social existence is imaginary and hypothetical. Montesquieu simply followed in their footsteps, using the state of nature for polemic purposes, but probably not believing in its existence. What of the religious objections to the state of nature – how did the School of Natural Law and Montesquieu answer these?

Pufendorf had been fully aware of the doubtful orthodoxy of the idea of a state of nature:[58]

il faut avouer que tout le genre humain à la fois ne s'est jamais trouvé dans l'état de nature, pur et simple; et que même cela ne pouvait point arriver, de la manière que les choses ont été disposées. Car, comme nous le croyons sur le témoignage incontestable de l'Écriture sainte, tous les hommes descendent de deux personnes unies par le lien conjugal.[59]

Perhaps with rather an uneasy conscience, he rejected the suggestion

[56] *An Essay on the Freedom of Wit and Humor*, p. 109.

[57] It is not mentioned either by Crisafulli, 'Parallels to Ideas in the *Lettres persanes*', or by Vernière in his edition of the *Lettres persanes*.

[58] When Bossuet referred to "le temps de la loi de nature", he was not thinking of the state of nature as we understand it, but of the time between the Fall and the giving of the Law, when "les hommes n'avaient pour se gouverner que la raison naturelle et les traditions de leurs ancêtres" (*Discours sur l'histoire universelle* [1681], I, *quatrième époque*, in *Œuvres complètes*, Lefèvre, Didot, 1836, vol. X, p. 136).

[59] *Dn.*, II, ii, 4, vol. I, p. 158. Like Pufendorf, Rousseau claimed to reject the factual existence of the state of nature on religious grounds, hence his famous "Commençons donc par écarter tous les faits" (*Discours sur l'inégalité*, p. 141). After this disclaimer he went on to talk about the state of nature as if it had existed.

that the state of nature is in contradiction with the Book of Genesis as pure calumny (*Dv.*, Preface, iii, pp. xxiv–xv). He even used the common origin of mankind, as told in the Bible, as an argument against Hobbes's state of war (*Dn.*, II, ii, 7, vol. I, pp. 162–3); but apart from this, he did not make much reference to Revelation in his discussion of the state of nature.

Montesquieu, in his account of the state of nature, went even further than Pufendorf, since he did not so much as mention the Book of Genesis. Worse still, he said that since primitive man would not have speculative notions, he would not have any knowledge of God: religion is the most important natural law, but not the first chronologically (*Lois*, I, ii, paragraph 2, N. I, i, p. 5, Pl. II, p. 235).

The abbé de La Roche was horrified by this suggestion, and unfavourably compared the *président*'s approach with that of Domat.[60] The author of the *Esprit des lois*, he implied, had been led astray by the pernicious example of the deists (*Examen critique*, pp. 119–20). He was perhaps not entirely wrong in this suspicion,[61] but Montesquieu's view was not so unorthodox as the Jansenist would have us think: the Sorbonne found no fault with this passage, nor did the *Lettre au P.J.B.*;[62] St. Thomas had argued that since man cannot understand "the essence of the uncreated substance", "it must be said simply that God is not the first object of our knowledge" (*S.t.*, I, Q. 88, A. 3, vol. IV, p. 235).[63] Montesquieu may also have derived his view from an application of the doctrine of sensualism to the concept of the state of nature. As he said in the *Défense de l'Esprit des lois*, he had simply been examining "quelle serait la première impression" in the mind of primitive man, and had concluded that "il aurait des sentiments, avant de faire des réflexions" (N. I, ii, p. 447, Pl. II, p. 1131).

It was not impossible in the eighteenth century to believe in sensualist psychology and yet to be a Christian, as the example of Samuel Clarke shows.[64] However, Montesquieu's main line of defence was to shelter behind precedent. The abbé de La Roche had alleged that Montes-

[60] Domat had scorned what he claimed to be the pagan notion of a state of nature (*op. cit.*, *Traité des lois*, i, 1, vol. I, p. i), and had shown that man's first natural law is to love God (*ibid.*, 6–7, p. ii); M. may indeed have been "expressly [...] opposing" Domat in *Lois*, I, ii, as Shackleton suggests (*M.*, p. 249).

[61] *Cf.* a passage in Shaftesbury's *Inquiry Concerning Virtue*, where the English deist denied that man "should, at the very first, be taken up with those speculations, or more refined sort of reflections" about God (*Characteristicks*, vol. II, p. 53).

[62] This letter was probably written by a Jesuit: see above, p. 10, n. 39.

[63] In the Latin: "Deus non est primum, quod a nobis cognoscitur" (*Summa totius theologiæ*, *Prima pars*, p. 195).

[64] *Cf. Discourse*, p. 615.

quieu was following "les païens" in talking about the state of nature (*Examen critique*, p. 119), but Montesquieu said he had been influenced by more recent philosophers:

Il ne lui [i.e. à l'auteur] a pas été défendu, plus qu'aux philosophes et aux écrivains du droit naturel, de considérer l'homme sous divers égards: il lui a été permis de supposer un homme comme tombé des nues, laissé à lui-même, et sans éducation, avant l'établissement des sociétés (*Défense*, N. I, ii, pp. 446–7, Pl. II, p. 1131).

Pufendorf had in fact used very similar expressions when he introduced the concept of the state of nature.[65] Montesquieu, in referring to that concept, was on the side of the School of Natural Law, and in opposition to the stricter elements within the Church. His answer to the religious objections was to lay the blame on his predecessors, and their answer, as in the case of the anthropological objections, had been that the state of nature is merely a hypothesis.

Unlike the state of nature, the original contract was sometimes regarded as a historical reality: Locke claimed to find several instances of a contract between ruler and ruled, especially in Antiquity (*T.T.*, II, viii, 100–103, pp. 351–4). What was Montesquieu's attitude to this idea, that was born in Greece,[66] that all but died in the Dark Ages,[67] that was revived by the School of Natural Law, and that seems to live in some of the democracies established since the Renaissance?

IV. The Original Contract and its Implications[68]

For the School of Natural Law, the original contract was an agreement whereby individual men, usually in a state of nature, renounce some of the rights they enjoyed in that state, and put themselves under a sovereign power, which may consist of one person or of many. The form and implications of the agreement depend on the political opinions of each theorist.

Grotius held ambiguous views on the original contract. He stated that since sovereign power is not usually in the hands of the people, they may not punish him if they think he has acted wrongly (*Dg.*, I,

[65] *Dn.*, II, ii, 2, vol. I, p. 149: "figurons-nous un homme *tombé*, si j'ose ainsi dire, *des nues*, et entièrement *abandonné à lui-même*" (our italics); *cf. Dv.*, Preface, iii, p. xxiv.

[66] A form of contract played a part in the theories of the Sophists and the Epicureans, in that they thought men had to agree to practise justice (*cf.* above, p. 69).

[67] On the contract in the Middle Ages, see Bréhier, *op. cit.*, vol. II, p. 150, and D'Entrèves, *op. cit.*, pp. 55–6.

[68] The best brief account of the theory of the original contract is probably Derathé's, *op. cit.*, pp. 27–48.

iii, 8–12, vol. I, pp. 121–41). However, he admitted that some governments are established by contract (*ibid.*, 13–17, pp. 141–51), and that in such cases, princes who break the contract

> peuvent non seulement être repoussés et mis à la raison par les voies de la force, mais encore punis de mort, s'il en est besoin (*ibid.*, iv, 8, p. 192).[69]

The consequence of such a concession is obvious: as soon as it is admitted that all, and not only some societies, are based on a contract, then the right to resist unjust rulers becomes universal.

Hobbes saw the danger of such concessions, and tried to nullify them by bringing a greater precision to the mechanism of the contract. He argued that when they left the state of nature, men agreed "every one, with every one" to obey the decision of the sovereign (*Leviathan*, II, xviii, p. 159), but that the sovereign himself made no agreement with the people (*ibid.*, p. 161); consequently, he is never accountable to the people for the way he governs (*ibid.*, pp. 161–70); further, he is not obliged to obey the natural law, or the laws of his country (*Leviathan*, II, xxvi, p. 253; *Tripos*: *De corpore politico*, II, viii, p. 205); he must not break the law of God, but he is the final arbiter, on earth at least, of what is or is not the law of God (*Tripos*: *De corpore politico*, II, vi, pp. 170–89). It is his duty to procure the benefit of his subjects (*ibid.*, ix, pp. 213–4), but they may not rebel against him if he does not (*ibid.*, viii, pp. 200–12), since any government, however bad, is better than the anarchy of the state of nature (*Leviathan*, II, xviii, p. 170).

Hobbes's specific purpose was to vindicate Charles I's rights against the Parliament that had executed him. Locke had quite a different purpose, in writing his *Two Treatises*: to justify the Revolution of 1688; hence his notion of the contract differed considerably from that of Hobbes. When man left the state of nature, he agreed with others to give up some of his natural rights "into the hands of the community" (*T.T.*, II, vii, 87, p. 342), which he then authorized "to make laws for him as the public good of the society shall require" (*ibid.*, 89, p. 343). The community, or a majority of its members, then decided on what form the government should take (*ibid.*, x, 132, p. 372). Though, as in Hobbes's contract, the "community" did not make a reciprocal agreement with the contractants, the latter delegated their power only "with this express or tacit trust, that it shall be employed for their good, and the preservation of their property" (*ibid.*, xv, 171, p. 399). Hence,

[69] It is difficult to agree with L. Crocker that Grotius did not accept the contract (*Nature and Culture*, p. 11).

the power of the government cannot be arbitrary or absolute (*ibid.*, vii, 90–3 and xi, 135, pp. 344–6 and 375–6).[70] With certain reservations (*ibid.*, II, xix, 225, p. 433), Locke claimed that if a king uses unjust force against his subjects, he puts himself and them back into the state of nature, where they have the right to retaliate in self-defence (*ibid.*, xviii, 205, p. 420).

The original contract is more part of the Protestant than of the Catholic tradition, and it finds its most absolute expression in the *Contrat social* of Jean-Jacques Rousseau, published in 1762. For the Citizen of Geneva, the contract secures "l'aliénation totale de chaque associé avec tous ses droits à toute la communauté";[71] he rather optimistically claimed that since the community is formed only of the contracting individuals,[72] it cannot go against their "volonté générale",[73] and that they remain as free as they were in the state of nature.[74]

Although most of the contractualists who influenced Rousseau were Protestants,[75] the theory of the contract also has certain affinities with Catholic thought. St. Thomas had argued that subjects should only obey just laws (*S.t.* II, ii, Q. 104, A. 6, rep. obj. 3, vol. XII, p. 39), and that since tyranny is "conducive to the private good of the ruler, and to the injury of the multitude", "there is no sedition in disturbing a government of this kind" (*ibid.*, Q. 42, A. 2, rep. obj. 3, vol. IX, p.518). Bossuet, in spite of the fact that he was writing in the reign of Louis XIV, nevertheless claimed that a king should always obey both the laws of nature and those of his own country.[76] However, neither St. Thomas nor Bossuet, believing as they did in the Divine Right of kings, made any specific reference to an original contract. Strangely enough, such a reference is to be found in an official defence of Louis XIV's

[70] Pufendorf's position is similar to that of Locke. He said that there are two contracts, the first by which all agreed to join together, the second by which they agreed to obey their rulers or ruler (*Dn.*, VII, ii, 7–8, vol. II, pp. 231–2). He also stated that "ceux qui sont revêtus [du] pouvoir, s'engagent à veiller avec soin au bien et à la sûreté publique, et [...] les autres, de leur côte, leur promettent une fidèle obéissance" (*ibid.*, 8, p. 232).

[71] *Du Contrat social*, I, vi, in *The Political Writings*, vol. II, p. 33.

[72] *Ibid.*, vii, p. 35.

[73] *Ibid.*, II, iii, p. 42: the "volonté générale" is distinguished from the "volonté de tous", which may be corrupt.

[74] *Ibid.*, I, vi, p. 32.

[75] For a thorough examination of the relation of Rousseau to the theorists of the contract, see Derathé, *op. cit.*, *passim*, esp. pp. 172–247. Faguet had claimed that Rousseau was influenced by the Calvinist Jurieu (*La Politique comparée de Montesquieu, Rousseau et Voltaire*, pp. 74–5), but Derathé denies this, *op. cit.*, pp. 120–22.

[76] *Politique tirée des propres paroles de l'Écriture sainte*, [1709], IV, i, 4, and VIII, i, 4, *Œuvres complètes*, vol. X, pp. 349 and 431.

claim to parts of the Spanish empire.[77] Of the Catholic writers of the age of Louis XIV, Fénelon came closest to accepting a contract. Looking back nostalgically at the relation which he supposed to exist between earlier kings of France and their subjects, he said:

> Le sacre consommait tout, parce que les peuples ne voulaient qu'un roi chrétien et catholique. – Contrat et serment dont la formule reste encore.[78]

This idea of a fundamental law, to be respected by the king, is also found in the work of Montesquieu, for he was appalled by the way in which the French monarchy had gradually arrogated to itself rights that traditionally belonged to other sections of the community. Chapter iv of Book II of the *Esprit des lois* opens with the words:

> Les pouvoirs intermédiaires subordonnés et dépendants constituent la nature du gouvernement monarchique, c'est à dire, de celui où un seul gouverne par des lois fondamentales (N. I, i, p. 20, Pl. II, p. 247).

The two powers he had in mind were of course the nobility, which he called "Le pouvoir intermédiaire subordonné le plus naturel", and which he believed could prevent monarchy from turning into despotism (N. I, i, pp. 20–21, Pl. II, p. 247), and the "dépôt de lois" vested in certain "corps politiques", namely the parlements, "qui annoncent les lois lorsqu'elles sont faites, et les rappellent lorsqu'on les oublie" (N. I, i, p. 22, Pl. II, p. 249).

In assigning a political as well as a juridical rôle to the parlements, Montesquieu was following a tradition of opposition to absolutism that dated back to the previous century.[79] The *parlementaires*, in their remonstrances, did not refer to the idea of a social contract, with its egalitarian associations. Instead, they used such phrases as *le droit de la nation*, in their attempts to prove that they were the proper channel through which *la voix des peuples* should make itself heard.[80] Montesquieu avoided such provocative phrases, for while he was certain that the parlements and the aristocracy were necessary to monarchy, he emphasized that they should be ultimately subordinate to the king.[81]

[77] This work, entitled *Traité des droits de la reine très chrétienne sur divers états de la monarchie d'Espagne*, Imprimerie royale, 1667, is referred to in the *Encyclopédie*, Briasson, etc., 1751–65, art. 'Autorité politique', *Errata*, vol. III, p. xvi, and in Rousseau's *Discours sur l'inégalité*, p. 186; *cf.* J. Proust, *Diderot et l'Encyclopédie*, Colin, 1962, pp. 345 and 375–6.

[78] *Plans de gouvernement*, in Fénelon, *Écrits et lettres politiques*, edited by C. Urbain, Bossard, 1920, p. 110.

[79] *Cf.* Henri Sée, *Les Idées politiques en France au XVIIIe siècle*, Giard, 1923, pp. 97–9, 116–8, 219–70; *L'Évolution de la pensée politique au XVIIIe siècle*, Alcan, 1925, pp. 315–39.

[80] *Cf.* Sée, *L'Évolution de la pensée politique*, pp. 318–22 and 330–1.

[81] He had already stated in the first edition of the *Lois*, that the prince is the source of all

In the eighteenth century, the majority of *parlementaires* were, like Montesquieu, members of the aristocracy, and some of them believed in the historical origin of the laws that supposedly protected the political rights of the nobility. The subject was highly controversial. The abbé Dubos, in his *Histoire critique de l'établissement de la monarchie française* (1734), had put forward the unusual but ingenious theory that the Franks had not conquered Gaul, but had entered it as a result of a treaty made with the Romans. Consequently, according to Dubos, the Merovingian kings were the legitimate successors to the Roman emperors, and inherited their absolute power. This justification of absolutism had been written partly as a refutation of the theories of le comte de Boulainvilliers. In the *État de France* (1727–8) and in the *Histoire de l'ancien gouvernement de la France* (1727), Boulainvilliers had argued that Gaul had been conquered by the Franks. Anxious to underline the rights of the ancient noble families of France, he showed that the Franks, being conquerors, had been superior in rights to the Gauls. Dubos, on the other hand, held that both Franks and Gauls were in the same position of inferiority with respect to the king. Boulainvilliers saw Clovis as having been chosen king by the Frankish conquerors, whereas Dubos, believing Clovis to have been appointed by the Romans, admitted no such choice.[82]

Montesquieu took up a position between that of Boulainvilliers and that of Dubos, but, being an aristocrat, and seeing himself as descended from "les Germains",[83] he tended to sympathize with the former:[84] Dubos, he insinuated, "ne voyait jamais dans cette histoire qu'une pension" (*P.* 795, Bkn. 915, N. II, p. 234, Pl. I, p. 1249). Most of the details of Montesquieu's account of the origins of the Frankish empire do not concern us here,[85] but one point is very relevant to the present discussion: Montesquieu agreed with Boulainvilliers that the Frankish kings had been chosen by the leaders of the nation:

> On a dit [...] que les peuples qui ne cultivent point les terres jouissaient d'une grande liberté. Les Germains furent dans ce cas. Tacite dit qu'ils

political and civil power; in the 1757 edition he added phrases stressing the subordination of the intermediary powers: see Brethe de la Gressaye, *Lois*, vol. I, p. 246, n. 33, to p. 45.

[82] *Cf.* É. Carcassonne, *Montesquieu et le problème de la constitution française au XVIIIe siècle*, Presses Universitaires de France, [1927], pp. 18–25 and 42–5.

[83] *Cf. Lois*, XIV, xiv, N. I, i, p. 321, Pl. II, p. 487.

[84] On M. and the fundamental law see Carcassonne, *op. cit.*, pp. 65–102; A. Lemaire, *Les lois fondamentales de la monarchie française, d'après les théoriciens de l'ancien régime*, Fontemoing, 1907, pp. 211–4; E. H. Price, 'Montesquieu's Historical Conception of the Fundamental Law', *Romanic Review*, 1947, pp. 234–42.

[85] For a fuller account of this question, see Shackleton, *M.*, pp. 328–33.

ne donnaient à leurs rois ou chefs qu'un pouvoir très modéré (*Lois*, XVIII, xxx, N. I, i, p. 407, Pl. II, p. 554).

He supported this claim with some lines from Tacitus' *Germania*, which are in fact a drastic truncation of the original:

Nec regibus libera aut infinita potestas. Cœterum neque animadvertere, neque vincire, neque verberare, &c.[86]

He cited the same work to show that there were further limits placed on the power of the Germanic kings: "Les princes [...] délibèrent sur les petites choses, toute la nation sur les grandes",[87] and added that "Cet usage se conserva après la conquête, comme on le voit dans tous les monuments", citing as proof an article from the Capitularies of Charles the Bald, "Lex consensu populi fit et constitutione regis" (*Lois*, XVIII, xxx, N. I, i, p. 408, Pl. II, p. 555).

A comparison between Locke and Montesquieu suggests itself here. Just as the Englishman sought historical examples of an original contract, in order to justify the powers of the English parliament, so the Frenchman sought historical proof of the way in which the powers of the French kings had been limited at the establishment of the French monarchy, and, by implication, of the way these powers were, or should have been limited in his own day. Of course, in Montesquieu's case, it was a contract made by the nobles, not by the common people; but then, the contractualists certainly did not envisage an agreement made by universal suffrage – only by the wise, as Gravina put it.

One significant difference between Montesquieu and Locke in this matter is apparently that while Locke's contract seems to apply to all governments, Montesquieu's remarks on the subject seem limited to the French monarchy. Do we find in the *président*'s work any references to a more universally operative contract, such as was propounded by the School of Natural Law?

There can be no doubt of the answer in so far as Montesquieu's early work is concerned, for in it he makes frequent allusions to the idea. The Troglodyte people had once been governed by "un roi d'une origine étrangère", whom they assassinated because he tried to "corriger la méchanceté de leur naturel". Then,

[86] *Lois*, XVIII, xxx, n. a, N. I, i, p. 407, Pl. II, p. 554; Tacitus, *Germania*, vii, p. 274; M. gave a fuller, but not complete version of the quotation in the next chapter, N. I, i, p. 408, Pl. II, p. 555.

[87] *Cf.* Tacitus, *Germania*, xi, p. 278.

Le coup étant fait, ils s'assemblèrent, pour choisir un gouvernement; et, après bien des dissensions, ils créèrent des magistrats (*L.p.* XI, N. I, iii, p. 27, Pl. I, p. 146),

who soon met the same fate as the king. In this contract there was apparently no agreement between the magistrates and the people and, while the analogy cannot be pushed too far, the contract resembles that of Hobbes, who held that there was no agreement between ruler and ruled. The resemblance could be intentional, since the wicked Troglodytes are meant to depict Hobbes's notion of self-preservation.

Later in the story there is a second contract. The virtuous Troglodytes

crurent qu'il était à propos de se choisir un roi; ils convinrent qu'il fallait déférer la couronne à celui qui était le plus juste; et ils jetèrent tous les yeux sur un vieillard vénérable par son âge et par une longue vertu (*L.p.* XIV, N. I, iii, p. 35, Pl. I, p. 152).

There is once again no mention of an agreement between the new ruler and the people. Indeed, the chosen man "n'avait pas voulu se trouver à cette assemblée" (*ibid.*). However, such an agreement was obviously unnecessary, since the Troglodytes had chosen a virtuous man. There is a similarity between both these contracts and the theory of Pufendorf. The Troglodytes apparently decided first upon the form of the government, then on who should be magistrate (or king). According to Pufendorf, the first agreement, that of joining together to form a society, is followed by a decree, made "d'un commun accord", on the form of the government; by a second "convention", the ruler or rulers are chosen (*Dn.*, VII, ii, 7–8, vol. II, pp. 231–2).

Of course, the story of the Troglodytes is only a fable. But Montesquieu was under no obligation to describe the way in which the two Troglodyte governments were chosen. The fact that he did so reveals his interest in the contract as a method of establishing political sovereignty. This interest is also revealed in two other places in the *Lettres persanes*.

In the early editions, Letter XCV contained the words:

Une société ne peut être fondée que sur la volonté des associés. Si elle est détruite par la conquête, le peuple redevient libre: il n'y a plus de nouvelle société et si le vainqueur en veut former, c'est une tyrannie.[88]

The indignant tone of this passage seems to show that at this time

[88] *Lettres persanes*, ed. Vernière, p. 375, n. c to p. 197; Pl. I, p. 1593.

Montesquieu believed quite fervently in the contract. The fact that in later editions this text was replaced by another where there is no allusion to the contract (N. I, iii, p. 190, Pl. I, p. 272), does not necessarily prove that he rejected the theory, but rather that he changed his mind regarding the right of conquest.[89]

There were no significant alterations to Letter CIV, where Usbek recounts certain political theories of the English. He tells us that according to the English, all governments are based on gratitude: subjects are obedient to their ruler only inasmuch as they are able to be grateful to him (N. I, iii, pp. 206–7, Pl. I, p. 284). This notion is clearly related to the theory of the contract: the ruler's right to rule depends on his giving satisfaction to his subjects by governing justly. The idea of "reconnaissance" was in fact a commonplace of contractual theory. According to Pufendorf, force is not sufficient to establish legitimate authority:

> il faut de plus [...] que celui qui veut assujettir l'autre à suivre sa volonté lui ait fait quelque bien considérable [...]. En effet, naturellement on ne peut qu'aimer celui de qui on a reçu plusieurs bienfaits (*Dn.*, I, vi, 12, vol. I, p. 100).[90]

According to Paul Vernière, Letter CIV is a psychological interpretation of the causes of English liberty, and is rather confused.[91] It is, however, possible to see it rather as a fairly clear, if bookish summary of the contractual doctrine – as a piece of abstract theorizing.

The same kind of theorizing is to be found in *Pensée* 224 (Bkn. 601), probably written between 1721 and 1731, which may be considered as a sequel to *Lettre persane* CIV. It confirms that in putting forward the notion of the contract in the *Lettres persanes*, Montesquieu was not just playing with ideas. The *Pensée* opens with a discussion of Hobbes's contract and its consequences:

> C'est un principe bien faux que celui de Hobbes: que, le peuple ayant autorisé le prince, les actions du prince sont les actions du peuple, et, par conséquent, le peuple ne peut pas se plaindre du prince, ni lui demander aucun compte de ses actions: parce que le peuple ne peut pas se plaindre du peuple.

As far as it goes, this is a reasonable account of Hobbes's contract, but it is a poor piece of argument, because it does not mention one vital

[89] See below, Ch. 6, IV.
[90] *Cf.* Burlamaqui, *Principes du droit naturel*, I, ix, 8, pp. 103–5.
[91] *Lettres persanes*, ed. Vernière, p. 216, n. 1.

point, namely the reason Hobbes gave for the unaccountability of the sovereign: the fact that he made no agreement with the people to govern as they wished. Hence the criticism of Hobbes in the remainder of the *Pensée* is irrelevant:

> Ainsi Hobbes a oublié son principe du droit naturel: *Pacta esse servanda.* Le peuple a autorisé le prince sous condition; [. . .] le prince ne représente le peuple que comme le peuple a voulu ou est censé avoir voulu qu'il le représentât.[92]

The last sentence reminds us of Locke's phrase: "with this express or tacit trust", and it makes us suspect that Montesquieu has confused Hobbes with Locke, or rather that he has rolled Hobbes and Locke into one, and then accused the resulting fictitious theorist of inconsistency.

Though Montesquieu's criticism of Hobbes – inadequate as it is – is based partly on abstract considerations,[93] it is also based on supposedly factual grounds. The words "Le peuple a autorisé le prince sous condition" seem to refer to a historical event – presumably to one that Montesquieu believed to occur at the start of every society.

This factual approach is also evident in the *Traité des devoirs*. Talking in the past tense (and not in the conditional that he was later to use in the *Esprit des lois*, I, i,) he described how the scattered but related families were obliged to become reunited "par des conventions" (*P.* 1267, Bkn. 616, N. II, p. 346, Pl. I, p. 1141). It is true, as Cotta says, that Montesquieu did not here say what form the conventions took: whether they were Hobbesian or Lockian; but Cotta is wrong to infer from this that Montesquieu did not fully accept the contract:[94] in *Pensée* 224, as has just been seen, Montesquieu believed that there is only one kind of contract, the Lockian one, and there is no reason to suppose that he held a different view at the time of the *Traité des devoirs*.

In the 1720's, then, Montesquieu believed in the original contract, regarding it as a historical reality and understanding its political implications; he did not however understand its technicalities, and his thought on the subject was not original.

If we believe the majority of critics, Montesquieu made no mention of the contract in his later works. C. E. Vaughan's chapter on Montes-

[92] N. II, p. 94, Pl. I, p. 1127. Hobbes did indeed say that contracts must be observed – it is his third law of nature (*Leviathan*, I, xv, p. 130; in *P.R.*, iii, 1, pp. 29–30 it is called the second law of nature), but he did not say that "Le peuple a autorisé le prince sous condition."

[93] The *Pensée* ends with a sentence – subsequently deleted – on how much power ruler and ruled are entitled to.

[94] *Montesquieu e la scienza della società*, p. 193.

quieu is entitled 'Eclipse of Contract'; according to both Sabine and Fletcher, Montesquieu "neglected" the contract; "Nul contrat" is Althusser's laconic comment on both the *Lettres persanes* and the *Esprit des lois*; Brethe de la Gressaye is equally sweeping: talking of Book I, iii, he says, "Montesquieu, à la différence des penseurs politiques des XVIIe et XVIIIe siècles, ne fait même pas allusion à l'idée [...] d'un contrat social".[95]

Now it is true that in his later years Montesquieu was not a contractualist in the full sense of the word. His originality lies in having devised other, though related, ways of ensuring political liberty. However, it would be surprising if his early interest in the contract had left no traces in the work of his maturity.

In *Pensée* 1908 (Bkn. 237), written in or after 1749, there is a reference to Grotius and an admission that there can be both mutual and one-sided contracts (N. II, p. 573, Pl. II, p. 1048): clearly his understanding of the question had deepened since *Pensée* 224. It is significant that at this date he should still have talked about the contract as if it were an event that often occurs.[96]

However, it is in the *Esprit des lois* that Montesquieu made the most pointed allusions to an original contract and it is difficult to see how critics can have overlooked them. The first allusion occurs almost at the start of the work, in Book I, iii, which deals with the origin of civil and political laws. After denying that Montesquieu alludes to a contract, Brethe de la Gressaye refers the reader to Book III, Chapters i and v of Gravina's *Origines iuris civilis*, as the source of Montesquieu's remarks on the origin of "l'état politique" and "l'état civil". There is in fact only a slight resemblance between these chapters of Gravina's work and the *Esprit des lois*.[97]

Montesquieu's remarks are based on another part of the *Origines iuris civilis*, where the Italian is postulating an original contract. In Book II, xvii, entitled 'De iure sapientis in ceteros', Gravina said that political society was established in order to prevent the anarchy that would result if men, who, with few exceptions, are not ruled by reason, were left to their own devices. This is a commonplace, but Gravina went

95 C. E. Vaughan, *Studies in the History of Political Philosophy*, vol. I, pp. 253–302, and esp. p. 258; Sabine, *op. cit.*, p. 551; Fletcher, *Montesquieu and English Politics*, p. 111; Althusser, *op. cit.*, p. 20; Brethe de la Gressaye, *Lois*, vol. I, p. 237, n. 9, to p. 24.

96 *Cf.* Benrekassa, *op. cit.*, p. 35.

97 Brethe de la Gressaye, *Lois*, vol. I, p. 239, n. 13, to p. 26. In the *Origines*, III, i, Gravina talked of civil law, and in III, v, of one kind of government. But there are few textual similarities between this part of Gravina's work and the *Lois*.

on to make an interesting distinction between political and civil law. Society originates with an agreement made by the wise, who resolve to establish and enforce laws:

> nihil est enim aliud civitas, quam publica multorum ad communem utilitatem, ac vitæ bonorumque tutamen instituta societas: quæ perpetuis publicarum pactionum vinculis, nempe legibus continetur. Quibus firmandis, atque constituendis suam quisque voluntatem contribuunt, propriasque in medium conferunt pro communi securitate vires. Atque his e voluntatibus, et viribus in unum confluentibus, publica voluntas conflatur, summaque potestas: quarum altera dicta lex est, sive communis ratio, vel civilis sapientia, et publica philosophia ; altera imperium, sive vis, et potestas universorum.[98]

Gravina thus distinguished between "lex", which is the result of the reason and will of the people, and "imperium," which is the result of their combined "potestas". He went on to show that the act of union safeguards the liberty of those who are a party to it, since "qui lege involvitur non aliena vi, sed sua voluntate, suaque imperii portione gubernatur" (*Origines iuris civilis*, II, xviii, p. 257).

Montesquieu, then, was not misinterpreting Gravina when he said that "l'*état politique*" is formed by "*La réunion de toutes les forces particulières*", and that

> Les forces particulières ne peuvent se réunir, sans que toutes les volontés se réunissent. *La réunion de ces volontés*, dit encore très bien Gravina, *est ce qu'on appelle l'état civil.*[99]

Though it is clear that on the previous page, at the beginning of his chapter on positive law, the *président* had envisaged society as having begun at a certain moment, and not as having always existed,[100] it is difficult to tell from his "translation" of Gravina whether he was giving a historical account of the origins of government (as the Italian was

[98] *Origines iuris civilis*, II, xvii, p. 256. In the translation by Requier, *Esprit des lois romaines*' Videcoq and Brière, 1821, p. 23, this passage reads as follows:

> Une ville n'est autre chose qu'une société publique, établie pour l'utilité de plusieurs, c'est à dire, pour la défense de leurs personnes et celle de leurs biens. Cette société est entretenue par des lois, au soutien desquelles chaque particulier contribue de sa volonté et de ses forces. De toutes ces volontés, de toutes ces forces réunies, naissent la volonté publique et la puissance suprême. La première a été nommée *loi*: on eût pu la nommer raison commune, science civile, philosophie publique. On a appelé l'autre *empire*: on eût pu l'appeler force et puissance de tous.

[99] *Lois*, I, iii, N. I, i, p. 8, Pl. II, p. 237. Pufendorf had already used terms similar to those Gravina and M. were to use: "C'est de cette union de volontés et de forces que résulte le corps politique" (*Dn.*, VII, ii, 5, vol. II, p. 230).

[100] Such at least is the impression conveyed by his use of the historic present in the first paragraph of *Lois*, I, iii: "Sitôt que les hommes sont en société, ils perdent le sentiment de leur faiblesse", etc.

doing), or whether he was simply analyzing the nature of government. However, this distinction does not affect the main issue, for whether his account was historical or analytic, whether the "réunion" is "express" or "tacit", he was undoubtedly telling his readers that all governments are composed of the will and power of each individual, that they are all based on a contract.

Not only does Montesquieu introduce the theory of the original contract in the third chapter of the *Esprit des lois,* he also refers to it at important moments in the body of the work. In particular his arguments against slavery are based partly on the idea of a contract: society is established for the benefit of all, hence slavery, which benefits the master and not the slave is wrong.[101] A similar allusion to the natural right of liberty also appears in Montesquieu's discussion of property, where, once more viewing the beginning of society as a historical event, he said:

> Comme les hommes ont renoncé à leur indépendance naturelle, pour vivre sous des lois politiques, ils ont renoncé à la communauté naturelle des biens, pour vivre sous des lois civiles.
>
> Ces premières lois leur acquièrent la liberté; les secondes, la propriété (*Lois,* XXVI, xv, N. I, ii, p. 147, Pl. II, p. 767).

Here once again, Montesquieu was leaning on the theorists of the conract, in this case perhaps on Locke.[102]

In spite of the many significant, but often neglected references in the *Esprit des lois* to an original contract, the work apparently holds but little hope for those who are aggrieved by their government. In the Preface, Montesquieu stated his intention of giving each subject new reasons why he should love his duties, his ruler, his country, and its laws; as we have shown, this is an invitation to gradual reform:[103] it is certainly not an invitation to rebellion. The reference to the contract in Book I, iii is not followed by a proclamation of the subjects' right to rebel if the contract is violated. This cautious attitude is all the more apparent when we compare the *Esprit des lois* with Montesquieu's earlier works.

His description, in the *Discours sur Cicéron,* of the killing of Cæsar as "cette grande action qui étonne encore aujourd'hui les tyrans" (N. III, p. 20, Pl. I, p. 97) could be dismissed as youthful enthusiasm,[104] were it not that a similar attitude can be discerned behind his discussion of

[101] See below, Ch. 6, II.
[102] See below, Ch. 6, III.
[103] See above, Ch. 2. III, pp. 40–41.
[104] This *Discours* was written when M. was about 20, *cf,* N.III, p. 15.

Brutus's action, in the *Considérations*. Here Montesquieu based the right of tyrannicide on

> un certain droit des gens, une opinion établie dans toutes les républiques de Grèce et d'Italie, qui faisait regarder comme un homme vertueux l'assassin de celui qui avait usurpé la souveraine puissance (Ch. XI, N. I, iii, p. 430, Pl. II, p. 131).

Nor can it be said that this attitude applied only to tyrannicide in Antiquity. In the *Lettres persanes*, we find Usbek summarizing what appears to be Locke's theory of rebellion:[105]

> si un prince, bien loin de faire vivre ses sujets heureux, veut les accabler et les détruire, le fondement de l'obéissance cesse; rien ne les lie, rien ne le, attache à lui; et ils rentrent dans leur liberté naturelle (*L.p.* CIV, N. Is iii, p. 207, Pl. I, p. 284).

It is perhaps not certain that Montesquieu endorsed this theory, since Usbek continued by giving an ironical account of the excuses made by the English for rebelling against Charles I: but the Persian is himself a tyrant, in his harem at least, and could not be expected to sympathize with revolutionaries; he is not always Montesquieu's mouthpiece. Tyrannicide is certainly advocated in *Pensée* 1252 (Bkn. 603), which is a fragment of the *Traité des devoirs*. Just as Usbek had done, Montesquieu, in this *Pensée*, attributed his arguments to the English. However, the tone of the passage indicates that the *président* was in fact stating his own views.

The discussion begins with a question: which is more useful to humanity, that authority should be blindly respected, or that it should be curbed, "lorsqu'elle devient destructive?" In terms that recall those of the *Discours sur Cicéron* or of the *Considérations*, Montesquieu answered that whoever freed men from the "superstition" of blind obedience, and taught them instead that there are certain "lois invariables et fondamentales" which princes must respect, would be a hero. The *Pensée* ends by showing that it is better to prefer the safety of the state to that of the prince, and to overthrow tyranny by civil war (N. II, pp. 332–3, Pl. I, pp. 1128–9).

The allusions here to fundamental laws and to "la Loi" are particularly significant. On the one hand, they take us back to the old controversy about whether or not the king is subject to the natural law, and to the civil law of his own country: clearly, Montesquieu opposed

[105] Usbek goes on to say, just as Locke had done (*T.T.*, II, iv, 23, p. 302), that no one can give to another more power than he has over himself.

Hobbes on this issue, and sided with Grotius, Bossuet and Locke.[106] On the other hand, these allusions take us forward to the *Esprit des lois*, where, as we have seen, Montesquieu was to work out the mechanism and implications of the fundamental law.

It is surely no accident that in the one place in the *Esprit des lois* where Montesquieu did praise rebellion, he based his argument precisely on the concept of fundamental law. In his second long chapter on the English Constitution, he is lead to talk of the Revolution of 1688, and his enthusiasm shows beneath the impartiality given to his words by the conditional tense:

> si les disputes étaient formées à l'occasion de la violation des lois fondamentales, et qu'une puissance étrangère parût; il y aurait une révolution qui ne changerait pas la forme du gouvernement, ni sa constitution: car les révolutions que forme la liberté ne sont qu'une confirmation de la liberté (*Lois*, XIX, xxvii, N. I, i, p. 435, Pl. II, p. 576).

To praise a historical event is not the same as believing that it should be repeated: Montesquieu was not in this passage implying that the remedy to the absolutism of the French monarchy was revolution. He was simply issuing a warning – just as Bossuet had done when he said that "Sans autoriser les rébellions, Dieu les permet".[107]

The claim made by many scholars that Montesquieu's attitude to the contract and to the state of nature was more empirical than that of his predecessors is based on a failure to appreciate the implications of the opening chapters especially of the *Esprit des lois*, and on a misunderstanding of the doctrine of natural law. By adopting the original contract as a guarantee of the right of liberty and of property, Montesquieu revealed both his own idealism, and his debt to earlier political philosophers.[108]

[106] Grotius and Locke believed that the sovereign should always obey the law of nature: *Dg.*, I, iii, 16, pp. 144–5; *T.T.*, II, xvi, 195, pp. 413–4; Bossuet believed he should obey the natural and the civil law, see above, p. 88.

[107] *Politique tirée de l'Écriture sainte*, VII, vi, 2, p. 424.

[108] For a different presentation of the argument of this chapter, see our article, 'Montesquieu et le problème de l'origine des sociétes', *Studi francesi*, 1969, pp. 235–46.

CHAPTER 5

MONTESQUIEU AND EMPIRICISM IN POSITIVE LAW: THE DIVERSITY OF GOVERNMENTS AND LAWS

A purely logical approach to the question of the origin of society might result in the following argument: if men in the state of nature are all equal, they are all the same; if they are all the same, then they all need identical governments and laws; yet there are several different kinds of government, and laws vary from country to country; either this diversity is inexplicable, or it results from the corruption of an ideal universally-valid legislation. This attitude, which seems to be fostered by the philosophy of natural law, did not appeal to Montesquieu. His very purpose in the *Esprit des lois* was to show why governments and laws are different from country to country. How far was he innovating?

I. The Diversity of Governments

It is often said that Montesquieu did not believe that any one kind of government is more natural than any other kind, and that in judging the worth of each régime he employed scientific rather than moral criteria.[1] This claim seems to find support in *Lettre persane* LXXX, where Usbek said:

> J'ai souvent recherché quel était le gouvernement le plus conforme à la raison. Il m'a semblé que le plus parfait est celui qui va à son but à moins de frais; de sorte que celui qui conduit les hommes de la manière qui convient le plus à leur penchant et à leur inclination, est le plus parfait.
>
> Si, dans un gouvernement doux, le peuple est aussi soumis que dans un gouvernement sévère; le premier est préférable, puisqu'il est plus conforme à la raison, et que la sévérité est un motif étranger (N. I, iii, p. 164, Pl. I, p. 252).

The standard by which Usbek here judges governments is reason, and

[1] *Cf. Montesquieu: Textes choisis et commentés* par F. Strowski, Plon, 1912, p. 97; Dedieu, *Montesquieu*, pp. 120–1; Delbos, *La Philosophie française*, p. 183; Mercier, 'La Notion de loi morale chez Montesquieu', p. 190.

it is based on a realization of the limits of human nature and on a belief that unnecessary cruelty is wrong. It is true that he did not say that one *kind* of government is more reasonable than another, only that some *governments* are more reasonable than others. But such a distinction is flimsy, and under the guise of a supposed impartiality, Usbek is praising certain kinds of régime and criticizing others. "Un gouvernement sévère" clearly refers to oriental despotisms, and to monarchies with despotic tendencies, while "un gouvernement doux" refers to some European governments. If the reasonable is the same as the natural,[2] then Usbek was in fact saying that moderate governments are more natural than severe ones.

In the *Esprit des lois*, Montesquieu wanted to be even more impartial than Usbek had tried to be. He wanted to give all men new reasons for loving their own country (Preface, N. I, i, p. lxi, Pl. II, p. 230); he argued that no one kind of government is particularly natural, but rather that

> le gouvernement le plus conforme à la nature est celui dont la disposition particulière se rapporte mieux à la disposition du peuple pour lequel il est établi (*Lois*, I, iii, N. I, i, p. 8, Pl. II, p. 237).

When this passage, which looks at first glance like the basis of an impartial scientific method, is examined in its context, it will be seen to have a polemic aim: in the previous paragraph, Montesquieu had argued against the theory – usually associated with absolutism – that the example of paternal power proves monarchy to be the most natural form of government.

The sixteenth-century magistrate Jean Bodin, though he was not an absolutist, argued that 'La royauté est plus conforme aux lois générales de la nature' since the family is "l'image authentique de l'État".[3] Similarly, Bossuet was later to claim that monarchy "a son fondement et son modèle dans l'empire paternel, c'est à dire dans la nature même".[4] One of the most extreme applications of this theory is in Sir Robert Filmer's *Patriarcha*, published in 1680, where absolute monarchy is derived from Adam's supposedly absolute power over his children.[5]

[2] *Cf.* R. Grimsley, 'The Idea of Nature in the *Lettres persanes*', *French Studies*, 1951, pp. 293–306.

[3] *La Méthode de l'histoire*, traduite et présentée par P. Mesnard, Les Belles Lettres, 1941, Book VI, p. 266; in spite of his claim that royal authority is absolute (*Les Six livres de la république*, I, viii, Lyons, Du Puys, 1579, p. 85), Bodin admitted that the monarch must obey the laws of nature (*ibid.*, p. 92).

[4] *Politique tirée de l'Écriture sainte*, II, i, 7, p. 332; *cf.* Domat, *op. cit.*, *Le Droit public*, I, i, vol. II, pp. 2–5.

[5] *Patriarcha and Other Political Writings*, pp. 57–8. Hobbes, on the other hand, had not been

This kind of unverified claim and far-fetched analogy did not appeal to the School of Natural Law: their eminently sensible refutations have already been examined in Chapter 3.

In the *Esprit des lois*, Montesquieu's refutation of the paternalist thesis is in the same spirit as that of Grotius, Pufendorf and Locke, since it is based on practical considerations:

> Quelques-uns ont pensé que la nature ayant établi le pouvoir paternel, le gouvernement d'un seul était le plus conforme à la nature. Mais l'exemple du pouvoir paternel ne prouve rien. Car, si le pouvoir du père a du rapport au gouvernement d'un seul; après la mort du père, le pouvoir des frères; ou, après la mort des frères, celui des cousins germains, ont du rapport au gouvernement de plusieurs (N. I, i, p. 8, Pl. II, p. 237).

Though this argument is logical, it is not very satisfactory, since the monarchists could retort that it is not usually "[les] frères" but *le frère aîné* or *le fils aîné* who take charge of a family when the father dies. One wonders why Montesquieu did not mention the natural limitations on paternal power that he had discussed in the *Traité des devoirs*.

Montesquieu's idea that no one kind of government is natural has struck many critics as being highly original. According to Durkheim, for example, political scientists before Montesquieu did not try to study societies as they are, but "s'efforçaient plutôt de nous faire admirer et imiter le modèle idéal d'une société parfaite".[6] Alengry makes a similar generalization:

> Les écrivains politiques antérieurs à Montesquieu, au lieu d'observer ce qui est, construisaient ce qui doit être; ils recherchaient quelle était la meilleure forme de gouvernement. En outre, après l'avoir construite *a priori*, ils la proclamaient valable pour tous les hommes.[7]

Dedieu quite rightly claims that "les théoriciens de la monarchie" believed monarchy to be the most natural form of government;[8] but he fails to mention that among Montesquieu's predecessors there were not a few political philosophers who were not monarchists.

The attitude of the positivists is strangely unpositivistic. Alengry omits Aristotle from his list of Montesquieu's precursors,[9] and yet Aristotle held that the three main types of government, namely the

very interested in the example of paternal power, *cf. Leviathan*, II, xx, pp. 186–7 and 190–1.

[6] *Thèse de Bordeaux*, p. 410; *cf.* p. 422; *cf.* also Comte, *Cours de philosophie positive*, vol. IV, p. 130, who talks of the "vain débordement d'utopies métaphysiques" of M.'s contemporaries, without mentioning the more empirical attitude of M.'s predecessors.

[7] *Op. cit.*, p. 396.

[8] *Montesquieu*, p. 167.

[9] *Op. cit.*, pp. 401–2.

monarchy, aristocracy and republic, though not the corruptions of each, are all natural.[10] This empirical approach is also characteristic of the School of Natural Law: it is a logical consequence of the hypothesis of the original contract that any form of government decided on by the community is legitimate. Grotius showed that the people may make a contract either with one man or with a group of men (*Dg.*, *Disc. prél.* xvi, vol. I, p. 12 and II, iii, 8, vol. I, pp. 121–2). Similarly, in Pufendorf's contract, immediately after the first agreement, the form of government is decided upon, and that form can be either monarchical, aristocratic or popular, each form having advantages and disadvantages (*Dn.*, VII, ii, 8, vol. II, pp. 232–4; *Dv.*, II, vi, 8–13, pp. 293–6 and II, viii, 2–8, pp. 304–8). Like Pufendorf's contract, Locke's did not specify any particular form of government to be natural: the form is decided on by the majority (*T.T.*, II, x, 132, p. 372).[11] Montesquieu simply followed the contractualists in this matter, when he said in Book I, iii: "La force générale peut être placée entre les mains d'un seul, ou entre les mains de plusieurs" (N. I, i, p. 8, Pl. II, p. 237).

Thus, when "Helvétius" criticized the *Esprit des lois* by saying:

> je n'ai jamais bien compris les subtiles distinctions sans cesse répétées sur les différentes formes de gouvernement. Je n'en connais que deux espèces: les bons et les mauvais (N. III, p. 1105),

and when Rousseau ruefully complained in his *Émile* that the *président* had not created political science, but "se contenta de traiter du droit positif des gouvernements établis",[12] they should have criticized the contractualists at the same time. The uncompromising idealism of "Helvétius" and Rousseau is not part of the pragmatic, Aristotelian tradition of natural law.

This tradition finds one of its clearest expressions in Corneille's *Cinna*. Maxime, in his effort to persuade Auguste to renounce the Empire and re-establish the Republic, agrees with the Emperor that the Romans consider any other form of government with hatred; he continues:

> J'ose dire, Seigneur, que par tous les climats
> Ne sont pas bien reçus toutes sortes d'États;
> Chaque peuple a le sien conforme à sa nature,
> Qu'on ne saurait changer sans lui faire une injure.

[10] *Politics*, III, xi, 10, pp. 269–71.
[11] *Cf.* also Gravina, *Origines iuris civilis*, II, xviii, p. 257.
[12] *Émile*, V, p. 836.

Cinna, on the other hand, who wants Auguste to remain Emperor, argues that the "génie" of each people varies "selon les temps, comme selon les lieux", and that the Romans have outgrown their Republicanism.[13] Though the motives of the conspirators differ, and though the facts they allege are at variance, they both agree that the form of the government should depend on the temperament of the people.

Montesquieu's superiority over common political wisdom, as here expressed by Corneille, and over the School of Natural Law, is not that he invented the theory that governments should vary according to local conditions, but that he developed its implications in such great detail, particularly in the first twenty-five books of the *Esprit des lois*. The philosophers of natural law had not been deeply interested in the question, which they had answered only in general terms, concentrating on the inclinations of the people and usually neglecting factors such as climate and size of territory.[14] When seen in its true proportion, Montesquieu's originality is great enough to make us wonder why the positivists felt obliged to exaggerate it.

For Grotius, Pufendorf and Locke, no one form of government is more natural than any other form, but they each had preferences. Grotius and Pufendorf thought that monarchy is usually the least unsatisfactory, but they were aware that each form, including monarchy, has certain disadvantages.[15] Locke preferred moderate monarchies where legislative and executive functions are in different hands (*T.T.*, II, xiv, 159, pp. 392–3).

Similarly, Montesquieu, while proclaiming his desire to be impartial, revealed that he had strong preferences for certain forms of government. A desire to conceal the *président*'s preferences leads the abbé Dedieu into contradicting himself. In one place, he admits that Montesquieu hated despotism,[16] and in another that he "ne pouvait

[13] *Cinna*, II, i, ll. 535–48, in *Œuvres de Corneille*, vol. III, p. 408–9. *Cf.* Fénelon, *Les Devoirs de la royauté*, in *Écrits et lettres politiques*, p. 94:

> Toutes sortes de gouvernements sont nécessairement imparfaites, puisqu'on ne peut confier l'autorité suprême qu'à des hommes; et toutes sortes de gouvernements sont bonnes, quand ceux qui gouvernent suivent la grande loi du bien public. Dans la théorie, certaines formes paraissent meilleures que d'autres; mais, dans la pratique, la faiblesse ou la corruption des hommes, sujets aux mêmes passions, exposent tous les États à des inconvenients à peu près égaux.

[14] Though Domat had established a relationship between the size of a country and its type of government, showing that republics are "restreintes à peu d'étendue" while monarchies need larger territories (*op. cit.*, *Le Droit public*, I, i, vol. II, p. 4); but he did not develop this idea.

[15] *Dg.*, I, iii, 8, vol. I, pp. 122–3; *Dn.*, VII, v, 9 and 22, vol. II, pp. 275 and 289; *Dv.*, II, viii, 4–8, pp. 305–8.

[16] *Montesquieu*, pp. 134–5.

s'empêcher de proclamer l'excellence du gouvernement monarchique".[17] But Dedieu asks us to forget these concessions a few pages later, when he claims that

> il ne serait juste ni d'interpréter ses sympathies ni de les confisquer au bénéfice de tel ou tel gouvernement. Quelles que fussent ses préférences intimes, Montesquieu n'a prétendu que faire l'anatomie de ces organismes vivants.[18]

We are thus asked to overlook Montesquieu's preferences in order to preserve the myth of his positive, impartial approach. More recently, Sergio Cotta has said of Montesquieu: "tutta la sua opera conferma [la] sua imparzialità di scrittore", adding that the fact that Montesquieu was willing to discuss despotism at all bears witness to that impartiality.[19]

Montesquieu's preferences are so obvious that it is impossible to overlook them. He disliked despotism – or rather, as Muriel Dodds has shown, he disliked a certain conception of despotism invented by himself and not corresponding very closely to historical fact[20] – for two main reasons. Firstly, because it is unstable:

> Le principe du gouvernement despotique se corrompt sans cesse, parce qu'il est corrompu par sa nature (*Lois*, VIII, x, N. I, i, p. 158, Pl. II, p. 357).

This could perhaps be described as a scientific criticism, since it could be argued that it is based not on personal prejudice but on an examination of *la nature des choses*.

No such empiricism is to be found in the second reason for which Montesquieu condemned despotism: he thought it to be unnatural, just as Aristotle had done,[21] thus applying an *a priori*, rationalistic standard. The despotic government "cause à la nature humaine des maux effroyables" (*Lois*, II, iv, N. I, i, p. 22, Pl. II, p. 248); in despotic countries, the prince may be held in check by religion, but not by natural law:

> On abandonnera son père, on le tuera même, si le prince l'ordonne: mais on ne boira pas du vin, s'il le veut et s'il l'ordonne. Les lois de la religion sont d'un précepte supérieur, parce qu'elles sont données sur la tête du

[17] *Montesquieu*, p. 133.
[18] *Ibid.*, pp. 136–7.
[19] *Montesquieu e la scienza della società*, pp. 342–3.
[20] *Op. cit.*, pp. 169–70.
[21] *Politics*, III, xi, 10, pp. 269–71.

prince, comme sur celles des sujets. Mais, quant au droit naturel, il n'en est pas de même; le prince est supposé n'être plus un homme (*Lois*, III, x, N. I, i, pp. 37–8, Pl. II, p. 260).

The style of these two passages indicates that Montesquieu was not impartial, but indignant. No subject of a despotic government could love his country more, after reading the *Esprit des lois*, unless the falsity of the picture Montesquieu had painted caused him to feel patriotic indignation.

Although Montesquieu thought despotism to be unnatural, he did not think monarchy to be particularly natural; but he still thought it to be the best government, just as Grotius, Pufendorf, and Locke had done. It is true that some scholars have argued that the *président* favoured democracy,[22] and there is no doubt that in Book III, v, for example, he gave a highly satirical account of the lack of virtue in monarchies. But the majority of the evidence indicates that he believed in the superiority of monarchy from all other points of view: it is clear from Book V, xi, entitled 'De l'excellence du gouvernement monarchique', that he preferred monarchy to despotism; from Chapter x of the same book, that he thought monarchy to be more practical than democracy; and from Book XI, iv, that since "La démocratie et l'aristocratie ne sont point des états libres par leur nature" (N. I, i, p. 206, Pl. II, p. 395), monarchy is most likely to produce political freedom – and for Montesquieu this fact gave it a most important advantage over other régimes.

Montesquieu held two particular monarchies, the English and the "Gothic", in especial favour, because of the amount of freedom they ensured for their subjects. He believed that in the case of the English Constitution, freedom was more or less protected by the limitations imposed on the monarch's power by the privileges of the nobility and of Parliament. Oudin's statement that

Il ne faut [. . .] pas prendre dans l'œuvre de Montesquieu la théorie de la constitution anglaise comme l'expression de ce qu'il considère comme le meilleur gouvernement en soi,[23]

[22] *Cf.* P. Janet, 'Comparaison des théories morales et sociales de Montesquieu et de Jean-Jacques Rousseau', *Revue politique et littéraire*, 1871, p. 558; this interpretation rests partly on a belief that the first eight books of the *Lois* were written before 1728, a theory for which there is no concrete evidence (*cf.* Brethe de la Gressaye, *Lois*, vol. I, pp. xvii–xix, and Shackleton, 'La Genèse de l'*Esprit des lois*', pp. 425–6 and 438). Janet's article proves less that M. thought monarchy to be the best government, than that he had great admiration for the republics of Antiquity: as Janet admits (p. 560) M. realized that such republics were no longer practical.

[23] *Le Spinozisme de Montesquieu*, p. 88.

is only partly true. Montesquieu did not specifically state that the English Constitution has produced one of the best governments in the world, and he denied that it is necessarily suitable for other countries (*Lois*, XI, vi, N. I, i, p. 221, Pl. II, p. 407). However, the fact that, in Book XI, vi, he spent so many pages on explaining its mechanism, and on denouncing the lack of liberty in countries where there are no limitations on the monarch's power, indicates that "en soi" it is a very good kind of government, and that he would have been happy to see the French monarchy adopt some of its features.

Towards the end of Book XI, vi, he claimed that the "beau système" of the English Constitution was derived from the government of certain Germanic tribes, as described by Tacitus (N. I, i, p. 221, Pl. II, p. 407). It is on this "Gothic" or feudal kind of government that Montesquieu bestowed his fullest praise.[24] He thought that the Germanic tribes which had conquered the Roman Empire were "très libres"; that when the conquest was completed, they established a kind of representative government containing a mixture of aristocratic and monarchical features; and that they gradually freed their serfs. He ended by exclaiming:

> il est admirable que la corruption du gouvernement d'un peuple conquérant ait formé la meilleure espèce de gouvernement que les hommes aient pu imaginer (*Lois*, XI, viii, N. I, i, pp. 223–4, Pl. II, p. 409).

Thus Montesquieu's ideal was apparently a kind of feudal monarchy tempered by certain parliamentary and individual rights; he believed that such a government had existed fairly generally in Europe in the Middle Ages, and that it was still to be found, in a modified form, in the England of his own day.

There is a close resemblance between Montesquieu and the philosophers of natural law on this question of the best government; neither he nor they believed monarchy to be more natural than democracy or aristocracy, but they all had preferences. The philosophers of natural law were in fact less idealistic, and Montesquieu less impartial, than the positivists believe.

Did this empiricism of Montesquieu's predecessors also extend to the realm of legislation, or did they believe that because natural law is the same everywhere, civil law should also be the same everywhere?

24 *Cf.* Barckhausen, *Montesquieu, ses idées et ses œuvres*, pp. 66–7.

II. The Diversity of Civil Law

The answer to this question will be divided into two parts, theory and practice, the latter being studied first. The laws concerned with marriage and related topics take up a large portion of the statute books of most countries. They also form a weighty section in the treatises of natural law. How much, in the laws on marriage, is within the province of the natural law, and how much within the province of the civil law?

We have seen in Chapter 3 that for most of the philosophers of natural law, whether religious or secular, the main purpose of marriage is obviously enough the begetting and upbringing of children. They further argue, as Montesquieu did in Book XXIII, ii of the *Esprit des lois*, that if human intercourse were not regulated by law, children would be neglected.[25] However, this did not mean that they believed that marriage should be regulated by identical laws in every country. According to Pufendorf, although all are obliged, by natural law, to marry, the civil law is entitled to stipulate on how far people should be forced, or allowed to marry, taking into account various material, social and political considerations (*Dn.*, VI, i, 6–8, vol. II, pp. 153–6).

Montesquieu made the same points, but his discussion, though based on the same principle, that is, the needs of the state which regulate a civil law, is much better than Pufendorf's. Though the German mentioned many of the examples that Montesquieu was later to give, he was very vague on the question of why particular countries should have needed to increase their population. Whereas Montesquieu gave a closely documented account of the problem, showing also how different climates, soils, political policies and religious doctrines have influenced the size of the population (*Lois*, XXIII, v–xxviii, N. I, ii, pp. 45–77, Pl. II, pp. 684–712). It is true that his rationalism occasionally caused him to make rather naïve comments,[26] but in general he was far more in command of his subject than Pufendorf.

A particularly controversial aspect of this question was celibacy chosen for religious motives. St. Thomas, while admitting that by both natural and divine law, "the precept of procreation regards the whole multitude of men", claimed that this precept does not apply to

[25] *Cf. S.t.*, II, ii, Q. 154, A. 2, vol. XIII, p. 135, and *Dn.*, VI, i, 5 and 15, vol. II, pp. 152–3 and 163–4.

[26] Eg. *Lois*, XXIII, xiii, N. I, ii, pp. 51–2, Pl. II, p. 690, on the effect that eating fish has on fertility.

every individual, and that those who abstain from procreation and "betake themselves to the contemplation of Divine things" are more worthy than those who "betake themselves to carnal procreation" (*S.t.*, II, ii, Q. 152, A. 2, rep. obj. 1, vol. XIII, p. 111). In the late seventeenth and early eighteenth centuries there was an onslaught by Protestant writers and others on the practice of celibacy, in the name of nature and of society,[27] and this attack was continued by the *philosophes*.[28] Montesquieu was likewise opposed to the view of the Catholic Church, though it is most unlikely that he was merely following the trend, as Jacques Vier suggests,[29] since his condemnation of excessive celibacy is a consequence of his belief that Europe's dwindling population must be increased. Though he probably did not believe that celibacy should be abolished altogether (*Lois*, XXV, iv, N. I, ii, p. 112, Pl. II, p. 740, and *Défense*, N. I, ii, pp. 469–71, Pl. II, pp. 1147–9), his choice of vocabulary seems to suggest that he considered the practice to have been predominantly harmful: it has caused the propagation of the human race to be "choquée" (*Lois*, XXIII, xxi, N. I, ii, p. 70, Pl. II, p. 706), and the religious legislator "fatigua la société" in order to favour it (*Lois*, XXIV, vii, N. I, ii, p. 88, Pl. II, p. 720). Montesquieu's views were unanimously condemned (on religious rather than moral grounds) by both mild and extremist religious critics.[30] Here, then, he was on the side of those who prefer natural law to divine law.

A related topic where Montesquieu took a similar view was divorce. In the *Lettres persanes*, Usbek had put forward a very ingenious theory: he saw the Christian doctrine of the indissolubility of marriage as one of the major causes of the depopulation of Europe; he argued that a couple who hate each other are not likely to have many children, whereas, if they were to divorce, and marry a more suitable partner, they would contribute to the propagation of the species. This rather flippant argument is another aspect of Montesquieu's obsessional worship of fertility. Usbek concluded by saying that it is difficult to see why divorce is forbidden among the Christians, since marriage is

[27] *Cf.* Lanson, 'Origines et premières manifestations de l'esprit philosophique dans la littérature française de 1674 à 1748', *Revue hebdomadaire des cours et conférences*, 1907–9, vol. XVI, ii, 1908, p. 152, and 'Formation et développement de l'esprit philosophique', vol. XVII, ii, p. 717. Pufendorf gave various causes for which legislators might prevent marriage, but he did not include religion among them (*Dn.*, VI, i, 8, vol. II, pp. 155–6).

[28] Eg. *Encyclopédie*, art. 'Célibat', vol. II, pp. 803–6.

[29] *Histoire de la littérature française, XVIIIe siècle*, vol. I, Colin, 1965, p. 142.

[30] *Lettre au P. J. B.*, pp. 109–10; *Examen critique*, pp. 128–30; 1750: 5th and 6th Propositions; 1752: 8th and 9th propositions: see Beyer, 'Montesquieu et la censure religieuse', p. 118, n. 3, p. 119, n. 1, p. 120, n. 7, and p. 125, n. 3.

only a contract (*L.p.* CXVI, N. I, iii, pp. 231–3, Pl. I, pp. 303–4).

Traces of this attitude remain in the *Esprit des lois*, but in an attenuated form. According to Usbek, divorce always helps to increase population. For the Montesquieu of the *Esprit des lois*, divorce is only acceptable if it increases population. This is clear from the remark that divorce should not be allowed in the case of a couple who wish to enter religion, since such a concession would shock "le principe fondamental du divorce, qui ne souffre la dissolution d'un mariage que dans l'espérance d'un autre" (*Lois*, XXVI, ix, N. I, ii, p. 138, Pl. II, p. 760). But an *only if* is not an absolute prohibition, and Montesquieu's critics were not slow to take him up on this remark and on various others, where it was implied that divorce might be suitable in some countries.

Catholic thought was undecided as to whether divorce was forbidden by Divine law only, or by natural law as well. In Chapter 3, we showed that St. Thomas had admitted that by natural law, marriage need not be lifelong. An objection in the *Supplement* to the *Summa theologica* developed this argument along the lines Usbek was later to adopt (*S.t.* III, *Supplement*, Q. 67, A. 1, obj. 4, vol. XIX, p. 358), but the author of the *Supplement*, intent on proving that divorce is unnatural as well as ungodly, claimed that the precept in Matthew, XIX, 6, forbidding divorce is based on natural law, firstly because natural law tells us to obey God, and secondly because parents should stay together for life in order to "lay up for their children" (*ibid.*, A. 1, p. 358). These arguments seem rather feeble, and in the next article, we find the author admitting that indissolubility of marriage is not part of "the first intention of nature" (*ibid.*, A. 2, p. 361). In their condemnation of Montesquieu's thought on this matter, the Sorbonne used such words as "hæretica" and "verbo Dei contraria", rather than referring to natural law,[31] and neither the *Lettre au P.J.B.* nor even the abbé de La Roche actually stated that divorce is forbidden by natural law.[32]

One remark that particularly displeased the Sorbonne was:

> La répudiation pour raison de la stérilité de la femme ne saurait avoir lieu que dans le cas d'une femme unique (*Lois*, XVI, xv, N. I, i, p. 363, Pl. II, p. 519).

[31] 1750: 1st Proposition, and 1752: 7th Proposition: see Beyer, 'Montesquieu et la censure religieuse', p. 110, n. 1; *cf.* however the condemnation of *Lois*, XVI, xv: 1750: 2nd Proposition: Beyer, *ibid.*, p. 125, n. 2.

[32] *Lettre au P. J. B.*, pp. 107–8 and 112–3; *Examen critique*, p. 127: the Jansenist merely said that M. was one of "ces messieurs de la religion naturelle" and that he was following "la nature corrompue".

In order to placate the theologians, Montesquieu added the following note, which first appeared in the 1757 posthumous edition:[33] "Cela ne signifie pas que la répudiation pour raison de la stérilité soit permise dans le christianisme". In fact, this footnote tells us nothing new, since it does not say that the Christian religion should not allow repudiation, only that it does not allow it. Nevertheless, Montesquieu had already shown, even in the 1748 edition, that he was aware of the disadvantages of divorce:

> Le divorce a ordinairement une grande utilité politique; et, quant à l'utilité civile, il est établi pour le mari et pour la femme, et n'est pas toujours favorable aux enfants (*Lois*, XVI, xv, N. I, i, p. 364, Pl. II, p. 520).

In spite of this remark, there is no absolute condemnation of divorce, and not even any explanation of why it is forbidden by Christianity.

Such an explanation is to be found in the work of Grotius and Pufendorf, but they were far from condemning divorce. In the notes to his translation of *De iure belli ac pacis*, Barbeyrac summarized the Dutch philosopher's final position: he did not see Christ's words in Matthew, V, 32 as an absolute condemnation of divorce in all cases except adultery, since "en vertu de l'équité naturelle" divorce must surely also be allowed for other offences of equal gravity, such as attempted poisoning of the marriage partner. Furthermore, since marriage is established not only for the propagation of the species, but also for "le secours mutuel qu'on espère de cette union", divorce might be permitted by Christ's law in cases where this "secours" is no longer to be found (*Dg.*, II, v, 9, n. 7, vol. I, pp. 283–5).

Pufendorf repeated many of Grotius's arguments, and added an account of Milton's *Doctrine and Discipline of Divorce*. He claimed that his attitude towards the Englishman's book was impartial, but it is easy to see where his sympathies lay, for, like Grotius, he used the idea of natural law in order to temper the rigorism of the Gospel:

> si les paroles de notre Seigneur au sujet du divorce sont susceptibles d'une interprétation favorable, il faut la suivre, comme plus conforme à l'esprit de douceur qui règne dans l'Évangile (*Dn.*, VI, i, 24, vol. II, pp. 173–6).

For Pufendorf, natural law allows divorce when "l'une des parties ne tient pas ses engagements" (*ibid.*, 21, p. 170).

Thus Grotius and Pufendorf were in favour of divorce, and they did not believe it to be contrary either to natural law or to God's law.

[33] *Lois, ibid.*; Brethe de la Gressaye, *Lois*, vol. II, p. 432, n. 45 to p. 257 and Pl. II, p. 1511; see also the *Réponses et explications*, N. III. p. 655, Pl. II, p. 1177.

Montesquieu's attitude seems to have been very close to theirs. His ecclesiastical critics condemned him mainly in the name of God's law, perhaps because they were uncertain of the ruling of the natural law. In the question of polygamy, another subject that was likely to cause offense to pious ears, we find a similar grouping of opinions.

Montesquieu's attitude to polygamy is characterized by a certain ambiguity. Neither the chapters of the *Esprit des lois* devoted to the problem, nor the long descriptions in the *Lettres persanes* of life in Usbek's harem, were prompted solely by scientific curiosity. It is true that Montesquieu sometimes condemns polygamy. Usbek tells Rica that plurality of wives tends to diminish natality (*L.p.* CXIV, N. I, iii, pp. 226–9, Pl. I, pp. 299–301). Similarly, Book XVI, vi of the *Esprit des lois* tries to prove that

> A regarder la polygamie en général, indépendamment des circonstances qui peuvent la faire un peu tolérer, elle n'est point utile au genre humain [...]. Elle n'est pas non plus utile aux enfants (N. I, i, p. 354, Pl. II, p. 512).

This passage had appeared in the first edition, in 1748,[34] but at the same time, the title of Chapter iv of the same book had what a recent critic calls "une allure provocante":[35] 'Que la loi de la polygamie est une affaire de calcul'.[36] By the phrase "affaire de calcul" Montesquieu meant that the incidence of polygamy in any country depends on the relative numbers of boys and girls born there, which in turn depends on the climate. Forseeing that such a theory might be considered deterministic and contrary to the principles of Christianity, he had taken the precaution of stating that

> *j'ai peine à croire* qu'il y ait beaucoup de pays où la disproportion soit assez grande, pour qu'elle exige qu'on y introduise la loi de plusieurs femmes, ou la loi de plusieurs maris. Cela veut dire seulement que la pluralité des femmes, ou même la pluralité des hommes, *est plus conforme à la nature* dans de certains pays que dans d'autres.
>
> [...]
>
> Dans tout ceci, je ne justifie pas les usages; mais j'en rends les raisons.[37]

In spite of these precautions, the tenor of Chapters iv and vi of Book XVI, in the 1748 edition, is undoubtedly that although polygamy may not

[34] Brethe de la Gressaye, *Lois*, vol. II, p. 429, n. 22, to p. 248.

[35] Beyer, 'Montesquieu et la censure religieuse', p. 109.

[36] Brethe de la Gressaye, *Lois*, vol. II, p. 426, n. 13, to p. 246; Pl. II, p. 1510.

[37] Brethe de la Gressaye, *Lois*, vol. II, pp. 427–8, nn. 18–20, together with pp. 246–7; Pl. II, p. 1510 does not give the 1748 version of this passage. The italics are ours and indicate words that M. subsequently altered.

be very useful, it is probably not unnatural, or, if it is unnatural, it is excusable, being the result of a necessary cause, the climate.

Did Montesquieu clarify his attitude in his replies to his critics? The notion that 'La loi de la polygamie est une affaire de calcul' was sharply condemned by the *Nouvelles ecclésiastiques*: the abbé de La Roche was particularly indignant that the author of the *Esprit des lois* had failed to make it clear that polyandry is worse than polygamy (*Examen critique*, p. 126). In fact, Montesquieu had criticized polyandry, as he pointed out in his *Défense* and as La Roche later admitted.[38] He went further, and tried to claim that in Chapter vi he had "établi que la polygamie était, par sa nature et en elle même, une chose mauvaise" (N. I, ii, p. 461, Pl. II, p. 1141). But the word *nature* is ambiguous here. Montesquieu no doubt wished his critic to think that he meant *par la nature*; by using the word *sa*, however, he was referring less to eternal morality than to utility and to *la nature des choses*.

The same ambiguity is to be found in one of the alterations he made to meet the criticisms by the Sorbonne concerning Chapter iv:[39] the title of the chapter became more matter-of-fact: 'De la polygamie. Ses diverses circonstances', and the phrase "est plus conforme à la nature" became "s'éloigne moins de la nature", thus implying that polygamy is always unnatural, whatever circumstances may cause it.[40] This implication is undermined by the fact that once again *nature* could refer to *la nature des choses* rather than to natural law.[41]

Though it could be argued that since Montesquieu was willing to alter his text, he did eventually accept that polygamy is unnatural, it could more plausibly be argued that the new formulae are still by no means categorical, and represent a change of expression rather than of opinion. However, both these points of view are perhaps too absolute. Not everything that is unnatural is equally evil – there are degrees of unnaturalness. Thus, though Montesquieu held that abortion is completely unnatural (*cf. Lois*, XXIII, xi, N. I, ii, p. 50, Pl. II, p. 689), he did not put polygamy in the same category: it may be unnatural, but only to a certain extent, since it is "plus conforme à la nature"

[38] M. had criticized polyandry in *Lois*, XVI, vi, N. I, i, p. 354, Pl. II, p. 512; he referred to this criticism in the *Défense*, N. I, ii, p. 464, Pl. II, p. 1144; La Roche admitted his mistake in the *Réponse à la Défense*, pp. 225–6.

[39] 1750: 11th Proposition; 1752: 6th Proposition: see Beyer, 'Montesquieu et la censure religieuse', p. 109, nn. 4 and 5.

[40] See N. I, i, pp. 352–3 and Pl. II, p. 511; Brethe de la Gressaye, *Lois*, vol. II, pp. 425–6, n. 13, to p. 246, and p. 427, n. 19 to p. 246; M. also changed "j'ai peine à croire" to "je ne crois pas", *ibid.*, p. 427, n. 18, to p. 246.

[41] *Cf.* Ehrard, *L'Idée de nature*, vol. II, pp. 734–5.

or "s'éloigne moins de la nature" (the wording makes but little difference) in countries where it is caused by the climate.

If Montesquieu took this moderate view of polygamy, he was not the only writer to have done so. According to Pierre Martino, polygamy and other oriental institutions "épouvantaient la morale commune, et faisaient gronder les théologiens";[42] similarly, Ehrard claims that polygamy is "*absolument* contraire à la morale naturelle";[43] both scholars are thus able to make Montesquieu appear very daring. Perhaps they have been misled by an *avocat* in one of Molière's plays, who sings:

> La polygamie est un cas,
> Est un cas pendable.[44]

The view of the Catholic Church on this question was by no means clear-cut. According to the *Supplement* of the *Summa theologica*, polygamy "is in a way against the law of nature, and in a way not against it": it is against it in that it hinders the second and third aims of marriage, that is companionship and the symbolic fulfilment of the union of Christ and His Church; but it is not against it in that it does not hinder the first aim of marriage, namely procreation (*S.t.*, III, *Supplement*, Q. 65, A. 1, vol. XIX, pp. 330–1). The theologian added a further qualification:

> It is more opposed to the natural law that a wife have several husbands than that a husband have several wives: wherefore the latter has sometimes been lawful, but the former never (*S.t.*, III, *Supplement*, Q. 62, A. 4, obj. 2, vol. XIX, p. 299).[45]

The concession in the second sentence of this quotation, aimed at saving the reputation of some of the Patriarchs, makes Montesquieu's opinions appear fairly orthodox. Even Crevier, one of the *président*'s severest critics, had to admit that the example of the Patriarchs, as well as "divers textes de l'Ancien Testament", "ne permettent pas de regarder la pluralité des femmes comme absolument contraire à la loi naturelle".[46] Among Montesquieu's other critics, only the theologians of the Sorbonne, in their condemnation of 1750, implied that polygamy is unnatural;[47] neither the *Lettre au P.J.B.*, nor the abbé de La Roche,

[42] *L'Orient dans la littérature française au XVIIe et au XVIIIe siècle*, Hachette, 1906, p. 326; *cf.* Durkheim, *Thèse de Bordeaux*, p. 421.

[43] *L'Idée de nature*, vol. II, p. 734, (Ehrard's italics).

[44] *Monsieur de Pourceaugnac*, II, xi, in *Œuvres de Molière*, Hachette, 1921–2, vol. VII, p. 316.

[45] This statement is the premise to the objection; although the theologican rejected the conclusion drawn from it, he did not reject the premise itself (*ibid.*, rep. obj. 2, p. 301).

[46] *Observations sur le livre de l'Esprit des lois*, p.216.

[47] 1750: 11th Proposition: Beyer, 'Montesquieu et la censure religieuse', p. 109, n. 4.

nor the Sorbonne in its condemnation of 1752 claimed that polygamy is contrary to the natural law: this expression is reserved by the Jansenist and the Sorbonne for polyandry.[48]

In view of the uncertainty which surrounded the question of polygamy, Pufendorf does not appear to have been particularly heretical when he began his discussion in his usual fashion, by stating that he could not see any strong reason why it should be contrary to natural law:

Les savants ne conviennent pas entre eux, si cette sorte de polygamie [i.e. polygamous marriage, as opposed to "la communauté des femmes"] est contraire, ou non, au droit naturel. Je vais rapporter les raisons, que l'on allègue de part et d'autre; et j'en laisserai le jugement au lecteur (*Dn.*, VI, i, 16, vol. II, p. 164).

His account is biased towards those who believe that polygamy is not unnatural, and in his justification of it, he mentioned the example of the Patriarchs and of the Moslems, and he tried to explain the decline of the practice among the Turks (*ibid.*, 17–19, pp. 164–8). He thus allowed just as much variation in the civil law on this point as Montesquieu was to do; the only important difference between the two philosophers is that Montesquieu showed much greater ingenuity in explaining the causes of polygamy, thus revealing his rationalism. His intention is praiseworthy, but most critics agree that he drastically over-simplified an intricate problem.[49]

This tendency towards over-simplification is much less apparent in Montesquieu's discussion of incest. We have already seen how Pufendorf remained unconvinced by the physical and moral reasons alleged by the Catholic Church against incest, and that Montesquieu did accept those reasons, in the *Esprit des lois*. However, this did not prevent him from saying that incest is sometimes dependent on custom, that is on whether or not certain relations inhabit the same house. In almost all countries, fathers and daughters, brothers and sisters live together in the same house: there is consequently a universal natural law against the violation of *pudeur* in these circumstances:

[48] The *Lettre au P. J. B.*, pp. 105–7, did not call either polyandry or polygamy unnatural; it merely disputed M.'s contention that they are "une affaire de calcul"; La Roche says that polyandry is "un désordre monstrueux" (*Examen critique*, p. 126); the 1752 condemnation by the Sorbonne says that polygamy is contrary to the Gospel and that polyandry is contrary to the Gospel and to natural law (6th Proposition: see Beyer, 'Montesquieu et la censure religieuse', p. 109, n. 5.

[49] *Cf.* Dedieu, *Montesquieu*, pp. 229–30; Brethe de la Gressaye, *Lois*, vol. II, p. 428, n. 20, to p. 247.

Ces causes sont si fortes et si naturelles, qu'elles ont agi presque par toute la terre, indépendamment d'aucune communication. [...]

Que si quelques peuples n'ont point rejeté les mariages entre les pères et les enfants, les sœurs et les frères, on a vu, dans le livre premier, que les êtres intelligents ne suivent pas toujours leurs lois (*Lois*, XXVI, xiv, N. I, ii, p. 144, Pl. II, p. 765).

In the case of other relations – cousins, brothers-in-law, sisters-in-law – inter-marriage is not forbidden when, by the customs of the country, they do not live in the same house:

Les lois civiles défendent les mariages, lorsque, par les usages reçus dans un certain pays, ils se trouvent être dans les mêmes circonstances que ceux qui sont défendus par les lois de la nature [...]. La défense des lois de la nature est invariable, parce qu'elle dépend d'une chose invariable; le père, la mère et les enfants habitant nécessairement dans la maison. Mais les défenses des lois civiles sont accidentelles, parce qu'elles dépendent d'une circonstance accidentelle; les cousins germains et autres habitant accidentellement dans la maison (*ibid.*, N. I, ii, p. 146, Pl. II, pp. 766–7).

The principle is clear, in spite of the rather involved wording: the civil law enforces the natural law. In some cases (those concerning parents and children) the natural law is universal; in other cases (those concerning other relations), it is not, because it depends on circumstances which are different from country to country. In the first case it is a primary natural law, derived from the nature of man (here, the cohabitation of the family); in the second case, it is a secondary natural law, depending upon some human custom.

Brethe de la Gressaye praises Montesquieu's use of the theory of cohabitation;[50] Werner Stark says the *président*'s argument "is already modern sociology almost in the technical sense";[51] both scholars fail to mention that the theory of cohabitation, like the theory of respect, is borrowed from Catholic theology. The *Supplement* of the *Summa theologica* tried to explain why "in the Old Law a man was forbidden to marry his father's sister but not his brother's daughter":

the old Law in debarring certain persons looked chiefly to the danger of concupiscence arising from cohabitation; and debarred those persons who were in closer intimacy with one another on account of their living together. Now it is more usual for a niece to live with her uncle than an aunt with her nephew. [...] Hence there was not the same reason for debarring a niece and an aunt (*S.t.*, III, *Supplement*, Q. 54, A. 4, obj. 7 and rep. obj. 7, vol. XIX, pp. 207 and 211).

[50] *Lois*, vol. III, p. 449, n. 42, to p. 313.
[51] *Op. cit.*, p. 68.

Once again, Montesquieu found support for his rationalism in Catholic dogma, but the idea that the civil law concerning incest may legitimately vary from country to country is also consistent with the attitude of the School of Natural Law, whose members failed to find any universal natural law prohibiting incest.

In the three topics just discussed, divorce, polygamy and incest the School of Natural Law had been unable to say clearly what was the ruling of the natural law, though they tended to favour divorce and were not very shocked by polygamy. They tended to allow these questions to be settled by custom and practice: only when a custom appears universal, as in the case of marriage, were they able to make a firm statement of principle. Thus, in spite of their apparent *a priorism*, their approach was as empirical as that of Montesquieu in the case of divorce and polygamy, and more empirical than his in the case of incest.

However, on one topic related to marriage, Montesquieu does seem to have been more empirical than his predecessors: he thought that not only political succession, but also private succession, are no concern of the natural law.

La loi naturelle ordonne aux pères de nourrir leurs enfants; mais elle n'oblige pas de les faire héritiers (*Lois*, XXVI, vi, N. I, ii, p. 132, Pl. II, p. 755).

On this question, Montesquieu appears to have disagreed both with the Church, which, as we have already seen, claimed (on the authority of 2 Corinthians, XII, 14) that parents should "lay up" for their children, and with the other philosophers of natural law. Pufendorf stressed that in intestate succession, the law should presume that the father wished to leave his possessions to his children: failure to follow this rule might result in public disturbance. He added, rather surprisingly if one imagines that he was only an *a priorist*, that

La raison, et la pratique constante de tous les peuples qui nous sont connus, concourent également à faire passer les enfants devant tous les autres;

and that apart from any principle of duty, "la tendresse paternelle" causes fathers to want to leave their possessions to their children. He thus based the natural law of succession on the two concepts of duty and of practice, which latter he related to a supposedly universal instinct.[52] Similarly, both Domat and Gravina were to appeal to uni-

[52] *Dn.*, IV, xi, 2–3, vol. I, pp. 575–6; also *ibid.*, x, 4, p. 568; *cf.* Locke, *T.T.*, I, ix, 88, pp. 224–5.

versal consent and to duty, in establishing the natural law of succession.[53]

Montesquieu, on the other hand, claimed to base succession purely on practice, and he did not see any one practice as universal. But it is difficult to take at its face-value his notion that succession is no concern of the natural law, when we read his discussion of the Roman *Lex Voconia*. This law, said Montesquieu, was aimed at restricting the amount of wealth that women could inherit. He told how certain citizens who wished to evade the law inscribed their name not in one of the first five categories of the *census*, to which it applied, but in the sixth and lowest category, to which it did not apply; alternatively, some fathers resorted to a *fidei-commissum*. Montesquieu's comment on the effects of this law is revealing:

> Telle était la force de la *nature*, que des pères, pour éluder la loi voconienne, consentaient à souffrir la honte d'être confondus dans la sixième classe avec les prolétaires [. . .].
>
> [. . .]
>
> C'est un malheur de la condition humaine, que les législateurs soient obligés de faire *des lois qui combattent les sentiments naturels mêmes*: telle fut la loi voconienne. C'est que les législateurs statuent plus sur la société que sur le citoyen, et sur le citoyen que sur l'homme. [. . .] la loi méprisait, dans le testateur, *les sentiments de la nature*.[54]

Montesquieu did not say that it was contrary to natural law, that the civil law should force parents to break the law in order to leave their possessions to their children, he simply said that it was "un malheur de la condition humaine". Hence, in one sense, he was true to his principle that succession depends only on the civil law. In another sense, however, he was false to that principle. His conception of a natural law is that of a command based on those instincts which relate to the preservation of life, freedom and "la pudeur". Therefore, since the instinct which makes parents leave their property to their children is related to the preservation of life, Montesquieu should logically have regarded it as the basis of a natural law. He might have argued in reply to such an objection that though it is always in society's interest to encourage say "la pudeur", it is not always in that interest to allow fathers to do what they want; and that in this case the *Lex Voconia* was consistent with the nature of the Roman government at the time, and

[53] Domat, *op. cit.*, Part II, Preface, iv, vol. I, p. 302; Gravina, *Origines iuris civilis*, II, xli, p. 322.

[54] *Lois*, XXVII, N. I, ii, pp. 167–70, Pl. II, pp. 783–6 (our italics); see Shackleton, *M.*, pp. 320–4, for a comparison of M.'s historical approach with the more descriptive approach of other writers to the Roman laws of succession.

in particular with its desire to eradicate excessive luxury. However, this argument is not entirely convincing: it reveals an unpractical attitude, since it advocates that civil law should not take account of human nature; it is in contradiction with Montesquieu's maxim that the best government is that which best suits the "disposition" of its people. In his discussion of succession, Montesquieu failed to reconcile his conception of natural law with his method of studying civil law.

His treatment of two much more controversial topics, suicide and usury, avoids this ambiguity; he was once more able to base his empiricism on that of his predecessors.

In the eighteenth century the age-old debate on the rights and wrongs of suicide came to a head. As Lester Crocker puts it, the act was seen by both traditionalists and *philosophes* as "a crucial test of man's freedom or his dependence on a superior force".[55] What was Montesquieu's attitude?

Suicide had been condemned by St. Thomas on three main grounds: that it is a crime against oneself, against society and against God.[56] In *Lettre persane* LXXVI, Usbek tried to justify suicide by answering, in effect, these three objections. To the first, he replied that he has the right to end his life when he is suffering (N. I, iii, p. 156, Pl. I, p. 246). To the second, he replied that

La société est fondée sur un avantage mutuel: mais, lorsqu'elle me devient onéreuse, qui m'empêche d'y renoncer? (N. I, iii, pp. 156–7, Pl. I, p. 246)

This argument is a blatant misuse of the theory of the original contract, since one cannot justly reject an agreement unless one has the consent of the other parties, and since in any case the contract did not guarantee happiness, only security. To the third objection, that by killing himself he would be upsetting God's laws, he replied in language tinged with Cartesian and even Spinozistic terms[57] that he has an absolute right to change anything in nature, including the relationship between his soul and his body, since the universe will still remain as perfect as before (N. I, iii, pp. 157–8, Pl. I, pp. 246–7).

[55] *An Age of Crisis*, p.12; see also 'The Discussion of Suicide in the Eighteenth Century', *Journal of the History of Ideas*, 1952, pp. 47–72.

[56] *S.t.*, II, ii, Q. 64, A. 5, vol. X, pp. 203–4; Aristotle insists on the crime against the state, *Ethics*, V, xi, 3, pp. 318–9, while Clarke is more concerned with the crime against God, *Discourse*, pp. 622–4.

[57] Cartesian terms: "les lois de la création et de la conservation", etc: *cf. Discours de la méthode*, V, p. 45; Spinozistic terms: Usbek's *right* to disturb the whole of nature reminds us of Spinoza's conception of right: "chaque type naturel a un droit souverain sur tout ce qui est en son pouvoir", *Tractatus theologico-politicus*, xvi, p. 881.

It would appear that at the time of the *Lettres persanes*, Montesquieu – who so often hides his views behind those of the sober Usbek – believed that suicide is not unnatural. Nevertheless, by the time of the 1754 edition of the *Lettres* he had either changed his belief or decided to disguise it more carefully: he added a new letter from Ibben to Usbek, showing that it is more obedient to God not to end one's life voluntarily, and that a civil law against suicide will help to prevent other crimes.[58] This concept of a civil law derived from the nature of society was accompanied, in a draft of the new letter, by a reference to man's instinctive horror of death, which is then made the basis of a moral natural law forbidding suicide:

Depuis que l'Etre suprême a uni nos âmes à nos corps, l'être composé a toujours une horreur secrète de la séparation des deux êtres simples: ce sentiment est une branche de la loi naturelle.[59]

This normative natural law derived from a certain instinct of self-preservation is entirely in keeping with Montesquieu's notion of natural law, but we cannot be sure that it represents his true belief: Usbek's letter in favour of suicide is much more fervent in tone than Ibben's refutation.

At the time of the *Considérations*, at least, Montesquieu was still in agreement with Usbek. In Chapter XII, he suggested that suicide is caused by a kind of "instinct naturel et obscur" which makes men love their reputation more than their lives. In a passage which was suppressed at the wish of the Censor, but which nevertheless appeared in some editions, he ended by lamenting that since this power that men have over their lives is no longer exercised, they have become less free and less courageous (N. I, iii, p. 436, Pl. II, pp. 136 and 1489–90).[60] It is paradoxical that in the unpublished corrections to the *Lettres persanes*, Montesquieu should have said that men have an instinctive horror of suicide, and in the *Considérations*, that they have an instinctive desire to end their life in certain circumstances. Such contradictions are perhaps the inevitable result of deriving natural law from instinct.

The question of suicide was clearly one that fascinated Montesquieu, for he discussed it again in the *Esprit des lois*: it was yet another of those exceptional phenomena that he wished to bring within the compass of

[58] N. I, iii, pp. 158–9, Pl. I, pp. 247–8; *Lettres persanes*, ed. Vernière, pp. 371–2, n. f, to p. 162 and Pl. I, p. 1591.

[59] See *Lettres persanes*, ed. Vernière, pp. 371–2, Pl. I, p. 1591 (not in N.).

[60] See Vian, 'Montesquieu et la censure', in Laboulaye, *Œuvres complètes de Montesquieu*, vol. VI, p. 325.

his "principes". In the case of the Romans, he alleged, suicide was the result of a moral cause, education; in the case of the English, it is the result of a physical cause, the climate (*Lois*, XIV, xii, N. I, i, p. 319, Pl. II, pp. 485–6). Discussing suicide as practised by the Romans, he said that "Du temps de la république, il n'y avait point de loi à Rome qui punît ceux qui se tuaient eux-mêmes", and that at that time suicide did not invalidate a man's will; he then explained how later certain Emperors, in order to enrich themselves, made a law by which the goods of those who committed suicide in order to escape punishment for a crime, were confiscated (*Lois*, XXIX, ix, N. I, ii, pp. 275–6, Pl. II, pp. 870–1).

With his psychological and historical approach to the problem, Montesquieu made, in the early editions, only the barest reference to the fact that suicide is usually condemned on moral grounds.[61] Nevertheless, the Sorbonne seems to have been more than usually naïve when it claimed that in saying there was no *law* against suicide in the Rome of the Republic, Montesquieu was implying that there was no *natural* law against it.[62] In his *Réponses et explications*, Montesquieu quite rightly argued that

> dire qu'il n'y avait point de loi à Rome ["contre ceux qui se tuaient eux-mêmes"], cela ne peut s'entendre que d'une loi civile, parce que la loi naturelle ne peut être une loi locale (N. III, p. 658, Pl. II, p. 1179).

He also stated that he had made certain changes in his text in order to meet the criticisms of the theologians, and in particular that he had added a footnote to Book XIV, xii, to the effect that "L'action de ceux qui se tuent eux-mêmes est contraire à la loi naturelle et à la religion révélée", and that he had changed some of the words in the chapter, in order to imply a stronger condemnation of suicide (N. III, pp. 657–8, Pl. II, p. 1179). These changes were in fact incorporated into the 1757 edition,[63] and they are consistent with the new *Lettre persane* from Ibben to Usbek added to the collection only a few years earlier. Never-

[61] "Il est clair que les lois civiles de quelques pays peuvent avoir eu des raisons pour flétrir l'homicide de soi-même", *Lois*, XIV, xii, in Brethe de la Gressaye, *Lois*, vol. II, p. 406, n. 48, to p. 203; Pl. II does not give this variant.

[62] 1750: 10th Proposition; 1752: 10th Proposition: see Beyer, 'Montesquieu et la censure religieuse', p. 109, n. 1 and p. 115, n. 5.

[63] *Cf.* N. I, i, p. 319, n. a, Pl. II, p. 485, n. b; see also N. I, i, p. 320, Pl. II, p. 486, where "peuvent avoir eu des raisons" has become "ont eu des raisons". *P.* 1890 (Bkn. 258), N. II, pp. 565–6, Pl. II, p. 1054), condemns suicide on the grounds that it is caused by pride. This *Pensée* was probably written after 1749, so Brethe de la Gressaye seems to be wrong when he says (*Lois*, vol. II, p. 406, n. 48) that it dates from long before the *Lois*; and that consequently M.'s opinions were orthodox even before 1748.

theless, the footnote to Book XIV, xii strikes the reader as very odd, since its dogmatic, moralizing tone is in complete contrast with the objective nature of the chapter itself.

It was not, however, Montesquieu's remarks on suicide in Rome that received the most publicity, but those on suicide in England. He asserted in this same Book XIV, xii that in England, suicide is caused solely by the climate, and hence that

> on ne peut pas plus le punir qu'on ne punit les effets de la démence (N. I, i, p. 320, Pl. II, p. 486).

Montesquieu's critics were unanimous in condemning this idea. The *Lettre au P.J.B.* suggested that the English were indeed guilty, since their frequent attempts at suicide were caused by a fashion resulting from their irreligion (pp. 104–5). The abbé de La Roche accused Montesquieu of whitewashing the English through a desire to absolve the "berceau" of natural religion.[64] In his witty reply to the Jansenist, Montesquieu spent five pages combating the charge of deism, but said nothing at all about suicide.[65] Even La Beaumelle, usually so anxious to justify Montesquieu, here disagreed with him.[66]

Though these critics disputed the facts that Montesquieu had mentioned and his interpretation of them, they did not dispute the principle underlying his argument: that no-one should be punished for an involuntary action. This notion was stated by Pufendorf in his discussion of suicide. He condemned the action when it is caused by "l'ennui des incommodités", but added that

> Il n'en est pas de même de ceux qui se tuent eux-mêmes dans l'accès d'une maladie qui leur ôte l'usage de la raison; car chacun voit qu'ils sont entièrement innocents (*Dn.*, II, iv, 19, vol. I, p. 252).

Though Montesquieu's application of this principle to suicide in England is rather far-fetched, the principle itself was commonly accepted.

Pufendorf was inclined to be lenient towards suicide. He mentioned that Samson and Saul had killed themselves in order to prevent the true religion from being mocked, and we have the impression that,

[64] *Examen critique*, p. 125; *cf.* La Porte, *op. cit.*, pp. 89–95.
[65] *Défense*, N. I, ii, pp. 450–4, Pl. II, pp. 1134–6; M. did however later justify himself on this point to the theologians of the Sorbonne, by claiming that his discussion of suicide in England was based on medical evidence (N. III, p. 659, Pl. II, p. 1180).
[66] *Op. cit.*, pp. 294–5.

unlike St. Thomas,[67] he believed that their example provided a precedent, especially as Barbeyrac felt obliged to add a footnote to the effect that "Cette raison n'excuse point l'homicide de soi-même" (*Dn.*, II, iv, 19, vol. I, p. 250 and *ibid.*, n. 3, p. 251). Pufendorf continued by giving an account of the argument prevalent in Antiquity, that suicide is only wrong if it harms society, and that if a man realizes that he is going to suffer a very painful death, he can assume he is already cut off from society and does no wrong to forestall his fate by killing himself. Pufendorf would seem to have agreed with this, for he finds nothing to say against it, concluding with a "Voilà ce qu'on dit là-dessus, et dont nous laissons le jugement au lecteur" (*ibid.*, pp. 251–2). Once more, Pufendorf reveals himself to be more empirical than Catholic theology: for the Sorbonne, suicide is contrary to divine and natural law,[68] but the German philosopher was unable to give a full account of the ruling of the natural law on this question.

Montesquieu's attitude was very similar to Pufendorf's; however, his willingness to incorporate conciliatory footnotes and textual changes seems to hint that he had no very profound reason for wishing to justify suicide, except on the one hand his admiration for Rome and the Stoics, and on the other his desire to show off his theory of climate. His remarks on suicide reveal his *a priori* mentality, his effort to bend the facts in order to make them fit his theory of climate, and, as in the *Lettres persanes*, a wish to play with provocative ideas.

Lester Crocker sees dangers in this kind of play. In his witch-hunt for early eighteenth-century nihilists, he claims that "Montesquieu's statement [in *Lettre persane* LXXVI] about a man's death not disturbing the universal order or perfection tallies exactly with Sade's defence of murder".[69] This assertion is not justified. It may be logically correct to say that from this *Lettre persane* we can deduce the idea that "All acts are reduced to equivalence and justified, at least from the viewpoint of nature and God",[70] but there is no evidence that Montesquieu accepted this deduction; indeed, he argued against it in the *Traité des devoirs* (as Crocker admits).[71] Crocker further states that in adding the

[67] St. Thomas (*S.t.*, II, ii, Q. 64, A. 5, rep. obj. 4, vol. X, p. 205) cited St. Augustine, who had said that not even Samson is to be excused for his action unless it was secretly inspired by God.

[68] The propositions extracted from *Lois* XIV and XXIX were held by the theologians to be "falsæ, legi naturali et divinæ contrariæ, verguntque in societatis detrimentum", 1752: 10th Proposition: see Beyer, 'Montesquieu et la censure religieuse', p. 109, n. 1.

[69] *An Age of Crisis*, p. 77.

[70] *Ibid.*

[71] *Ibid.*, p. 82; *cf. P.* 1266 (Bkn. 615), N. II, p. 343, Pl. I, pp. 1138–9.

letter from Ibben to Usbek, "Montesquieu seeks to elude the consequence by positing a providential order",[72] but again there is no evidence for this statement: it is much more likely that Montesquieu added the letter in order to placate religious opinion already outraged by his discussion of suicide in the *Esprit des lois*. In short, there may possibly be "the seed of moral nihilism"[73] in the position of Montesquieu, but he did not consciously sow that seed.

Montesquieu's justification of suicide in the *Lettres persanes* springs primarily from his humanitarianism: Usbek does not conceal his righteous indignation in the first two paragraphs of *Lettre persane* LXXVI. Montesquieu's justification of usury, on the other hand, is more the result of his practical sense.

Catholic thought on the subject of usury had two main sources: Aristotle and the Gospel. Aristotle had argued that since the purpose of money is exchange, not increase, it is wrong to receive interest on money lent.[74] St. Thomas developed Aristotle's theory (*S.t.*, II, ii, Q. 78, A. 1, vol. X, pp. 329–33), in which he found confirmation of the Gospels' rejection of usury (*cf.* Luke, VI, 34).

The Protestant School of Natural Law accepted neither the religious interdiction, nor that based on natural law. Grotius simply put a limit on rates of interest (*Dg.*, II, xii, 20–22, vol. I, pp. 432–7). Pufendorf thought that it is not wrong to charge interest, provided that the loan is not "accompagné d'extorsion ni d'inhumanité envers les pauvres" and that the rate of interest is moderate (*Dn.*, V, vii, 9, vol. II, p. 75). For Barbeyrac, the prohibition of interest is the result of a "vain scrupule" and of a "piété mal entendue".[75]

In the late seventeenth century, certain Catholics made concessions to meet the growing feeling that usury is not always wrong;[76] it is perhaps significant that in their criticism of Montesquieu's views on the subject, neither the Jansenist La Roche (in spite of the precedent provided by Domat)[77] nor the Sorbonne alleged that usury is unnatural, though they both said it is contrary to Divine law.[78] Montesquieu had

[72] *An Age of Crisis*, p. 77.

[73] *Ibid.*

[74] *Politics*, I, iii, 23; in the Loeb edition, pp. 50–51.

[75] *Discours sur la permission des lois, où l'on fait voir, que ce qui est permis par les lois, n'est pas toujours juste et honnête*, Geneva, Fabri et Barrillot, 1715, p. 14.

[76] *Cf.* Lanson, 'Formation et développement de l'esprit philosophique', vol. XVII, ii, 1909, p. 717.

[77] For Domat, usury is contrary both to Divine and natural law, *op. cit.*, Part I, I, vi, vol. I, pp. 68–73.

[78] La Roche, *Examen critique*, pp. 127–8; also *Réponse à la Défense*, pp. 231–6. 1750: 3rd and 4th Propositions: see Beyer, 'Montesquieu et la censure religieuse', p. 111, nn. 1 and 2,

argued, from a historical point of view, that the principles of the Scholastics, borrowed from Aristotle, had led to commerce being abandoned in the Middle Ages (*Lois*, XXI, xx, N. I, i, pp. 513–6, Pl. II, pp. 639–41); he had also shown in general terms the ill effects resulting from the interdiction of usury: if money is not lent at interest, then none will be lent at all, at least for commercial purposes, and commerce will dwindle. Alternatively, money will be lent illegally, at extortionate rates; in this case, commerce will still dwindle, since merchants will have to pay more for their money than they can gain by their ventures. In normal cases, therefore, interest rates should be moderate (*Lois*, XXII, xix, N. I, ii, pp. 33–4, Pl. II, p. 675). When the risk is very great, the rate of interest can legitimately be increased (*ibid.*, xx, N. I, ii, p. 34, Pl. II, p. 676).

From a practical point of view, then, Montesquieu saw usury as justified. He also believed that it is not morally wrong. He implied that Aristotle's arguments are not valid, and that usury is "une chose naturellement permise ou nécessaire" (*Lois*, XXI, xx, N. I, i, pp. 513–4, Pl. II, p. 639). He accepted that usury is forbidden by Divine law (*ibid.*), but felt that this interdiction has no place in the world of commerce:

> C'est bien une action très bonne de prêter à un autre son argent sans intérêt: mais on sent que ce ne peut être qu'un conseil de religion, et non une loi civile (*Lois*, XXII, xix, N. I, ii, p. 33, Pl. II, p. 675).

It is significant of his attitude that although he said in his reply to the Sorbonne that he would remove this passage, he did not in fact do so.[79]

Montesquieu's views on usury are probably the result of his own experience. He was not only a legal man, but also a business man, who relied for part of his income on the wine-trade, and who lived near a prosperous port. He no doubt agreed with Bayle, who lived for much of his life in the port of Rotterdam, that

> Le seul article de l'usure observé selon les règles des casuistes rigides nuirait infiniment au commerce, et par conséquent au bien essentiel de l'état.[80]

and p. 118.

79 *Réponses et explications*, N. III, p. 667, Pl. II, p. 1188; *cf.* Brethe de la Gressaye, *Lois*, vol. III, pp. 396–7, n. 70. to p. 173, and Beyer, 'Montesquieu et la censure religieuse', pp. 128–9.

80 *Réponses aux questions d'un provincial*, III, xxviii, p. 980. In this connection it is interesting to note that M.'s intense dislike of Bayle's theories led him to contradict himself. He particularly deplored Bayle's suggestion (*Réponses aux questions d'un provincial*, III, xxvi–xxviii, pp. 972–83; *Continuation des pensées diverses* [1704], cxxiv, *Œuvres diverses*, III, i, pp. 359–61) that

On the subject of usury, as in most of the topics that have been discussed in this section, Montesquieu's apparently controversial views were built on an empirical foundation similar to that which had already been accepted by the School of Natural Law. They had admitted that in these difficult questions – divorce, polygamy, suicide and usury, precisely those topics on which the *Esprit des lois* was to be censured – the natural law gives no clear ruling. They thus implied that laws and customs connected with these topics may legitimately vary from country to country. Their empiricism (or relativism) had prepared the way for that of Montesquieu, though in some cases, notably that of incest, the *président* was anything but empirical, and closely followed the teaching of the Church.

Did this practical empiricism of the philosophers of natural law have any theoretical basis, or was it in contradiction with the principles they professed?

Many Montesquieu scholars, in their discussion of his method, have compared it with that of the School of Natural Law, and the latter is always put in an unfavourable light. On reading these scholars we have the impression that whereas Montesquieu studied positive law impartially, the School of Natural Law, and in general, those who believed in natural law, had their eyes fixed on nothing but eternal truths, and were quite unable to explain why civil law is different in different countries.

This contrast is made by many of Montesquieu's most eminent interpreters, and not least by two of his editors. Édouard Laboulaye tells readers of the *Esprit des lois* that of all the philosophers who "s'amusaient à bâtir des systèmes de droit naturel", "aucun [...] ne doutait qu'on ne pût faire une législation applicable à tous les peuples de la terre".[81] More recently, Brethe de la Gressaye has made the same point: the philosophy of natural law, he says,

> n'explique pas comment, l'homme étant partout et toujours le même, les lois positives sont si diverses, si variables, relatives et contingentes.[82]

a state composed solely of Christians would not survive, and tried to refute it in the *Lois* (XXIV, vi, N. I, ii, pp. 86–7, Pl. II, p. 719): he maintained that the absolute honesty of the inhabitants of such a state, together with their sense of duty, would enable them to survive. Yet it has just been seen that M. considered commerce, and particularly usury, absolutely vital to the preservation of an economically viable state. Hence we must either assume that M. did not really believe that Christianity forbids usury, and that the first paragraph of *Lois*, XXI, xx, is not to be taken too seriously; or else, that he conveniently forgot about usury when he refuted Bayle.

[81] 'Introduction à l'*Esprit des lois*', in *Œuvres complètes*, vol. III, p. vi.

[82] *Lois*, vol. I, p. xciii.

The contrast between Montesquieu and the philosophers of natural law is in fact a commonplace,[83] it is the obvious way to show Montesquieu's originality, it is expressible in a neat formula so that it can be remembered by students. It is, however, false.

It would seem that all the scholars who see an almost complete disagreement between Montesquieu and his predecessors on this question are viewing the idea of natural law through the eyes of idealists such as "Helvétius" (that is, the author of the letters to Montesquieu and Saurin), Rousseau and Condorcet. It is the latter philosopher who gives the clearest summary of the idealist position:

> Comme la vérité, la raison, la justice, les droits des hommes, l'intérêt de la propriété, de la liberté, de la sûreté, sont les mêmes partout, on ne voit pas pourquoi toutes les provinces d'un état, ou même tous les États, n'auraient pas les mêmes lois criminelles, les mêmes lois civiles, les mêmes lois de commerce, etc. Une bonne loi doit être bonne pour tous les hommes, comme une proposition vraie est vraie pour tous.[84]

This passage was intended as a condemnation of the *Esprit des lois*: Condorcet had evidently failed to appreciate Montesquieu's purpose in writing the book, but his idealistic conception of legislation, like the idealistic conception of government we examined earlier, is akin to the Platonic tradition of natural law, rather than to the more practical Aristotelian tradition.

Aristotle was not dismayed by the fact that different countries have different laws: he believed that the latter should be "adapted to the constitution", and that it is right to change them in certain circumstances.[85] He thus accepted that positive law can vary, so long as it is not unjust. Aristotle's theory was adopted by Christian theologians. St. Augustine, for example, while holding that "there is nothing just or legitimate in temporal law save what men have derived from the eternal law", argued that the proper definition of a temporal law is one

> which, though it be just, may be justly changed to suit altered circumstances.[86]

St. Thomas also seems to have followed Aristotle in this matter. He

[83] *Cf.* Janet, *Histoire de la science politique*, vol. II, pp. 331–2; Dedieu, *Montesquieu*, pp. 60-66; Vaughan, *Studies in the History of Political Philosophy*, vol. I, pp. 260–61; Bréhier, *op. cit.*, vol. II, pp. 373–4; Dimoff, 'Cicéron, Hobbes et Montesquieu', pp. 43–4; Cotta, *Montesquieu e la scienza della società*, pp. 160–72 and 370–72; Courtney, 'Montesquieu', p. 38.

[84] *Observations sur le vingt-neuvième livre de l'Esprit des lois*, p. 418.

[85] *Politics*, III, vi, 13, p. 231 and II, v, 10–14, pp. 127–33.

[86] *On Free Will*, I, vi, 14, in *Augustine, Earlier Writings*, Library of Christian Classics, S.C.M. Press, vol. VI, 1953, pp. 120–1.

quoted the idealist objection:

> It would seem that human law should not be changed in any way at all. Because human law is derived from the natural law [. . .]. But the natural law endures unchangeably. Therefore human law should also remain without any change (*S.t.*, II, i, Q. 97, A. 1, obj. 1, vol. VIII, p. 76).

His reply began with words that recall those Montesquieu was to write many centuries later in Book I, iii of the *Esprit des lois*:

> human law is a dictate of reason, whereby human acts are directed;

consequently, he argued, human law can be changed on two grounds. Firstly, if reason changes: this is quite possible, since man is continually making advances in the speculative sciences, and in political science too. Secondly, if society changes:

> the law can be rightly changed on account of the changed condition of man, to whom different things are expedient according to the difference of his condition (*S.t.*, II, i, Q. 97, A. 1, vol. VIII, p. 77).

He did not think that human law should be changed lightly, whenever a better law occurs to someone (*ibid.*, A. 2, p. 79), but, as D'Entrèves puts it, "The largest possible allowance is made for historical circumstances".[87]

A later religious writer, Domat, in spite of the fact that his outlook was generally stricter than Catholic orthodoxy required, saw no objection to positive laws being changed where necessary: whereas natural law is essential to the order of society, and is always the same,

> les lois arbitraires étant indifférentes à ces fondements de l'ordre de la société; de sorte qu'il n'y en a aucune qui ne puisse être changée ou abolie sans les renverser; la justice de ces lois consiste dans l'utilité particulière qui se trouve à les établir, selon que les temps et les lieux peuvent y obliger.[88]

He saw the origin of the laws of Rome as a mixture of empiricism and idealism. The jurists began with the "principes naturels et immuables de l'équité", but they could only create their codes of law after "une infinité d'événements pendant plusieurs siècles", which taught them to "former des règles sur ces principes".[89]

[87] *Op. cit.*, p. 44. As D. J. O'Connor shows (*op. cit.*, p. 78), St. Thomas's theory that human law may be altered is quite compatible with his probable belief that human nature is unchangeable.

[88] *Op. cit.*, *Traité des lois*, xi, 20, vol. I, p. xvii.

[89] *Op. cit.*, *Préface*, vol. I [this general preface is not paginated but these words occur some seven sides after the title page].

Among the secular jurists who believed in natural law, Bodin is often referred to as a precursor of Montesquieu. In his *République*, there is a chapter entitled 'Du règlement qu'il faut tenir pour accommoder la forme de république à la diversité des hommes', where he emphasized the influence of climate, education, laws and customs on the character of each people.[90] Here, in germ, is a theory similar to that of Montesquieu. What scholars often fail to note is that the same theory is in germ in the writings of the School of Natural Law.

It is true, as has already been seen, that Grotius claimed to be unable to explain the diversity of human laws, saying that they are not "susceptibles de système méthodique" (*Dg.*, *Disc. prél.*, xxxi, vol. I, p. 21). In fact, there was not in the Dutch philosopher's mind such a clear distinction between these laws and the laws of nature, since in many cases his conception of a natural law was any human law that he decided was "universally" observed: this is particularly true of his discussion of war and slavery.[91] Hence his treatise is partly a manual on the causes of various positive laws. The difference between a pragmatist like Grotius and an idealist like Rousseau, is clearly illustrated by the latter's criticism of the former: "Sa plus constante manière de raisonner est d'établir toujours le droit par le fait" (*Du Contrat social*, I, ii, p. 25).[92]

Nevertheless, in spite of his pragmatism, Grotius did not offer any general explanation of why human laws vary. Gravina, on the other hand, writing nearly a hundred years later, did offer such an explanation. In the chapter of his *Origines* entitled 'De variarum regionum legibus, et earum origine', he showed how law, enforced by the magistrates, is established by the jurisconsults, and that

> Hanc autem universam rationem publicæ tranquillitatis prudentissimi legum latores, ut populorum natura ferebat, formarunt, atque flexerunt, et ad suos cuiusque regionis, et temporis mores derivarunt.

This explains, Gravina continued, why "discrepantes sunt inter se leges", even though the concept of *honestas* is universal (*Origines iuris civilis*, II, xxi, p. 262).

Gravina's relativism had been anticipated by Pufendorf. Like all those who believed in natural law, he held that no positive law should contradict the natural law. On the other hand, he argued that it is

90 *République*, V, i, pp. 461–88.
91 See below, Ch. 6, II and IV.
92 *Cf.* Derathé, *op. cit.*, p. 72.

essential to the well-being of a state that its laws should be in keeping with its nature:

> Pour les défauts du gouvernement, ils se remarquent en général lorsque les lois et les coutumes de l'État ne sont pas conformes au naturel du peuple qui doit s'y soumettre, ou aux qualités et à la situation du pays (*Dn.*, VII, v, 10, vol. II, p. 276).

We note that the factors mentioned by Pufendorf – the "naturel du peuple", the "qualités" and the "situation" of the country – are some of those which Montesquieu was to name in his definition of "l'esprit général" (*Lois*, XIX, iv, N. I, i, p. 412, Pl. II, p. 558).

Not only did Pufendorf make this general statement, he also showed, in a number of places in his work, that it is up to the civil law to decide on details when the ruling of the natural law is unclear. This is apparent from his account of the various topics discussed earlier in this chapter. It is also apparent from his account of prescription, restitution, wealth,[93] and punishment. In the case of punishments, he specifically stated that they should vary according to "le naturel de chaque peuple, et les intérêts de chaque État" (*Dn.*, VIII, iii, 26, vol. II, p. 406). To imply, as Althusser does, that political theorists before Montesquieu held the diverse nature of penal laws to be unexplainable,[94] is unfair to Pufendorf. Not that the German jurist made any brillant new discovery when he said that criminal law should vary to suit the nature of each people: the idea is perfectly obvious, and was well established in Roman law (*Digest*, XLVIII, xix, 16, p. 815). Why, one wonders, should critics be so keen to give Montesquieu the credit of inventing a commonplace? Does it really enhance his reputation?

Dedieu is a little fairer to Pufendorf, who, he says,

> se rapproche [...] de la réalité, et, faisant des lois l'expression rationnelle de la nature des choses, n'est pas éloigné d'admettre que les variétés des législations s'expliquent par la diversité de la nature des choses.[95]

The words "n'est pas éloigné de" are an understatement. Dedieu seems to have been unaware that the German did not *almost admit* that legislation should vary with *la nature des choses*: he said that it *should* vary. It is difficult to see why Dedieu should not want to give Pufendorf

[93] Prescription: *Dn.*, IV, xii, 9, vol. I, p. 598 and *Dv.*, I, xii, 12, pp. 195–6; restitution: *Dv.*, II, xii, 5, p. 335; wealth: *Dn.*, VIII, v, 3, vol. II, pp. 443–5 and *Dv.*, II, xv, 2, p. 358.

[94] *Op. cit.*, p. 42. The wording of this passage in Althusser is a little vague, but this is the implication he seems to be making.

[95] *Montesquieu*, p. 66.

the credit he deserves, for having outlined the theory that Montesquieu was later to develop. Montesquieu's achievement is in no way diminished by that of his predecessors, since there is a considerable difference between just outlining a theory, as Aristotle, St. Thomas, Bodin, Pufendorf and Gravina did, and working out its implications in detail: only Montesquieu did this.

Dedieu makes another sweeping statement about the School of Natural Law, and in particular about Grotius, Pufendorf and Domat:

> Ils n'ont pas songé à mettre une séparation radicale entre la morale individuelle et la morale sociale. Le citoyen ne se distingue pas, à leurs yeux, de l'homme, et l'homme reste la créature religieuse, soumise à des obligations d'origine religieuse.[96]

Dedieu further claims that Montesquieu is different to these philosophers in that he does not judge the moral life of the peoples he is studying,[97] and in that he is not interested in "l'idée métaphysique et religieuse du bien, du devoir, de la volonté divine."[98] These assertions are untrue. Firstly, it is untrue that the School of Natural Law saw man as "la créature religieuse". The "idée métaphysique" in which Dedieu, like another abbé de La Roche, sees the foundation of ethics, is in fact the old voluntaristic concept of morality, to which the philosophers of natural law, including St. Thomas himself, have always been opposed.[99]

Secondly, it is untrue that the philosophers of natural law were unaware of a distinction between individual and social morality: their belief in an *a priori* natural law did not result in an exclusively moralistic view of legislation. Pufendorf, in particular, like Montesquieu, was sceptical about the efficacy of reason on the individual level. He believed that although natural law is essential to the holding together of society, it is not, by itself, sufficient for that task, and needs to be reinforced by the cruder and more obvious threats of the civil law (*Dv.*, II, xii, 3, p. 334 and II, v, 8, p. 286).

Then again, just as Montesquieu held that it is wise to tolerate certain abuses in the legal system of a country (*P.* 19, Bkn. 1921, N. II, p. 5, Pl. I, p. 1461), so Grotius, Pufendorf and Barbeyrac had all been of the opinion that it would be stupid for the civil law to punish every

[96] *Montesquieu*, pp. 186–7; *cf. Montesquieu l'homme et l'œuvre*, pp. 132–3 and Oudin, *Le Spinozisme de Montesquieu*, pp. 55 and 63.
[97] *Montesquieu*, p. 187.
[98] *Ibid.*, p. 184.
[99] See below, Ch. 7, III.

infringement of the natural law: only those crimes that affect public safety should be repressed.[100] On this matter the School of Natural Law was at one with the view of the Catholic Church (*S.t.*, II, i, Q. 91, A. 4, vol. VIII, p. 16), and even with that of a Jansenist such as Domat.[101] It is consequently ridiculous to suppose, with Dedieu, that Montesquieu was the first political theorist to separate social and individual morality. Montesquieu's originality lies not in the fact that he made this separation, but in his application of it in the theory of the "principes": such a systematic examination of the different kinds of social morality needed in different régimes had not been attempted by his predecessors.[102]

One critic has denied that there are any important similarities between Montesquieu and the School of Natural Law, by claiming that the latter were only interested in propounding "une théorie abstraite sur le fondement et les limites du pouvoir".[103] This statement is false for two reasons. Firstly, because the theory of the original contract, which appears at first sight to be a mere abstraction, was compatible with a realistic and fairly impartial assessment of the advantages and disadvantages of different kinds of government. Secondly, it is false because, quite apart from their political theories, the School of Natural Law were also interested in the same legal and social problems that were later to attract the attention of Montesquieu.

It is only when it is made clear that there is no fundamental difference between Montesquieu and the School of Natural Law, in their attitude to the variation of positive law, that the *président*'s true originality can be seen. Montesquieu did not pioneer a new method, but rather developed and completed an ancient tradition. Both he and the philosophers of natural law believed that positive law should not contradict natural law, but that it may vary according to circumstances. However, whereas the philosophers of natural law, in their accounts of this variation, confined themselves to generalities, Montesquieu concentrated his attention on this very problem. He examined and concluded where they had only glanced and suggested.

[100] Grotius, *Dg.*, II, xx, 20, vol. II, p. 596; Pufendorf, *Dn.*, VIII, iii, 14, vol. II, pp. 388–9; Barbeyrac, *Discours sur la permission des lois*, pp. 10–13.

[101] *Op. cit.*, *Le Droit public*, III, i, vol. II, p. 196; also the introduction to *Le Droit public*, III, p. 193.

[102] The theory of the "principes" is exposed in *Lois*, III, and its consequences in Books IV–VIII.

[103] Brethe de la Gressaye, *Lois*, vol. I, p. 231, n. 12, to p. 13.

If the School of Natural Law had really been so abstract and rationalistic as the positivists and others suggest, why is it that in their discussion of the controversial topics of divorce, polygamy, incest, suicide and usury, they were often content to tell their readers what happens and happened in different countries, without reaching any firm conclusion as to the ruling of the natural law? In fact, the philosophy of natural law was consistent, both in theory and in practice, with considerable empiricism, in civil and political matters.

However, it has also been seen that the empiricism of the School of Natural Law tended towards liberalism: to say that there is no natural law against divorce and usury, for example, is to imply that it is unwise for governments to try to prevent these practices. In the next Chapter, we shall examine Montesquieu's attitude to other "liberal" themes, by comparing it with that of his predecessors.

CHAPTER 6

RATIONALISM IN POSITIVE LAW: MONTESQUIEU THE REFORMER

In spite of the importance accorded by certain philosophers to the state of nature and the original contract, the doctrine of natural law is not basically dependent on either of these concepts. Grotius and Burlamaqui managed to found their theories without much reference to the state of nature, and Burlamaqui was not interested in the original contract either. Neither hypothesis features prominently in the work of Cicero or of Aristotle, and yet it cannot be said that they disbelieved in natural law.

The principle foundation of the doctrine of natural law is the conviction that there are certain basic rights and laws, discovered by reason, which must be preserved and observed in relations between a man and his fellows, between men and their government, and between different states. The existence of these rights and laws is not dependent on a contract, but on the nature of man and of society, both of which are fundamentally the same, in spite of differences caused by climate and temperament.

It has already been seen that Montesquieu accepted, in theory, that civil law should be the expression of natural law. In this Chapter, we propose to see how far he put this theory into practice in his discussion of certain vital issues, namely the criminal law, property, slavery and war. We shall then be in a position to say how far Montesquieu may be called a reformer, and how far he believed in progress.

I. *The Criminal Law*

In the *Esprit des lois*, one of Montesquieu's unstated aims was to show how the maximum amount of political and civil liberty could be obtained within a monarchical constitution. Political liberty he believed could be ensured by what is now called the *separation of powers*: in his analysis of the English Constitution, in Book XI, vi, he showed that there are two kinds of separation, one between the legislative, executive and judiciary, the other between the people, the nobility and the monarch. The separation of powers did not mean, for Montesquieu, antagonism, but rather co-operation or "collaboration":[1] each "puissance" is dependent on the others in some respects, hence "par le mouvement nécessaire des choses [...] elles seront forcées d'aller de concert" (N. I, i, p. 219, Pl. II, p. 405); at the same time, this dependence prevents each power from acting in an arbitrary or absolute fashion. In the matter of political liberty, Montesquieu's superiority over his predecessors is clear: though both Montesquieu and the School of Natural Law referred to a contract as a means of guaranteeing liberty, he went further and described the separation of powers as a more practical safeguard. No such account of the mechanism of political liberty is to be found in the work of Grotius, Pufendorf or Gravina; it is, however, to be found, in somewhat similar terms, in Locke's *Two Treatises* (*T.T.*, II, xi–xiv, 134–168, pp. 373–98), but his analysis is less clear than that of Montesquieu, who seems, as Shackleton suggests, to have merely "sought theoretical support in Locke for an analysis which he had already formed on the basis of observation".[2]

Montesquieu was confident that in protecting political liberty, the separation of powers would also protect individual liberty,[3] but he considered that careful attention to the administration of justice and to the contents of the statute-book is also necessary if the liberty of the subject is to be safeguarded.

He struck a balance between formality and simplicity in legal procedure. He claimed that formalities are an antidote to despotism and that they are particularly valuable in moderate governments (*Lois*, VI, ii, N. I, i, pp. 99–101, Pl. II, pp. 309–11). However, he was also aware of the abuses to which an excessive observance of formalities could lead. Talking, in Book XXIX, i, not of one particular kind of government, but presumably of all, he said:

> Les formalités de la justice sont nécessaires à la liberté. Mais le nombre en pourrait être si grand, qu'il choquerait le but des lois mêmes qui les auraient établies: les affaires n'auraient point de fin; la propriété des biens resterait incertaine [...].

[1] *Cf.* Barckhausen, *Montesquieu, ses idées et ses œuvres*, p. 95.

[2] *M.*, p. 287. On the influence of Locke, see also Dedieu, *Montesquieu et la tradition politique anglaise*, pp. 160–91. Bolingbroke's *Dissertation on Parties* is another possible source of M.'s theory (*cf.* Shackleton, *M.*, pp. 296–301 and 'Montesquieu, Bolingbroke, and the Separation of Powers', *French Studies*, 1949, pp. 25–38).

[3] *Cf.* the passage devoted to 'La liberté politique, dans un citoyen', in Book XI, vi, N. I, i, p. 208, Pl. II, p. 397).

Les citoyens perdraient leur liberté et leur sûreté; les accusateurs n'auraient plus les moyens de convaincre, ni les accusés le moyen de se justifier (N. I, ii, p. 269, Pl. II, pp. 865–6).

The natural right of liberty is the inspiration behind this passage, and Montesquieu saw it as implemented by an equitable approach to legal formalities.

Equity also demands that laws be simple. One aspect of this simplicity was, for Montesquieu, that civil law should be confined to generalities. Usbek had claimed that most legislators were "des hommes bornés" who "se sont jetés dans des détails inutiles" (*L.p.* CXXIX, N. I, iii, p. 257, Pl. I, p. 322). In the *Esprit des lois*, Montesquieu was more explicit as to his dislike of "les exceptions, limitations, modifications": when they are unnecessary, "De pareils détails jettent dans de nouveaux détails" (*Lois*, XXIX, xvi, N. I, ii, p. 285, Pl. II, p. 878). It could well be argued that Montesquieu here opened the door to injustice, since according to some philosophers, the main purpose of the civil law is to decide on points left obscure by the natural law;[4] hence it is bound to be concerned with details and exceptions.

Not only did Montesquieu think that laws should be concerned only with generalities, he also believed that they should be simple in style and intention – he had been a judge, not an *avocat*. Usbek had criticized legislators further for not using everyday language, for having made laws "trop subtiles", and for having followed "des idées logiciennes, plutôt que l'équité naturelle" (*L.p.* CXXIX, N. I, iii, p. 258, Pl. I, p. 323). According to Usbek, then, civil laws should be simply the expression of equity. The same function was assigned to civil law by the Montesquieu of the *Esprit des lois*. Talking once again not just of one kind of régime, but of all, he said:

'Choses à observer dans la composition des lois.'

[. . .]

Le style en doit être concis. [. . .]

Le style des lois doit être simple [. . .].

Il est essentiel que les paroles des lois réveillent chez tous les hommes les mêmes idées.

And in words that echo those of Usbek, he continued:

Les lois ne doivent point être subtiles: elles sont faites pour des gens de médiocre entendement: elles ne sont point un art de logique, mais la

[4] *Cf.* Pufendorf, *Dv.*, II, xii, 6–7, pp. 336–7; Domat, *op. cit.*, *Traité des lois*, xi, 6, vol. I, p. xv.

raison simple d'un père de famille (*Lois*, XXIX, xvi, N. I, ii, pp. 283 and 285, Pl. II, pp. 876–8).

These views, although they are laudable, seem rather impractical, since legal disputes often arise from the imprecision of everyday language; they also seem to have little relevance to the preceding books of the *Esprit des lois*, where the art of legislation is shown to be highly sophisticated, and where, in particular, we are often made aware that the obvious purpose of any law is not necessarily its real purpose.[5] Montesquieu's opinions are here in contradiction with his method; they are in keeping with the idealistic tradition of natural law, as represented for example by Sir Thomas More: he believed that ideally there is no need for "attorneis, proctours, and sergeauntes at the lawe", no excuse for having more laws "than be hable to be read" or for using language which prevents them being understood easily by all.[6] Perhaps, in this matter, Montesquieu was reacting against his legal training.

The barriers which Montesquieu believed to be presented to injustice by legal formalities and by relative simplicity of legislation are useless unless they are supplemented by a respect on the part of those who make or administer the criminal law for the proper relationship between crime and punishment. Here, Montesquieu's views are in keeping both with the doctrine of natural law and with the broad outlines of modern criminology; they also reveal that he would like to have seen many reforms put into practice.

What, according to natural law, is the purpose of punishment? It is certainly not revenge, which is inspired either by anger or by an abstract kind of morality.[7] The true purpose of punishment is the preservation of society and nothing more. Consequently, unnecessarily cruel punishments are contrary to natural law. As Pufendorf put it:

Que celui qui a fait du mal, en souffre, il n'y a rien là d'injuste, à ne regarder que l'action en elle-même. Cependant les hommes ne doivent jamais punir, à moins qu'il n'en revienne quelque utilité. [...] on doit [...] prendre garde de ne pas faire souffrir sans nécessité un homme, coupable à la vérité, mais toujours uni avec nous par les liens de l'humanité com-

[5] *Cf.* the phrase "La politique est une lime sourde, qui use et qui parvient lentement à sa fin" (*Lois*, XIV, xiii, N. I, i, p. 321, Pl. II, p. 487).

[6] *Utopia* [1515–16], translated by R. Robynson, edited by J. R. Lumby, Cambridge University Press, 1897, pp. 126–7 (original spelling).

[7] In an early *Pensée*, M. condemned revenge, on the grounds that it is ineffective in procuring its "but naturel" or "vrai but", namely the ending of vicious intentions in the offender (*P.* 29, Bkn. 1102, N. II, p. 8, Pl. I, p. 1286). Grotius had similarly condemned revenge (*Dg.*, II, xx, 5, vol. II, p. 572).

mune, pour une action qui ne saurait plus être redressée (*Dn.*, VIII, iii, 8, vol. II, p. 383).[8]

Montesquieu neatly summed up this doctrine in Book XIX, xiv of the *Esprit des lois*: "Toute peine qui ne dérive pas de la nécessité est tyrannique. La loi n'est pas un pur acte de puissance" (N. I, i, p. 421, Pl. II, p. 565).

It is pertinent to ask whether the preservation of society is always best achieved simply by a suitably severe punishment, or whether it is sometimes better to try to amend the criminal. Eighteenth-century French law made no attempt to do the latter,[9] but the philosophers of natural law, such as Grotius, Pufendorf, and even Hobbes, believed that reform of the criminal was one aim of a good penal code.[10] Montesquieu seems to have agreed with their idea, and to have implicitly criticized the practice prevailing in his own country, when he commented on certain violent punishments administered in Japan:

Il n'est pas question de corriger le coupable, mais de venger le prince. Ces idées sont tirées de la servitude (*Lois*, VI, xiii, N. I, i, p. 115, Pl. II, p. 322).

Here, as so often, the idea of cruelty is associated with that of despotism.

The question of punishment in despotic countries is in fact the touchstone of Montesquieu's attitude. In Book VI, ix of the *Esprit des lois*, he had the intention of examining the problem in the light of his system. Thus

La sévérité des peines convient mieux au gouvernement despotique, dont le principe est la terreur, qu'à la monarchie et à la république, qui ont pour ressort l'honneur et la vertu (N. I, i, p. 109, Pl. II, p. 318).

He then claimed that a direct correlation can be established between the severity of punishments and the degree of political liberty in any country (N. I, i, p. 110, Pl. II, p. 318). The reference to liberty should at once make us suspect that Montesquieu was no longer applying his system. We realize that when he said that severe punishment "convient mieux au gouvernement despotique", he did not mean that it is essential to have such punishments in a despotism, but simply that one would expect to find them there, together with all the other manifestations of tyranny. The remark was not a statement of fact – it was an

[8] *Cf.* Grotius, *Dg.*, II, xx, 20 and 34, vol. II, pp. 596 and 608–9.

[9] *Cf.* R. Anchel, *Crimes et châtiments au XVIIIe siècle*, Perrin, 1933, p. 4.

[10] Pufendorf, *Dn.*, VIII, iii, 9, vol. II, p. 384; Grotius, *Dg.*, II, xx, 7, vol. II, p. 574; Hobbes, *The Questions Concerning Liberty, Necessity and Chance*, p. 177; Domat, on the other hand, here out of tune with the trend of natural law at his time, also emphasized the need to revenge society, *op. cit.*, *Le Droit public*, III, vol. II, p. 192.

insult to Eastern countries and a warning to the French. This impression is confirmed by the wording of the chapter, for Montesquieu chose emotive rather than descriptive terms. Thus, in connection with despotism, he used such words as "terreur" (rather than "crainte"), "malheureux", "exorbitant", "outragé", "cruel", "justice atroce", "douleur", "les maux de la nature humaine"; whereas, in connection with moderate governments, he used terms connoting approval: "mœurs", "liberté", "douceur", "pitié", and of course "modérés" (N. I, i, pp. 109–11, Pl. II, pp. 318–9). It is impossible to claim that Montesquieu even attempted to be impartial in this chapter.

Not that he was content simply to use emotive terms, without supplementing them with argument, for he showed convincingly that "un bon législateur" will be more concerned with preventing crime, by encouraging the right "mœurs", than with punishing. This reasoning is taken up three chapters later, where, abandoning all semblance of impartiality, he appealed for moderation in the name of nature. Just as Usbek had done (*L.p.* LXXX, N. I, iii, pp. 164–5, Pl. I, pp. 252–3), he claimed that the effectiveness of a punishment does not depend on its severity, but on the state of mind of the person on whom it is inflicted. Having given examples to prove his point, he added:

> Il ne faut point mener les hommes par les voies extrêmes; on doit être ménager des moyens que la nature nous donne pour les conduire. [...]
> Suivons la nature, qui a donné aux hommes la honte comme leur fléau; et que la plus grande partie de la peine soit l'infamie de la souffrir (*Lois*, VI, xii, N. I, i, pp. 113–4, Pl. II, p. 321).

The word "nature" in this context is particularly enlightening as to Montesquieu's attitude. It has here two related meanings. Firstly, it refers to man's physical and psychological characteristics: Montesquieu had shown that whereas the body soon becomes accustomed to cruelty, the conscience does not become accustomed to shame; "la nature", in this sense, is associated with what is expedient: a violent punishment "use le ressort du gouvernement" (N. I, i, p. 113, Pl. II, p. 321). Secondly, "la nature" refers to morality. Instead of tritely stating that unnecessarily cruel punishments are unjust – a fact that both he and his readers knew already – he implied it, both by his vocabulary ("tyrannie", "supplices cruels", "la violence du gouvernement", "les esprits sont corrompus"), and by the fact that he felt obliged not simply to state that severe punishments are unwise, but also to exhort governments to abandon them. In the same way, Usbek had argued that a moderate government is preferable to a severe one, "puisqu'il est plus conforme à la raison, et que la sévérité est un motif étranger" (*loc. cit.*).

A particular class of criminal laws that are unjust as well as being unwise are those which violate the natural law of *la pudeur*. They are unwise, so Montesquieu tells us, because they destroy "les mœurs"; they are unjust because they shock man's instinctive sense of right and wrong: when "la magistrature japonaise" enforced such punishments, "elle a fait frémir la pudeur" and "elle a fait frémir la nature même" (*Lois*, XII, xiv, N. I, i, p. 268, Pl. II, p. 445). Clearly, Montesquieu's feelings were aroused by such an injustice, but it would be wrong to think that his reaction was purely emotional, and that while he *felt* such punishments were wrong, even in a despotism, he *believed* them to be suitable there. His first reaction was undoubtedly emotional, but he went on to rationalize this emotion with arguments drawn from the concepts of utility and self-defence. In condemning punishments which violate *la pudeur*, Montesquieu was partly innovating. There seems to have been no specific reference to their injustice by writers in Antiquity, or by Grotius and Pufendorf. Montesquieu's conviction perhaps springs ultimately from the principles of the Christian religion, but at the same time, he was pushing to their logical conclusion arguments drawn from the philosophy of natural law.[11]

Less original, though no less praiseworthy, are Montesquieu's arguments against torture. In *Pensée* 643 (Bkn. 1954), written between 1734 and 1738, he commented on the inventiveness of man in devising new methods, "la plupart absurdes", of extracting confessions from criminals. Torture does not, he claimed, usually succeed in revealing the truth. Drawing on his personal experience as a judge, he continued:

> J'ai remarqué que, de dix personnes condamnées à la question, il y en a neuf qui la souffrent. Si tant d'innocents ont été condamnés à une si grande peine, quelle cruauté! Si tant de criminels ont échappé à la mort, quelle injustice! (N. II, p. 202, Pl. I, p. 1475)

In these words, he was expressing rather more pompously, but with equal conviction, an argument similar to that used by La Bruyère:

> La question est une invention merveilleuse et tout à fait sûre pour perdre un innocent qui a la complexion faible, et pour sauver un coupable qui est né robuste.[12]

From the literary point of view, La Bruyère's irony was, on this

[11] See above, Chapter 3, I.

[12] *Les Caractères* [1688–94], XIV, 51, in *Œuvres de La Bruyère*, Hachette, 1922, vol. III, i, p. 188.

occasion, more successful than Montesquieu's indignation; but the *président* did not rest content with indignation, for he backed it up by logic. He went on to answer the objection of the pragmatists, that a practice "autorisée par tant de lois" cannot be wrong, by showing that if such reasoning were legitimate, then trial by boiling water, for example, would never have been abolished. This *Pensée* proves once again that Montesquieu did not think that laws should never be changed.

Reform was obviously the aim of his arguments against torture in the *Esprit des lois*, too. Having shown that it is generally ineffective, and by implication, unjust, since "une nation très bien policé", namely England, managed without it, he went on to apply his system, and to see whether it might be suitable in despotic countries:

J'allais dire qu'elle [*sc.* cette pratique] pourrait convenir dans les gouvernements despotiques, où tout ce qui inspire la crainte entre plus dans les ressorts du gouvernement: j'allais dire que les esclaves, chez les Grecs et chez les Romains .... Mais j'entends la voix de la nature qui crie contre moi (*Lois*, VI, xvii, N. I, i, pp. 123–4, Pl. II, p. 329).

Whereupon Barthélemy Saint-Hilaire feels justified in saying that Montesquieu only protested "assez timidement" against torture.[13] This passage is one of the three principal places in the *Esprit des lois* where the *président* apparently stopped arguing, and referred instead to "la nature" or to his heart,[14] but this does not mean that he could find no arguments other than sentimental ones. In all three cases, this appeal to the emotions comes at the end of the chapter, after the reasoning: it is presumably placed in such a position for rhetorical effect. Thus, in the case of the chapter on torture, the appeal to nature is meant to convey the idea that *even* in despotisms, torture is wrong; therefore, by implication, it is all the more unjust in moderate régimes – such as that of France. It is unfortunate that critics should have mistaken a stylistic effect for timidity. Janet points to their error when he says: "dire que la torture peut convenir au despotisme, est-ce justifier la torture, ou flétrir le despotisme?"[15]

Another reason why Montesquieu did not produce any further reasons for abolishing torture, besides saying that it is not "nécessaire par sa nature" and that it is contrary to nature, is, as he said, because

[13] *Politique d'Aristote*, pp. cii–ciii; *cf.* Destutt de Tracy, *Commentaire sur l'Esprit des lois*, p. 77.

[14] The three places are: *Lois*, XII, xiv, N. I, i, pp. 267–8, Pl. II, pp. 444–5 (on *la pudeur*, already discussed); *Lois*, VI, xvii, N. I, i, pp. 123–4, Pl. II, p. 329 (on torture); *Lois*, XV, viii, N. I, i, pp. 333–4, Pl. II, pp. 496–7 (on slavery, see below, pp. 160–1).

[15] *Histoire de la science politique*, vol. II, p. 380.

> Tant d'habiles gens et tant de beaux génies ont écrit contre cette pratique, que je n'ose parler après eux (*Lois*, VI, xvii, N. I, i, p. 123, Pl. II, p. 329).

If he is timid, then, it is because of his modesty. In referring to the "habiles gens" and the "beaux génies", he simply endorsed the pleas of such philosophers as Montaigne, Grotius and Bayle.[16] In any case, his "timidity" was not ineffective, for it is partly because of the efforts of such writers as Montesquieu and Voltaire that the various forms of torture used in France were abolished later in the eighteenth century.[17]

If he is judged by modern standards, Montesquieu will not always appear as a reformer. He was quite certain, for instance, that the death penalty is legitimate for the crime of murder:

> Ce qui fait que la mort d'un criminel est une chose licite, c'est que la loi qui le punit a été faite en sa faveur. Un meurtrier, par exemple, a joui de la loi qui le condamne; elle lui a conservé la vie à tous les instants: il ne peut donc pas réclamer contre elle (*Lois*, XV, ii, N. I, i, p. 327, Pl. II, p. 492).

Like Montesquieu the philosophers of natural law based the death-penalty on the preservation of society. However, whereas St. Thomas (*S.t.*, II, ii, Q. 64, A. 2, vol. X, p. 198) and Pufendorf (*Dn.*, VIII, iii, 26, vol. II, p. 406) examined the question only from the point of view of the community, Montesquieu was also concerned with the right of the murderer, who is shown to have benefited from the law that eventually punishes him. Admittedly, there is only a difference of emphasis, but it seems that Montesquieu's attitude is more humane, and that of the earlier philosophers more utilitarian.

At the same time, though, Montesquieu's belief that it is right to punish murder with death is also a result of his acceptance of the utilitarian argument ("Cette peine de mort est comme le remède de la société malade"), and even of a vindictive principle, namely the law of the talion (*Lois*, XII, iv, N. I, i, p. 255–6, Pl. II, p. 435). As regards most other crimes, he thought, as Grotius (*Dg.*, II, xx, 32, vol. II, pp. 607–8) and Pufendorf (*Dn.*, VIII, iii, 27, vol. II, p. 407) had done, that it is not a very practical or expedient method of punishment – except, as he ironically added, that it is frequently used by

[16] Some of those who condemned torture are listed in *Dn.*, VIII, iii, 4, n. 10, vol. II, pp. 376–7. L. M. Levin says that writers in Antiquity had not condemned torture (*The Political Doctrine of Montesquieu's Esprit des lois*, New York, Institute of French Studies, [1936], pp. 229–30); however, the *Digest* had advised the greatest caution in its use (XLVIII, xviii, pp. 811–13).

[17] *Cf.* A. Chéruel, *Dictionnaire historique des institutions, mœurs et coutumes de la France*, Hachette, 1874, vol. II, pp. 1219–20; also R. Anchel, *op. cit.*, p. 139.

despotic governments, "qui aiment les lois simples" (*Lois* ,VI, xix, N. I, i, p. 124, Pl. II, p. 330).

The question of the appropriate punishment for theft was one in which Montesquieu's thought wavered between utility and humanity. Pufendorf's attitude had been purely utilitarian:

> on peut légitimement décerner la peine de mort contre les voleurs, lorsqu'on a de bonnes raisons pour en user avec cette rigueur (*Dn.*, VIII, iii, 26, vol. II, p. 407).

In Book XII, iv, Montesquieu seems to have agreed with Pufendorf, saying that "Lorsqu'on viole la sûreté à l'égard des biens, il peut y avoir des raisons pour que la peine soit capitale", especially in countries where wealth is not evenly distributed, since it would be the only way of protecting the rich; but he seems to have realized that even the harsh law of the talion could not justify such a punishment:

> il vaudrait peut-être mieux, et il serait plus de la nature, que la peine des crimes contre la sûreté des biens fût punie par la perte des biens (N. I, i, p. 256, Pl. II, p. 435).

Moreover, in Book VI, xvi, he had argued with more conviction that it is wrong to punish highwaymen who rob and kill, in the same way as those who simply rob, since such indiscriminate punishment encourages murder (N. I, i, p. 122, Pl. II, p. 328). How Book VI can be reconciled in this respect with Book XII, is difficult to see. Montesquieu's attitude is certainly not so unambiguous as that of Thomas More or Grotius.[18]

In this matter, then, the *président*'s approach tended to be utilitarian, as Pufendorf's had been. The German had put forward as a general principle that

> dans les tribunaux civils, il n'y a point de justice vindicative, qui impose à chaque crime et à chaque délit une certaine peine invariablement déterminée par la nature, et que l'on doive toujours infliger nécessairement: [...] la véritable et juste mesure des peines, parmi les hommes, c'est l'utilité publique, en vue de quoi la prudence du gouvernement oblige à augmenter ou à diminuer la rigueur de la punition, selon que l'un ou l'autre est plus à propos pour arriver à ce but; en sorte néanmoins que le degré des peines est susceptible d'une grande étendue (*Dn.*, VIII, iii, 24, vol. II, p. 404).[19]

This relativism with regard to the severity of punishments, he supple-

[18] *Cf. Utopia*, pp. 28 and 37–9; *Dg.*, II, i, 14, vol. I, pp. 219–20.
[19] *Cf.* Grotius, *Dg.*, II, xx, 35, vol. II, p. 610.

mented with a further relativism, with regard to the criminal: "la même peine ne faisant pas les mêmes impressions sur toutes sortes de gens", punishment must depend on "la personne même du coupable", on age, sex, status, wealth and health (*ibid.*, 25, p. 405). According to Dedieu, Montesquieu was the first writer to make punishment depend on political factors rather than moral ones[20] – but there is nothing moralistic about Pufendorf's approach.

In fact, Pufendorf's utilitarian attitude, his principle that punishment depends entirely on the needs of the state, remind us strongly of Montesquieu's method. But whereas Montesquieu refused to accept the full consequences of his method, and appealed openly for moderation in all régimes, Pufendorf did not so clearly temper his method with charity, even though he did hold, with Montesquieu, that unnecessarily cruel punishments are wrong. This is the first difference between the two men. The second is that Montesquieu was more interested than Pufendorf in the precise relationship between different kinds of crime and punishment: he wished to explain, where Pufendorf had tended to leave the question open.

Though the idea that the punishment should fit the crime is a commonplace,[21] it is possible that Montesquieu, in his treatment of the subject, was following Domat, who had written several pages on "les règles de la proportion des peines aux crimes".[22] But Montesquieu was more incisive than the Jansenist, and while the latter had his mind fixed above all on the religious aspects of his subject, the former aimed to produce liberty on earth, partly by keeping religion within certain bounds. In Book XII, iv, Montesquieu stated:

> C'est le triomphe de la liberté, lorsque les lois criminelles tirent chaque peine de la nature particulière du crime. Tout l'arbitraire cesse; la peine ne descend point du caprice du législateur, mais de la nature de la chose; et ce n'est point l'homme qui fait violence à l'homme (N. I, i, p. 253, Pl. II, p. 433).

Although this chapter of the *Esprit des lois* is ostensibly concerned with criminal law in moderate governments, one soon realizes that Montesquieu regarded the system he outlined in it as the ideal one – as "le triomphe de la liberté". The principles behind this system seem obvious enough to the present-day reader, though more than a little

[20] *Montesquieu*, pp. 221–2.
[21] *Cf.* Deuteronomy, XXV, 2; *Digest*, XLVIII, xix, 11, p. 815; *S.t.*, II, ii, Q. 99, A. 4, vol. XI, p. 248.
[22] *Op. cit.*, *Le Droit public*, III, vol. II, p. 194; *cf. ibid.*, tit. 1, pp. 196–200.

harsh in places; but at the time, French criminal law was far from corresponding to Montesquieu's ideal: for example, it still punished by death crimes such as sacrilege and even petty theft.[23] He divided crimes into four classes, and described what he considered to be the appropriate punishment for each. Crimes against religion should only be punished by ecclesiastical courts, with no temporal powers, and punishment should be limited to "la privation de tous les avantages que donne la religion"; crimes against morality should be punished with infamy; those against public order, with prison or exile; and those against public safety, with death or by fining the criminal (N. I, i, pp. 253–6, Pl. II, pp. 433–5). The whole argument of this chapter was based on Montesquieu's conception of nature as both a moral and a utilitarian principle: "Tout ce que je dis est puisé dans la nature, et est très favorable à la liberté du citoyen" (N. I, i, p. 256, Pl. II, p. 435).

In other chapters of the same book, Montesquieu discussed further points of criminal law, and in many instances he came to conclusions that he obviously considered to be valid for all kinds of government. He believed that where the accused's life is at stake, there should always be more than one witness (*Lois*, XII, iii, N. I, i, p. 252, Pl. II, p. 432) – in this he was following the ruling of the Bible and of natural law;[24] that "il faut être très circonspect dans la poursuite de la magie et de l'hérésie" (*ibid.*, v, N. I, i, p. 256, Pl. II, p. 435); and that freedom of thought and speech should be allowed (*ibid.*, xi–xii, N. I, i, pp. 264–6, Pl. II, pp. 441–3): the former of these two freedoms is of course a fundamental tenet of natural law.[25]

Montesquieu's belief that in certain respects the criminal law should be the same in all régimes gave him a further opportunity to criticize despotism. Thus many chapters of Book XII are devoted to showing that the crime of lese-majesty should be very clearly defined, and preferably limited to actions that undoubtedly injure the sovereign, otherwise the law will be open to abuse: he illustrated this idea with anecdotes drawn from the history of various despotic countries (*ibid.*, vii–xviii, N. I, i, pp. 259–72, Pl. II, pp. 438–48). Towards the end of Book XII, he reintroduced his method, showing how liberty is greater or lesser in different régimes, but often pleading that more should be introduced (*ibid.*, xix–xxx, N. I, i, pp. 272–84, Pl. II, pp. 448–58). In one in-

[23] *Cf.* Chéruel, *op. cit.*, vol. II, pp. 963–5 and 1122–3; also Anchel, *op. cit.*, *passim*, and Brethe de la Gressaye, *Lois*, vol. II, pp. 372–3, n. 10, to p. 112.

[24] Deuteronomy, XVII, 6; *S.t.*, II, ii, Q. 70, A. 2, vol. X, pp. 267–8; *Dn.*, V, xiii, 9, vol. II, p. 147.

[25] *Cf. Dg.*, II, xx, 18, vol. II, pp. 593–4; *Dn.*, VIII, iii, 14, vol. II, p. 388.

stance, however, his caution was greater than his love of liberty, since he decided to suppress a chapter written against the abuse of *les lettres de cachet* (N. III, pp. 590–1, Pl. II, pp. 998–9).

A particular aspect of Montesquieu's discussion of the punishment of crime is the question of religious intolerance. We have already seen how his application of the theory that the punishment should fit the crime led him to advocate that penalties for crimes against religion should be less harsh. How far did he in fact condemn intolerance, and on what grounds?

Firstly, he condemned it on moralistic grounds, because of its inhumanity. In Book XII, iv, he claimed that "il faut faire honorer la divinité, et ne la venger jamais"; that for the magistrate to punish "le sacrilège caché" would lead to an infringement of "la liberté des citoyens" and to boundless cruelty exercised in the name of an infinite being (N. I, i, p. 254, Pl. II, pp. 433–4). Book XXV, xiii, the 'Très humble remontrance aux inquisiteurs d'Espagne et de Portugal' is one of those imaginative chapters of the *Esprit des lois* where the argument is brought home to the reader by the use of indignation and irony. Speaking through the mouth of a Jew, Montesquieu proves that the Inquisition, as well as being unchristian, is contrary to the natural law of charity and of *do as you would be done by*: "traitez-nous", pleads the Jew,

comme vous feriez, si, n'ayant que ces faibles lumières de justice que la nature nous donne, vous n'aviez point une religion pour vous conduire, et une révélation pour vous éclairer (N. I, ii, p. 122, Pl. II, p. 748).

In the second place, Montesquieu condemned intolerance because it is not useful to society. Usbek had argued that it is a good idea for there to be several different religions in each state, on the grounds that the rival sects will vie with each other in meritorious actions; intolerance, on the other hand, could have disastrous economic consequences, as the story of the Armenians (Huguenots) shows (*L.p.* LXXXV, N. I, iii, pp. 172–3, Pl. I, pp. 258–9). Montesquieu again insisted on the evil social consequences of intolerance in his *Mémoire sur la constitution unigenitus*, which was probably written some thirty years after the appearance of the *Lettres persanes*.[26] The Papal Bull of 1713, condemning Jansenism, had continued to provoke hate and dissension in France until well into the 1750's. Montesquieu, in the *Mémoire*, advocated that the whole affair should be buried, and that in the interests of "le salut

[26] See N. III, pp. 469–70.

de l'État", the king should outwardly tolerate unorthodox religious opinions in France, even if he did not approve of them inwardly (N. III, pp. 472–6, Pl. II, pp. 1217–21). It is interesting that, whether or not he was influenced by the *président*'s advice, the king did follow this course of action in 1753.[27]

In the *Esprit des lois*, this same principle of *le salut de l'État* appears to have led Montesquieu from advocating complete toleration, to suggesting that intolerance has certain advantages. In Book XXV, ix, he showed that it is essential for the state to ensure that different religions "ne se troublent pas entre elles" (N. I, ii, p. 117, Pl. II, p. 744); in the next chapter, he added that the surest way of preventing discord is to keep the number of different religions in a state as low as possible:

Quand on est maître de recevoir, dans un État, une nouvelle religion, ou de ne la pas recevoir, il ne faut pas l'y établir; quand elle y est établie, il faut la tolérer (N. I, ii, p. 118, Pl. II, p. 744).

This remark displeases two kinds of people. The advocates of toleration say that it opens the door to religious persecution, for how else can one prevent the growth of a new sect except by some form of inquisition?[28]

We believe that this was not at all Montesquieu's intention, and would suggest that in this passage he was merely arguing that a new religion must not be given official encouragement or recognition: this, surely, is the sense of "recevoir" and "établir". Whereas Usbek, in advocating the multiplicity of religions, was probably thinking of Europe, Montesquieu, in Book XXV, x, was probably thinking of certain countries in the far east where the rivalries of different Christian sects had caused public disturbance.[29] To prevent the establishment of a new religion, a government would simply have to refuse entry to foreign missionaries. Such a policy cannot be called persecution, and does not violate natural rights, but it would of course be considered unwarranted by the missionaries themselves. Hence the displeasure shown by Montesquieu's religious critics, who are the second category of people to be offended by Book XXV, x.[30]

In order to placate the Sorbonne, Montesquieu added a note to

[27] See N. III, p. 470 and p. 476, n. a.

[28] *Cf.* Faguet, *La Politique comparée de Montesquieu, Rousseau et Voltaire*, p. 174.

[29] *Cf. Lois*, XXV, xi, N. I, ii, pp. 124–5, Pl. II, pp. 749–50; also the satirical letter from "Le roi du Thibet", denouncing the activities of Christian missionaries, perhaps intended for the *Lois*: Brethe de la Gressaye, *Lois*, vol. III, pp. 440–1, n. 43.

[30] La Roche, *Examen critique*, pp. 135–6 and *Réponse à la Défense*, pp. 226–9; 1750: 7th Proposition, and 1752: 2nd Proposition: see Beyer, 'Montesquieu et la censure religieuse', p. 115, n. 1.

Book XXV, x, excluding the Christian religion.[31] On the other hand, he did not attenuate or remove any of the passages where the Inquisition was criticized, and it was probably this intransigence that lead to the work's being put on the Index in 1751.[32]

On the question of religious toleration, Montesquieu has many predecessors: Spinoza,[33] Bayle,[34] and Locke,[35] as well as Grotius and, to a lesser extent, Pufendorf. Both philosophers of natural law believed it is wrong to punish people for offences that do not disturb public order (*Dg.*, II xx, 18 and 20, vol. II, pp. 583–4 and 596; *Dn.*, VIII, iii, 14, vol. II, pp. 388–9). On these grounds, Grotius claimed that the only punishable religious offence, apart from blasphemy, is atheism (*Dg.*, II, xx, 46, vol. II, p. 624). He did not think that the beliefs of any one sect of Christians are so obviously true as to give it the right to persecute those who interpret Christianity differently (*ibid.*, 50, pp. 629–32), nor did he think that the Christian religion itself is so obvious as to make it right for Christians to make war on non-Christians in order to convert them (*ibid.*, 48, pp. 626–8). He thus implicitly condemned the Crusades and the reason put forward by the Spanish for their conquest of South America.

According to Dedieu, Montesquieu is "le premier grand publiciste qui, en glorifiant la tolérance, l'ait solidement fondée en raison",[36] but in fact the writers just mentioned had, between them, produced all the *reasons* that Montesquieu was later to adopt. His originality lies not in the ideas he expressed on toleration, but in the way he expressed them: his arguments are put more forcefully and with more emotion than those of Grotius, and more succinctly than those of Bayle and Locke. None of Montesquieu's predecessors could have written the 'Très humble remontrance'.

Montesquieu's views on the punishment of crime owe much to his predecessors, the philosophers of natural law. Like them, he believed in two ultimately contradictory maxims, that the severity of any

[31] N. I, ii, p. 118, n. a, Pl. II, p. 744, n. a; *cf.* Brethe de la Gressaye, *Lois*, vol. III, p. 437, n. 34, to p. 277, and Pl. II, p. 1526.

[32] *Cf.* Bérard, 'L'*Esprit des lois* devant la Congrégation de l'Index', pp. 623–4.

[33] *Cf.* Vernière, *Spinoza et la pensée française*, vol. II, p. 457; Spinoza, *Tractatus theologico-politicus*, xx, pp. 952–64.

[34] *Commentaire philosophique sur ces paroles de Jésus-Christ, Contrains-les d'entrer*, [1686–7], in *Œuvres diverses*, vol. II, pp. 355–560.

[35] *Letters Concerning Toleration* [1689–1706], in *Works*, Strahan, etc., 1777, vol. II, pp. 313–681.

[36] *Montesquieu*, p. 292.

punishment should depend on the needs of the state, and that it should fit the crime. He went further than his predecessors in showing how different punishments are suitable for different crimes, and more particularly in arguing in favour of liberty, even in harsh régimes, thus taking to its logical conclusion the principle of natural law that no-one should be punished unnecessarily, and helping to promote the more enlightened attitude towards the punishment of crime that began to prevail in the later decades of the eighteenth century.[37]

Montesquieu's constant warnings against arbitrariness are based on his conception of the rights of the individual. This libertarian attitude also inspired his ideas on the subject of slavery.

II. Slavery

It is not necessary to give a complete account of the history of the literature concerned with the rights and wrongs of slavery, since this has already been done by R. P. Jameson in his admirable *Montesquieu et l'esclavage*.[38] Dedieu has given a useful historical survey of the evolution of Montesquieu's attitude: he claims that between 1721 and 1733, the *président* opposed slavery partly on moral, but mostly on sentimental grounds; that in the *Pensées* and the *Esprit des lois*, he condemned slavery both on moral and utilitarian grounds; and that he finally condemned it completely on the grounds that it is selfish.[39] In attempting to be concise, however, Dedieu has somewhat oversimplified the picture.[40] Rather than following Dedieu's approach, it is better to give an analytic presentation, with dates wherever possible, of the various arguments used by Montesquieu in connection with slavery, to see how far they derive from the philosophy of natural law and of natural rights.

Firstly, it is important to see what was his attitude to the question

[37] On the development of this attitude, see Shelby T. McCloy, *The Humanitarian Movement in Eighteenth-Century France*, University of Kentucky Press, 1957, pp. 172–209.

[38] Hachette, 1911.

[39] *Montesquieu*, pp. 200–10.

[40] The following examples show the uncertainty of Dedieu's conjectures: in *L.p.* LXXV, N. I, iii, pp. 155–6, Pl. I, p. 245, Usbek showed that the Christians started by freeing their slaves, because all men are equal, but ended by enslaving the negroes in order to cultivate land in the colonies. It is difficult to say how far this ironical criticism is sentimental or rational. In *L.p.* XXXIV, N. I, iii, p. 71, Pl. I, p. 180, Usbek showed that slaves have a bad effect on their masters: this argument is utilitarian, not sentimental. Dedieu conjectured that *P.* 174 (Bkn. 1935) and *P.* 2194 (Bkn. 171) were written after 1733 (*Montesquieu*, p. 204). In fact, though he was right about *P.* 2194 (after 1749), he was wrong about *P.* 174, which was probably written as early as 1721–31. Thus it is not correct to say that between 1721–33, M. "obéit [...] plus au sentiment qu'à la raison" (*Montesquieu*, p. 202). Dedieu did not of course have any positive means of dating the *Pensées*.

of equality. This question is complicated by the fact that when he talked about slavery, he had two different concepts in mind. On the one hand he was thinking of political slavery, the result of tyranny or arbitrary government; and on the other hand, of personal slavery, the absolute power of one citizen over another.

Hobbes had been an advocate of what Montesquieu obviously considered to be political slavery, and the *président* opposed him from the start of the *Esprit des lois*, in particular when he examined the concept of equality. He claimed, against Hobbes,[41] that in the state of nature, "chacun se sent inférieur; à peine chacun se sent-il égal" (*Lois*, I, ii, N. I, i, p. 5, Pl. II, p. 235). This phrase does not mean that Montesquieu denied natural men's equality: he only denied their wish to exploit that equality. For Montesquieu, equality is a fact in the state of nature, but it is not necessarily a fact in society:

> Sitôt que les hommes sont en société, ils perdent le sentiment de leur faiblesse; l'égalité qui était entre eux cesse, et l'état de guerre commence (*Lois*, I, iii, N. I, i, p. 7, Pl. II, p. 236).

Nevertheless, positive laws are soon established in order to bring this Hobbesian state of war to an end; they should ensure both natural liberty:

> les hommes ont renoncé à leur indépendance naturelle, pour vivre sous des lois politiques [. . .].
>
> Ces [. . .] lois leur acquièrent la liberté (*Lois*, XXVI, xv, N. I, ii, p. 147, Pl. II, p. 767),

and natural equality:

> Dans l'état de nature, les hommes naissent bien dans l'égalité: mais ils n'y sauraient rester. La société la leur fait perdre, et ils ne redeviennent égaux que par les lois (*Lois*, VIII, iii, N. I, i, p. 152, Pl. II, p. 352).

Thus the original aim of positive law, according to Montesquieu, is to ensure natural equality and liberty. Exactly the same aim is assigned to positive law by Locke (*T.T.*, II, iv, 22, pp. 301–2, and II, vi, 54, p. 322). But Montesquieu, again like Locke (*T.T.*, II, vi, 54, p. 322), did not believe in absolute equality, even in democracies (*Lois*, VIII, ii–iii, N. I, i, pp. 149–53, Pl. II, pp. 349–52).

Thus the purpose of law is not to make all citizens absolutely equal, but simply to ensure that no man becomes the slave – either in the political or the personal sense – of another. To achieve this aim, a

[41] See above, p. 61, n. 38.

certain amount of inequality is necessary:

> Le Goth Jornandez a appelé le nord de l'Europe la fabrique du genre humain. Je l'appellerai plutôt la fabrique des instruments qui brisent les fers forgés au midi. C'est là que se forment ces nations vaillantes, qui sortent de leur pays pour détruire les tyrans et les esclaves, et apprendre aux hommes que, la nature les ayant faits égaux, la raison n'a pu les rendre dépendants que pour leur bonheur (*Lois*, XVII, v, N. I, i, p. 375, Pl. II, p. 528).

It was in this memorable and poetic way[42] that Montesquieu adapted the theory of natural law to suit his belief that he was descended from the Germanic tribes that conquered France: but his aristocratic outlook never led him to deny natural liberty or equality.[43] Oudin thinks that Montesquieu did not consider men to be, by nature, equal.[44] Of course, the *président* thought that men have some physical and mental inequalities, especially those caused by climate; but from the passages just quoted, it is clear he believed in their right to equality, that is, in their natural equality. Oudin is able to present this travesty of Montesquieu's opinion only because he fails to distinguish between equality as a fact and equality as a right.

When, in his commentary on Jornandes, Montesquieu used the expression "la nature les ayant faits égaux", he was referring to equality as a right. This same concept also served him in his refutation of the second kind of slavery, personal slavery, where he was no longer arguing against Hobbes or discrediting Louis XIV, but disagreeing with the School of Natural Law or with Aristotle.

Personal slavery has, broadly speaking, been justified on two grounds. Firstly by empirical arguments intended to prove that men are physically and mentally unequal; secondly by legal arguments intended to prove that certain of them have forfeited such rights as they may have had to equality. We shall examine these justifications in turn, and see how Montesquieu reacted to them.

The Sophists appear to have believed that equality is natural, and that consequently slavery is a result only of the positive law;[45] this view is also found in the *Digest*, where it is attributed to Ulpian (I, i, 4, p. 1). Aristotle was probably arguing against the Sophists when he affirmed that in spite of some instances that seem to prove the contrary,

[42] See P. van Tieghem, *Le Préromantisme*, SFELT, 1948, vol. I, pp. 110–11 and 165–6, for a discussion of the influence of this idea.

[43] *Cf.* Ehrard, *L'Idée de nature*, vol. II, pp. 509–15.

[44] *Le Spinozisme de Montesquieu*, pp. 58–61.

[45] *Cf.* Coplestone, *op. cit.*, vol. I, pp. 94–5.

"there are cases of people of whom some are freemen and the others slaves by nature".[46]

Such a theory, resulting as it does from Aristotle's rather chauvinistic disdain for the barbarians, was bound to displease Montesquieu, who believed in the community of mankind, and who had written in about 1730–1733, that Peter the Great

> excusait ses cruautés sur ce que sa nation était faite pour être traitée ainsi, mais les hommes se ressemblent partout. Ils ne sont pas ici des bêtes, là des anges. C'est la faute du législateur s'ils ne valent pas mieux (*Spicilège* 551, N. II, p. 845, Pl. II, p. 1366).

In his arguments against Aristotle, in the *Esprit des lois*, Montesquieu appealed to natural law. He had just shown that one kind of slavery originated in certain very hot countries, where men will not work unless they are threatened with violence. He continued:

> Aristote veut prouver qu'il y a des esclaves par nature; et ce qu'il dit ne le prouve guère. Je crois que, s'il y en a de tels, ce sont ceux dont je viens de parler.
>
> Mais, comme tous les hommes naissent égaux, il faut dire que l'esclavage est contre la nature, quoique, dans certains pays, il soit fondé sur une raison naturelle (*Lois*, *XV*, vii, N. I, i, p. 332, Pl. II, p. 496).

The "raison naturelle" is the climate, but in this passage, at least, it is shown to be inferior to "la nature".

It is difficult to find any justification for Cotta's contention that when Montesquieu said slavery is unnatural, he was referring to

> un dato immutabile ed universalmente cogente dal punto di vista del contenuto, si richiama alla natura fisiologico-istintiva dell'uomo, la quale è universalmente immutabile, e non all'elemento razionale come volevano invece i giusnaturalisti.[47]

On the contrary, it is the "raison naturelle" which is based on man's physical and instinctive nature, while the words "contre la nature" refer to a rational natural law similar to that of the School of Natural Law. Pufendorf, for example, admitted that men are not all mentally and physically equal, but in his opinion this did not alter the fact that "chacun doit estimer et traiter les autres comme lui étant naturellement égaux"; no *inégalité de fait* can destroy man's "égalité de droit" (*Dn.*, III, ii, 2, vol. I, pp. 309–11).

[46] *Politics*, I, ii, 14–15, pp. 23–5; *cf. ibid.*, 19–20, pp. 27–9.
[47] *Montesquieu e la scienza della società*, p. 370.

Thus when Montesquieu ironically said in his famous chapter on 'l'esclavage des nègres', that

> Il est impossible que nous supposions que ces gens-là soient des hommes; parce que, si nous les supposions des hommes, on commencerait à croire que nous ne sommes pas nous-mêmes chrétiens (*Lois*, XV, v, N. I, i, pp. 330–1, Pl. II, p. 494),

he was obviouly not trying to tell his readers that men are equal because they have two arms and two legs, but because they have the same rights.

Montesquieu was a strong advocate of the humane treatment of slaves. He was not necessarily unusual in this respect, since many of those who were in favour of slavery advocated the same thing.[48] Sometimes his arguments, like theirs, were predominantly utilitarian, as for example when he suggested that "L'humanité que l'on aura pour les esclaves" might prevent them from revolting (*Lois*, XV, xvi, N. 1, i, p. 340, Pl. II, p. 502). In the main, however, he was more concerned than his predecessors had been with the rights of the slaves, both in Antiquity, and, by implication, in modern times, when, in spite of the infamous *Code noir*, slaves in the colonies were often treated very cruelly.[49] His criticisms of the Romans' attitude to the family life of their slaves (*P.* 2194, Bkn. 171, N. II, p. 659, Pl. II, p. 220), of Plato's law whereby slaves who kill in self-defence are treated as parricides (*Lois*, XXVI, iii, N. I, ii, p. 128, Pl. II, p. 752), and of the Mosaic law which was lax about punishing the murder of a slave (*Lois*, XV, xvii, N. I, i, p. 343, Pl. II, p. 504)[50] were all based on the concept of natural rights.

In his arguments against those who thought there is some factual justification for slavery, Montesquieu only had to refer to certain basic tenets of natural law. When he came to discuss the legal theories put forward in defence of slavery, his reasoning became more complicated, but it was still inspired by the same principles.

Both in the *Esprit des lois*, and much earlier, in *Pensée* 174 (Bkn. 1935), Montesquieu examined the three ways in which it has been claimed that slavery is legitimately established: a contract, by which a man sells himself to another; enslavement of prisoners of war, instead of

[48] *Cf.* Aristotle, *Politics*, I, ii, 20–21, p. 29; *Digest*, I, vi, 1, p. 8; Pufendorf, *Dn.*, VI, iii, 7–8, vol. II, pp. 204–6; see also Levin, *op. cit.*, pp. 262–4.

[49] See Jameson, *op. cit.*, pp. 59–66.

[50] Exodus, XXI, 20–21. Barbeyrac discussed this law (*Dn.*, VI, iii, 4, n. 3, vol. II, p. 203) in the sort of impartial tone that the positivists pretend to find in M., whereas M.'s criticism was expressed in emotive terms.

killing them; enslavement of the children of slaves. He disagreed with all three arguments.

According to Pufendorf, "la servitude" (he did not here use the term *esclavage*) originated when men agreed to serve others, "moyennant un certain salaire"; then, both masters and servants having found the arrangement satisfactory, the latter "se résolurent insensiblement à entrer pour toujours dans la famille des premiers, à condition que ceux-ci leur fourniraient la nourriture et toutes les autres choses nécessaires à la vie". The cruelty associated with slavery only began with the maltreatment of those made slaves in war (*Dn.*, VI, iii, 4–5, vol. II, pp. 202–3).

Locke attacked the kind of explanation put forward by Pufendorf:[51]

> a man, not having the power of his own life, cannot, by compact, or his own consent, enslave himself to anyone [. . .]. Nobody can give more power than he has himself (*T.T.*, II, iv, 23, p. 302).

In *Pensée* 174 Montesquieu seems to have taken Locke's theory, which was directed against political slavery, and applied it to personal slavery:

> qui ne voit qu'un contrat civil ne saurait déroger au droit naturel, par lequel les hommes sont aussi essentiellement libres que raisonnables? (N. II, p. 57, Pl. I, p. 1467).

He added another, more legalistic reason: contracts of enslavement are not proper contracts because, a slave having no possessions, he cannot keep the money he receives for the sale of his liberty; further, no man can sell his citizenship since "La nature l'a fait citoyen" (N. II, pp. 57–8, Pl. I, p. 1467, subsequently deleted).

In Book XV, ii, of the *Esprit des lois*, Montesquieu repeated these ideas, and especially developed the theory that no man can sell his liberty, because it has no price (N. I, i, pp. 326–7, Pl. II, pp. 491–2). Derathé compares Montesquieu's reasoning in this chapter with Rousseau's, and claims that whereas for the latter, to sell oneself into slavery is to sell one's "qualité d'homme", for Montesquieu, it is to sell one's "qualité de citoyen".[52] However, this contrast holds good only for this chapter of the *Esprit des lois*; in Chapter vii, the *président* condemned slavery as being "contre la nature", that is, against the natural rights of the individual.

[51] Locke was probably refuting Hobbes, eg. *Leviathan*, II, xviii, pp. 159–70: he was principally concerned with the political implications of the theory.

[52] *Op. cit.*, p. 202, n. 1.

The second[53] ground upon which slavery had been justified was the *ius gentium*: "Le droit des gens a voulu que les prisonniers fussent esclaves, pour qu'on ne les tuât pas" (*Lois*, XV, ii, N. I, i, p. 326, Pl. II, p. 491). When Aristotle discussed slavery, he was quite certain that nature has made some to command, some to obey, but he was not at all certain that it is right to enslave prisoners of war, because the justice of this enslavement depends on such aleatory factors as the justice of the war, which in turn depends on whether those who win are fit to command, or only fit to obey.[54] Such considerations did not weigh very heavily with those who fought wars in Antiquity, for it was very common practice for prisoners of war to be enslaved,[55] and the custom was sanctioned by the *Corpus*.[56]

Grotius, too, accepted the custom as the basis of a natural law. Nowhere is one more aware of the equivocal nature of his conception of right, than in his discussion of the origins of slavery: he held that in war, many actions are permissible, not because they are just, but because they cannot be prevented; this is the main reason why it is permissible to kill one's enemies (*Dg.*, III, iv, 2–5, vol. II, pp. 766–71), under which term are included not only soldiers and male civilians, but also women, children, and captives. In the case of captives, it is both lawful and prudent to kill them, because they have threatened our lives and may do so again; but it is also possible to sell them into slavery (*ibid.*, 9–10, pp. 773–5). Hence it is true to say that captives taken in war are, by the law of nature, slaves, even though, by nature, no man is slave to another (*ibid.*, vii, 1, pp. 820–1). Pufendorf likewise accepted this origin of slavery (*Dn.*, VI, iii, 5–6, vol. II, pp. 203–4), so did Locke, though he was careful to emphasize that the war must be a just one (*T.T.*, II, xvi, 180, p. 406), and so did the Catholic theorists.[57]

One of the few writers before Montesquieu to point out the injustice of this kind of slavery was Bodin. He first gave a convincing account of the arguments in favour of slavery, but then proceeded to give an even more convincing one of those against it. In particular, he thought that to make slaves of prisoners of war is to apply thieves' justice, since war gives victory to the strongest, not to the wisest; he

[53] Following the order of *P.* 174; in *Lois*, XV, ii, this argument comes first.
[54] *Politics*, I, ii, 16–18, pp. 25–7.
[55] Jameson, *op. cit.*, p. 9.
[56] Eg. *Institutes*, I, iii, 2–3, p. 2.
[57] St. Thomas, *S.t.*, II, ii, Q. 57, A. 3, rep. obj. 2, vol. X, p. 110; Domat, *op. cit.*, *Livre préliminaire*, ii, 2, paragraph 3, vol. I, p. 14. See Jameson, *op. cit.*, pp. 82–212 for a full account of this question.

showed that it is not charity which causes this kind of enslavement, as some have claimed, since the victor hopes to gain by the work of the slaves.[58]

Montesquieu was no doubt aware of Bodin's refutation, but his own is based on a rather different approach:

Il est faux qu'il soit permis de tuer dans la guerre, autrement que dans le cas de nécessité: mais, dès qu'un homme en a fait un autre esclave, on ne peut pas dire qu'il ait été dans la nécessité de le tuer, puisqu'il ne l'a pas fait. Tout le droit que la guerre peut donner sur les captifs, est de s'assurer tellement de leur personne, qu'ils ne puissent plus nuire. Les homicides faits de sang froid par les soldats, et après la chaleur de l'action, sont rejetés de toutes les nations du monde (*Lois*, XV, ii, N. I, i, p. 326, Pl. II, p. 491).

As a piece of reasoning, this passage is not entirely satisfactory,[59] but it is nevertheless pertinent, since it uses two principles of natural law, namely self-defence, admitted by both Grotius and Pufendorf, and universal consent, admitted by Grotius, in order to refute these jurists, as well as those of Antiquity.

The third manner in which slavery is said to come about is by birth. Grotius (*Dg.*, III, vii, 2, vol. II, p. 821) and Domat[60] held this view, and so did Pufendorf, though he made certain reservations; in particular, he claimed that the children of those who sell themselves into slavery, are not automatically slaves, unless this has been stipulated in the contract of enslavement (*Dn.*, VI, iii, 9, vol. II, pp. 207–8). Rousseau was later to go even further, denying that parents have any right to sell their children (*Discours sur l'inégalité*, II, p. 187). Locke had been almost alone in arguing that conquerors have no right over the children of their prisoners (*T.T.*, II, xvi, 182, pp. 407–8).

Montesquieu seems to have taken what is enlightened from each of these theories, and to have rejected the rest:

si un homme n'a pu se vendre, encore moins a-t-il pu vendre son fils qui n'était pas né: si un prisonnier de guerre ne peut être réduit en servitude, encore moins ses enfants (*Lois*, XV, ii, N. I, i, p. 327, Pl. II, p. 492).

Once again, this reasoning is drawn from natural law, from the principle that a man cannot sell his natural liberty. Another argument that

[58] *République*, I, v, pp. 32–47.

[59] The jurists did not say that it was necessarily in order to prevent an enemy from killing a soldier at the moment of capture, that the former was enslaved, but rather in order to prevent him from returning home and then renewing the war. M. does not, in this passage, say how it is possible to "s'assurer de [la] personne [des captifs], qu'ils ne puissent plus nuire", without enslaving them permanently.

[60] *Op. cit., loc. cit.*

had been used to justify the enslavement of the children of slaves captured in war, was that the expense of feeding them, before they are old enough to work, is sufficient to give their master a right of property over them (Pufendorf, *Dn.*, VI, iii, 9, vol. II, p. 207). Montesquieu, rather surprisingly, did not reply that loss of liberty is no way to pay for food: instead he claimed that the master has not been put to much expense (*Lois*, XV, ii, N. I, i, p. 328, Pl. II, p. 492) – arguing less on juristic grounds than on those of charity.

Having answered these theories of the jurists, Montesquieu also produced further reasons of his own, to show that slavery is wrong. Both Aristotle[61] and Pufendorf (*Dn.*, VI, iii, 4, vol. II, p. 202) had suggested that slavery is useful not only to the master, but also to the slave, since without a master he would be incapable of looking after himself. Montesquieu denied that slavery can ever be useful to the slave, since the law of slavery is

> dans tous les cas, contre lui, sans jamais être pour lui; ce qui est contraire au principe fondamental de toutes les sociétés (*Lois*, XV, ii, N. I, i, pp. 327–8, Pl. II, p. 492).

This is yet another reference to the natural rights of man: Montesquieu was asserting that in all societies, and not only in moderate monarchies, laws are established for the benefit of all, and not for that of a particular group. He was implicitly basing his argument on the idea of an original contract.

The principle that society must benefit all its members was put forward by Montesquieu in two other places, in connection with slavery. He first developed it in a letter he wrote in 1750 (N. III, p. 1294), and it appeared in its final form in the 1757 edition of the *Esprit des lois*:[62] replying to those theorists, such as his fellow-bordelais Melon,[63] who advocated the introduction of slavery into France, he pointed to the fact that they themselves would not want to become slaves:

> Le cri pour l'esclavage est donc le cri du luxe et de la volupté, et non pas celui de l'amour de la félicité publique. [. . .] Dans ces choses, voulez-vous savoir si les désirs de chacun sont légitimes? examinez les désirs de tous (*Lois*, XV, ix, N. I, i, p. 334, Pl. II, p. 497).

The basic maxim of natural law and of the Gospel, *do as you would be done by*, is the inspiration behind this passage.

61 *Politics*, I, ii, 20–21, p. 29.
62 See Brethe de la Gressaye, *Lois*, vol. II, p. 418, n. 45, to p. 224; Pl. II, p. 1510.
63 *Cf.* Dedieu, *Montesquieu*, pp. 204–5 and 207.

The School of Natural Law thought that slaves have the right to escape if they are maltreated (*Dg.*, II, v, 29, vol. I, pp. 310–11; *Dn.*, VI, iii, 11, vol. II, p. 210). Montesquieu went further and claimed, true to the principle just examined, that

> L'esclavage est [...] aussi opposé au droit civil qu'au droit naturel. Quelle loi civile pourrait empêcher un esclave de fuir, lui qui n'est point dans la société, et que par conséquent aucunes lois civiles ne concernent? (*Lois*, XV, ii, N. I, i, p. 328, Pl. II, p. 492).

He had already made the same point many years earlier, in *Pensée* 174, where he had also expressed his approval of Spartacus's revolt (N. II, p. 59, Pl. I, pp. 1468–9).

From the evidence just examined, Montesquieu would seem to have been one of the first abolitionists. But this is not the complete picture. It has been alleged by Jameson and others that although Montesquieu's humanity and love of justice caused him to see that slavery is contrary to reason and that it should not be allowed in Europe, his conservatism, or some other cause, prevented him from outspokenly demanding its complete abolition.[64]

Three chapters in Book XV of the *Esprit des lois* could be said to justify this view. However, one of them, Chapter v, on 'l'esclavage des nègres', can only have this interpretation placed on it if the reader is unable to recognize irony and indignation behind the feeble reasons that Montesquieu finds in support of slavery: sugar would be too expensive if it were not produced by slaves; negroes have no soul because God would not create one in a black body. The chapter ends with a plea to the princes of Europe to make a "convention" "en faveur de la miséricorde et de la pitié [...]" (N. I, i, pp. 330–1, Pl. II, p. 494): presumably, this would be an agreement to end slave trading, and to release those who are slaves. How then can Brethe de la Gressaye say that Montesquieu "n'a pas envisagé l'abolition de l'esclavage"?[65]

Chapter vi, entitled 'Véritable origine du droit de l'esclavage', which deals with slavery in despotic countries, and Chapter vii, on slavery in hot climates, present more serious difficulties to those who would like to think that Montesquieu always opposed slavery. In Chapter vi, he said that slavery is founded on "la nature des choses" when the government is such that "l'esclavage politique [...] anéantit, en

[64] Jameson, *op. cit.*, pp. 318–9; *cf.* Dedieu, *Montesquieu*, p. 207; Dodds, *op. cit.*, pp. 120–3; Levin, *op. cit.*, p. 251; Brethe de la Gressaye, *Lois*, vol. II, p. 212; Crocker, *Nature and Culture*, p. 321.

[65] *Loc. cit.*

quelque façon, la liberté civile"; thus, "les hommes libres, trop faibles contre le gouvernement, cherchent à devenir les esclaves de ceux qui tyrannisent le gouvernement" (N. I, i, pp. 331–2, Pl. II, p. 495). Here, then, in what seems suspiciously like a piece of wishful thinking, he claimed that personal slavery is a means of mitigating the effects of political slavery.

In Chapter vii, he tried to show that slavery can be "fondé sur une raison naturelle" because

> Il y a des pays où la chaleur énerve le corps, et affaiblit si fort le courage, que les hommes ne sont portés à un devoir pénible que par la crainte du châtiment: l'esclavage y choque donc moins la raison (N. I, i, p. 332, Pl. II, pp. 495–6).

Thus, in Chapter vi slavery is seen as the result of a free choice by the slave, while in Chapter vii it is seen as the result of force.

In putting forward these explanations, Montesquieu contradicted some of the principles by which he had condemned slavery. Firstly, by saying in Chapter vi that in certain despotisms, slavery is based on "le *choix libre* qu'un homme, *pour son utilité*, se fait d'un maître" (N. I, i, p. 332, Pl. II, p. 495, our italics), he contradicted the principles he had put forward in Chapter ii, namely that a free man cannot sell himself, and that slavery can never be useful to the slave. Secondly, by saying in Chapter vii that in certain hot climates men are so lazy that they will only work under threat of punishment, he contradicted the principle he put forward in the same chapter, that there are no "esclaves par nature".

Thirdly – and this is the most serious inconsistency – by saying in Chapter vi that when men sell themselves into personal slavery in order to harass the government,

> C'est là l'origine *juste*, et *conforme à la raison*, de ce droit d'esclavage très doux que l'on trouve dans quelques pays (N. I, i, p. 332, Pl. II, p. 495, our italics),

he contradicted the principle he put forward both in Chapter ii, where he said that slavery is "aussi opposé au droit civil qu'au droit naturel", and in Chapter vii, where slavery is said to be "contre la nature".

Thus it appears that Montesquieu believed slavery to be both unnatural and natural, in accordance with reason and contrary to reason. This contradictory state of affairs, of which he does not seem to have been fully aware, is to be explained by his method. He was certain that slavery, like all other institutions, must have explainable causes:

Il est temps de chercher la vraie origine du droit de l'esclavage. Il doit être fondé sur la nature des choses (*Lois*, XV, vi, N. I, i, p. 331, Pl. II, p. 495).

Now two of his "hobby-horses", in the *Esprit des lois*, are despotism and climate, the former being in his opinion the result of the latter.[66] It is precisely these factors which come into play in his discussion of slavery. One of the reasons why he considered despotism to be evil was because it does nothing to combat the bad effects of the climate (*Lois*, XIV, v–vi, N. I, i, pp. 311–3, Pl. II, pp. 479–80). As he said in Book XV, viii:

Parce que les lois étaient mal faites, on a trouvé des hommes paresseux; parce que ces hommes étaient paresseux, on les a mis dans l'esclavage (N. I, i, p. 334, Pl. II, p. 497).

As in the case of torture, Montesquieu's discussion of slavery is less the justification of a certain abuse than an indictment of despotism. Nevertheless, it is quite true that he was not as outspoken as one would have hoped.

Having applied his method in Chapters vi and vii, he went on to show, in Chapter viii, that "Il faut [...] borner la servitude naturelle à de certains pays particuliers de la terre", since in all others,

quelques pénibles que soient les travaux que la société y exige, on peut tout faire avec des hommes libres (N. I, i, p. 333, Pl. II, p. 496).

He ended the chapter in quite a different tone, with a personal admission, which is not found in the manuscript and seems to have been added at the last moment:[67]

Je ne sais si c'est l'esprit ou le cœur qui me dicte cet article-ci. Il n'y a peut-être pas de climat sur la terre où l'on ne pût engager au travail des hommes libres (N. I, i, p. 334, Pl. II, p. 497).

It would be wrong to take this too literally. It is not true that there is a complete gulf between Montesquieu's "esprit" and his "cœur", in his discussion of slavery, since the emotion revealed in this passage is in tune with his previous arguments showing that slavery is contrary to reason. If there was any conflict, it was between both his heart and his mind, on the one hand, when they argued against slavery, and his mind, on the other, when it forgot about natural law and showed how

[66] *Cf. Lois*, XVII, ii, N. I, ii, pp. 368–9, Pl. II, pp. 523–4: hot climates turn people into political slaves; also *Lois*, V, xv, N. I, i, p. 85, Pl. II, p. 297.
[67] Brethe de la Gressaye, *Lois*, vol. II, p. 417, n. 42, to p. 224.

slavery arises from "la nature des choses". Montesquieu's dislike of slavery – like that of his contemporary Buffon[68] – was neither purely emotional nor purely intellectual: it was the result of a powerful combination of reason and emotion.[69] Thus those scholars, such as Starobinski and Shelby T. McCloy, who claim that the *président*'s study of slavery was purely objective and devoid of emotion,[70] are seriously misrepresenting his attitude.

Those other scholars who emphasize the equivocalness of his thought are also perhaps slightly misrepresenting him: of the first eight chapters of Book XV, only two in any sense justify slavery; here, in spite of his explanations, he still implied or stated that it is wrong, though not so wrong as in the other cases. Chapters ii, v, and vii contain arguments valid against all forms of slavery, and so does Chapter ix, even though it purports to concern only those nations in which 'la liberté politique est généralement établie' (N. I, i, p. 334, Pl. II, p. 497). In the remaining chapters of Book XV, Montesquieu went on to examine how civil law may overcome the abuses and dangers of slavery; here, obviously, he had to talk about it as an established fact, but this does not invalidate his previous criticisms of the institution.

It is easy for twentieth-century critics, living in an age when slavery is officially unknown and survives unofficially in only a few places, to say that Montesquieu should have demanded its abolition in more outspoken terms. He was indeed the first major European writer to oppose all forms of slavery, but he did not believe in reforming abuses overnight; he thought it wise first to study the causes of those abuses, so as to prevent them more effectively; his weapon against them was not declamation but irony based on fact, irony that effectively showed slavery to be the result of greed, selfishness and bad government.

In so far as Montesquieu may be said to have excused certain forms of slavery, he was merely following the example set by his predecessors, and particularly that of the School of Natural Law. Far from believing, as Cotta implies when he talks of the "elemento razionale" of the *giusnaturalisti*, in a natural law forbidding slavery, they were intent on justifying the institution. If the question of slavery made Montesquieu feel uneasy, it embarrasses his positivistic admirers even more. In many of the topics where the *président* tended to deny the existence of

[68] See the *Histoire naturelle de l'homme* of 1749, in *Œuvres philosophiques*, pp. 312–3, where Buffon, deploring the maltreatment of the negroes, clearly reveals his personal emotions.

[69] *Cf.* Fletcher, *Montesquieu and English Politics*, p. 228: "Never do we see his powers of reason and feeling more closely mated".

[70] Starobinski, *op. cit.*, p. 109; Shelby T. McCloy, *op. cit.*, p. 86.

a universal natural law – suicide, usury, divorce, for example – the climate of modern opinion is often on his side; hence the positivists can praise him for his non-moralistic approach without too great a risk of incurring the reader's displeasure. But modern opinion does generally believe that slavery is wrong. Therefore, to praise Montesquieu for having discussed it in non-moralistic fashion, is probably to diminish his stature in the eyes of the reader. What then are the positivists to do? Will they imply that there is no moral law against slavery; or will they introduce such a law, contrary to the principles of their method?

Dedieu evidently shrinks from the first alternative, and this puts him in a very awkward position. He has previously asserted that Montesquieu's principal achievement is to have divorced social science from morality, whereas Grotius, Pufendorf and Domat considered laws and customs from a moralistic point of view.[71] Yet it is plain that in their discussion of slavery, these philosophers were doing precisely what Dedieu praises Montesquieu for doing in social science, namely finding explanations for existing institutions, without regard to morality. When Dedieu praises the *président* for his attack on slavery, he turns the tables on the School of Natural Law, criticising them for the very same empirical approach he had previously praised in Montesquieu, and praising Montesquieu for the rationalistic approach he had previously criticized in the School of Natural Law.[72] Such a *volte-face* no doubt helps to produce a flattering portrait of the *président*, but it is a portrait that lacks consistency. To be consistent, Dedieu should praise the School of Natural Law and Montesquieu for having justified slavery, and condemn Montesquieu when he tried to show that slavery is wrong. Such are the contradictions in wishing to see Montesquieu both as a positivist and as a humanitarian.

In the question of slavery, his true originality was rather that he was more moralistic than the School of Natural Law had been. The same cannot be said of his attitude to another thorny problem, property.

III. Property

The fact that the School of Natural Law discussed the existence of property in the state of nature has tended to obscure, for the modern reader, the true character of their thought on this question. In order to provide a more secure basis for the right of property, Locke argued that man in the state of nature could own things, or rather that he

[71] *Montesquieu*, pp. 186–7; *Montesquieu l'homme et l'oeuvre*, pp. 132–3.
[72] *Montesquieu*, p. 210; *Montesquieu l'homme et l'oeuvre*, p. 163.

could acquire them by work (*T.T.*, II, v, 26–36, pp. 304–11). On the other hand, Pufendorf denied the existence of property in the state of nature, and claimed that it owes its origin entirely to convention (*Dn.*, IV, iv, 4, vol. I, pp. 494–5). As regards the right of property in society, however, there is very little difference between Locke and Pufendorf.

Locke insisted that

> the supreme power cannot take from any man any part of his property without his own consent. For the preservation of property being the end of government, [...] it necessarily supposes and requires, that the people should have property (*T.T.*, II, xi, 138, p. 378).

Why, one might ask, if property existed in the state of nature, was it necessary to enter into society in order to preserve it? Locke's answer was that in the state of nature the right of property is uncertain, and that men formed societies in order to have "a secure enjoyment of their properties" (*T.T.*, II, viii, 95, p. 349). Pufendorf's reasoning is almost identical: property is a natural law because it is necessary in order to prevent society from degenerating into anarchy (*Dn.*, IV, iv, 14, vol. I, pp. 510–11). Both philosophers, in claiming that property is a natural law, derived it from the nature of society; in addition, Locke also derived it from the nature of man; for Pufendorf, property is a secondary natural law, for Locke, it is both a primary and a secondary natural law.

Montesquieu seems to have agreed with Pufendorf, rather than Locke, on the question of whether property existed in the state of nature, since, in Book XXVI, xv, he talks of "la communauté naturelle des biens" (N. I, ii, p. 147, Pl. II, p. 767). However, he shared with both of them the view that men in society should have property; his insistence on the rights of property-owners reminds us particularly of Locke:

> C'est un paralogisme de dire que le bien particulier doit céder au bien public: cela n'a lieu que dans les cas où il s'agit de l'empire de la cité, c'est à dire, de la liberté du citoyen: cela n'a pas lieu dans ceux où il est question de la propriété des biens, parce que le bien public est toujours que chacun conserve invariablement la propriété que lui donnent les lois civiles (*Lois*, XXVI, xv, N. I, ii, pp. 147–8, Pl. II, pp. 767–8).

This general statement of principle also happens, of course, to be in accordance with Montesquieu's position as an important landowner occasionally involved in litigation with other landowners and with the town of Bordeaux, and in quarrels with the Intendants. Nevertheless, it amounts to a proclamation of the natural right of property, based on the nature of man in society: Montesquieu thus believed in that right as much as Pufendorf or Locke had done. Oudin's claim that the *président* was original in that he derived property from the "conditions essentielles d'existence qu'il trouve dans la vie sociale" rather than from the "nature propre de l'individu", is the result of a misunderstanding of natural law.[73]

The claims of Montesquieu's conservative critics are no less misguided. The philosophy of natural law is generally anti-revolutionary in its ruling on the right of property,[74] and we have shown that Montesquieu was no exception in this respect. It is perhaps not surprising that those nineteenth- and twentieth-century critics, such as Vian, Barckhausen and Charmont who, again because of a misunderstanding of the doctrine as it was known in the seventeenth and eighteenth centuries, reproached Montesquieu with not having made property a natural law,[75] were themselves conservative in outlook: Vian in particular is annoyed with Montesquieu for having influenced "les socialistes en 1848". Barckhausen avoids showing his prejudices quite so openly, and instead quibbles with Book I, ii of the *Esprit des lois*: if primitive man has a natural desire to feed himself, how, asks Barckhausen, can he do this without an "appropriation préalable"?

This difficulty can be solved by reference to Pufendorf. He did not deny that people could possess things in the state of nature, he simply showed that such possession is not secure until society is established (*Dn.*, IV, iv, 4 and 14, vol. I, pp. 494 and 510–11). Montesquieu probably reasoned in a similar way, in spite of the fact that he would not have agreed with Pufendorf about the insecurity of the state of nature. He no doubt felt that since there was no question of competition interfering with primitive man's search for food, there was not much point in talking about a right of property in the state of nature; that this right only becomes important when society begins, causing a state of war which might jeopardize the liberty of the individual unless proper laws are established.

[73] *Le Spinozisme de Montesquieu*, p. 80; *cf.* a similar statement in Fletcher, *Montesquieu and English Politics*, p. 194.

[74] A notable exception to this tendency was the eighteenth-century philoshopher Morelly: *cf.* his *Code de la nature* [1755], edited by G. Chinard, 1950, pp. 206–7; on Morelly, see R. N. C. Coe, 'A la recherche de Morelly', *RHLF*, 1957, pp. 321–34 and 515–23.

[75] Vian, *op. cit.*, p. 316; Barckhausen, *Montesquieu, ses idées et ses œuvres*, p. 42; Charmont, *op. cit.*, p. 40.

Property, then, for Montesquieu, was a natural right; it was one aspect of the right of liberty. But true to the conservative tradition, he believed it to be a right that implies certain duties, and this is how, in spite of his conservatism, he may still be called a progressive.

Louis XIV had considered that he had "la disposition pleine et entière" of all the property in his kingdom.[76] With one eye on France, Montesquieu criticized those states where "Le clergé, le prince, les villes, les grands" have become "propriétaires de toute la contrée", on the grounds that the people are discouraged from working and remain poor (*Lois*, XXIII, xxviii–xxix, N. I, ii, pp. 76–9, Pl. II, pp. 711–12). He then showed that especially in industrialized countries, the government must help the old, the infirm, and orphans, and provide work and training for those who need it. He made the following statement of principle:

> Quelques aumônes que l'on fait à un homme nu, dans les rues, ne remplissent point les obligations de l'État, qui doit à tous les citoyens une subsistance assurée, la nourriture, un vêtement convenable, et un genre de vie qui ne soit point contraire à la santé (*Lois*, XXIII, xxix, N. I, ii, p. 78, Pl. II, p. 712).

Montesquieu's idea of charity goes further than that of Pufendorf. The German had stated that the sovereign must do all he can to encourage commerce and industry, that he should have "un soin particulier" of those who are needy through no fault of their own, but that he "n'est pas obligé de nourrir ses sujets" (*Dn.*, VII, ix, 11, vol. II, p. 349). However, it is not so much the ideas of Pufendorf and Montesquieu that differ here, as their temperament. Pufendorf's discussion of this question is as usual dry and legalistic; Montesquieu's, in the published version of the *Esprit des lois*, reveals sympathy for the poor, though not much emotion. In a fragment of the work, however, his tone becomes emotional:

> Si la famine vient, la suprême loi, c'est le salut du peuple. Tous vos engagements sont suspendus, parce que le salut du peuple peut seul vous mettre en état de maintenir vos engagements. Donnez, répandez, prodiguez (N. III, p. 622, Pl. II, p. 1021).

The numerous critics who think that Montesquieu had an icy temperament[77] take no account of lines such as these: the sentiment revealed

[76] Sée, *Les Idées politiques*, p. 137.

[77] Eg. Vian, *op. cit.*, pp. 337–8; Sorel, *op. cit.*, p. 164; Sabine, *op. cit.*, p. 551. This view has been convincingly challenged by A. Laborde-Milaá, 'La Sensibilité de Montesquieu', *Revue des études historiques*, 1908, pp. 333–40. It is time somebody pointed out that M.'s refusal

in them appears all the more sincere when we realize that he put these charitable precepts into practice, helping the poor of his district in time of famine.[78]

It might at first sight appear that Montesquieu's sympathy for the poor and his desire to help them, are socialistic. But his theory of the rights of property, in Book XXVI, xv of the *Esprit des lois*, and even the wording of the fragment just quoted ("Donnez, répandez, prodiguez"), indicate a man more inspired by a realization of his duties as a *seigneur*, than by any theory of civil equality. His conviction that men are naturally equal made him dislike exploitation of the weaker members of the community, but it did not make him believe in any kind of communism.[79] His "socialism" is in reality paternalism,[80] and it may well have been inspired by the principles of Christianity. Domat's remarks on "les hôpitaux" are very similar to those of Montesquieu. All, said the Jansenist, are entitled to food, lodging and clothing, "afin que tous soient dans l'État des membres du corps de la société"; those who cannot work and who lack the necessities of life "ont un titre et un droit naturel qui leur affecte la part nécessaire".[81] Natural law and Christianity are by no means always incompatible.

In Montesquieu's opinion, commerce and industry serve a two-fold purpose. Firstly, they ensure the prosperity of a state and of all the people in it, even the poorest: Usbek had put forward this argument in his defence of *le luxe* (*L.p.* CVI, N. I, iii, pp. 211–4, Pl. I, pp. 288–90). Secondly, they help to promote understanding between different nations:

> L'effet naturel du commerce est de porter à la paix (*Lois*, XX, ii, N. I, i, p. 446, Pl. II, p. 585).

In the philosophy of natural law, questions of war and peace come under the jurisdiction of the law of nature and of nations. What was Montesquieu's attitude to this question?

to reveal his identity to the *batelier* whose father's ransom he paid, indicates not so much "un caractère de bonté dédaigneuse" (Vian, *loc. cit.*), as modesty or timidity – M. admitted that timidity had been "le fléau de toute ma vie" (*P.* 1005, Bkn. 7, N. II, p. 278, Pl. I, p. 980).

[78] *Cf.* Shackleton, *M.*, p. 203.

[79] Edgar Zévort is surely mistaken when he claims that M. "restera [...] jusqu'à la fin, le partisan du communisme" (*Montesquieu*, Lecène et Oudin, 1888, p. 109).

[80] *Cf.* Sorel, *op. cit.*, p. 128; Ehrard, *Politique de Montesquieu*, p. 241.

[81] *Op. cit.*, *Le Droit public*, I, xviii, vol. II, pp. 131–2.

IV. International Relations

It has often been suggested that the behaviour of states towards each other resembles that of men in the state of nature, since in neither case is there any superior power to enforce laws: thus, it is said, states are in a state of nature with each other. Just as there was controversy over whether man in the state of nature was at war or at peace with his neighbours, so there was over whether states are naturally at war or at peace with each other.

The theory that nations are in a state of peace could probably be traced back at least as far as the Greek Stoics;[82] that they are in a state of war is an opinion of equal antiquity,[83] but in the seventeenth century one of its main exponents was Hobbes. In his sonorous prose he conjured up a grim picture of international relations:

in all times, kings, and persons of sovereign authority, because of their independency, are in continual jealousies, and in the state and posture of gladiators; having their weapons pointing, and their eyes fixed on one another; that is, their forts, garrisons, and guns upon the frontiers of their kingdoms; and continual spies upon their neighbours; which is a posture of war (*Leviathan*, I, xiii, p. 115).

Although Montesquieu strongly disagreed with Hobbes's suggestion that the state of nature is a state of war, he still seems to have agreed with him that the primary relationship between nations – that is, the relationship that would prevail if there were no international agreements – is one of war:

Sitôt que les hommes sont en société, ils perdent le sentiment de leur faiblesse; l'égalité qui était entre eux cesse, et l'état de guerre commence.
Chaque société particulière vient à sentir sa force; ce qui produit un état de guerre de nation à nation (*Lois*, I, iii, N. I, i, p. 7, Pl. II, p. 236).

Force is always the most important factor in international relations: rulers are "gouvernés par la force; ils peuvent continuellement forcer ou être forcés" (*Lois*, XXVI, xx, N. I, ii, p. 153, Pl. II, pp. 772–3).

Montesquieu nevertheless tempered this Hobbesian realism with a certain idealism. The two states of war, between different individuals and between different societies, are suspended, according to Montes-

[82] See below, p. 174.

[83] *Cf.* Plato, *Laws*, I, 626a, vol. I, p. 7, where one speaker says that each Greek state is "by a law of nature, engaged perpetually in an informal war with every other state". See also Levin, *op. cit.*, pp. 48–9.

quieu, by two different kinds of law: the first state of war is ended by civil and political law, the second by the law of nations:

> Considérés comme habitants d'une si grande planète, qu'il est nécessaire qu'il y ait différents peuples, [les hommes] ont des lois dans le rapport que ces peuples ont entre eux; et c'est le droit des gens (*Lois*, I, iii, N. I, i, p. 7, Pl. II, p. 236).

For Montesquieu the law of nations is partly an idealistic concept: he did not say that each nation should strive to surpass its neighbours; rather he claimed that the fundamental principle of the law of nations is that "les diverses nations doivent se faire dans la paix le plus de bien, et dans la guerre le moins de mal qu'il est possible, sans nuire à leurs véritables intérêts" (*ibid.*, N. I, i, p. 7, Pl. II, pp. 236–7). The final qualification shows that Montesquieu has not forgotten the realities of international affairs, and indeed he also thought of the law of nations as an empirical concept, since he said it is "le droit civil de l'univers, dans le sens que chaque peuple en est un citoyen" (*Lois*, XXVI, i, N. I, ii, p. 126, Pl. II, p. 751). But even this "droit civil" has idealistic undertones, since the notion that each state is a citizen of the universe is reminiscent of the idealistic doctrines of the Stoics.

In Book XXI, xxi, Montesquieu linked the two aspects, idealistic and empirical, of the law of nations, when he said that

> Les nations, qui sont à l'égard de tout l'univers ce que les particuliers sont dans un État, se gouvernent, comme eux, par le droit naturel et par les lois qu'elles se sont faites (N. I, i, p. 519, Pl. II, p. 644).

How can the positivists, and in general those who deny the *président*'s belief in natural law, have overlooked this passage? What clearer evidence could there be that he accepted the age-old idea that natural law should play its part, alongside positive law, in the political life of a nation?

In the *Lettres persanes*, Montesquieu accorded an even larger rôle to natural law in the law of nations: at the end of an excessively optimistic letter showing how easily international disputes can be settled, Usbek exclaimed "voila le droit des gens, ou plutôt celui de la raison" (*L.p.* XCV, N. I, iii, p. 190, Pl. I, p. 272). In later years, Montesquieu became more cynical, but he always retained something of Usbek's idealistic approach to international relations.

However, this idealism never went as far as pacificism. Bayle had suggested that a society composed solely of true Christians could not survive in the face of foreign aggression, because the Gospel forbids men to repel violence with violence and fraud with fraud; in support of this interpretation of the Gospel, he claimed that its teaching on the subject of war had been corrupted by the casuists with arguments drawn from the natural law of self-defence.[84] This rigorism did not appeal to Montesquieu; in his refutation of Bayle he distinguished between precepts and counsels. Precepts belong to the world of politics, and must be obeyed; counsels, such as the Gospel's injunction to love our enemies, belong to the world of religion, and need only be obeyed by those who seek perfection (*Lois*, XXIV, vi–vii, N. I, ii, pp. 87–8, Pl. II, pp. 719–20). This distinction is quite orthodox;[85] indeed, the concept of the just war was sanctioned by Catholic theology,[86] and Protestants less extreme than Bayle also thought that war is not necessarily unchristian.[87]

Montesquieu, then, felt that war could be in accordance with justice: "Le droit de la guerre dérive [...] de la nécessité et du juste rigide" (*Lois*, X, ii, N. I, i, p. 183, Pl. II, p. 378). Just as primitive man would think above all of his own preservation (*Lois*, I, ii, N. I, i, p. 5, Pl. II, p. 235), so the aim of every state is to stay in existence (*Lois*, XI, v, N. I, i, p. 206, Pl. II, p. 396); every state, by the very fact that it exists, has the right to continue in existence, and to preserve itself, by war if necessary:

> La vie des États est comme celle des hommes. Ceux-ci ont droit de tuer, dans le cas de la défense naturelle; ceux-là ont droit de faire la guerre pour leur propre conservation (*Lois*, X, ii, N. I, i, p. 182, Pl. II, p. 377).

Moreover, it is necessary to the well-being of the universe that each state should stay in existence (*P.* 1814, Bkn. 390, N. II, p. 538, Pl. II, p. 1100).

Montesquieu's justification of war reminds us strongly of that of Grotius:

> Si l'on considère les premières impressions de la nature, on n'y trouve rien qui tende à condamner la guerre, et tout, au contraire, en favorise la permission. Car on fait la guerre pour la conservation de sa vie ou de ses membres, et pour maintenir ou acquérir la possession des choses utiles à la vie; ce qui est très conforme aux premiers mouvements de la nature. Et il n'y a rien qui y soit contraire, à employer pour cet effet, s'il en est

[84] *Continuation des pensées diverses*, cxxiv–cxxv, pp. 359–62.

[85] *Cf. S.t.*, II, ii, Q. 25, A. 9, vol. IX, p. 324: "charity does not require us to do that which belongs to its perfection. Therefore charity does not require us to show the signs and effects of love to our enemies".

[86] *Ibid.*, Q. 40. A. 1, vol. IX, pp. 500–503.

[87] *Cf.* Grotius, *Dg.*, I, ii, 6–10, vol. I, pp. 76–106.

besoin, les voies même de la force; puisque la nature n'a donné des forces à chaque animal, qu'afin qu'il s'en serve pour sa défense et pour son utilité (*Dg.*, I, ii, 1, vol. I, p. 68).

If both Montesquieu and Grotius justified war partly by reference to the instinct of self-preservation, neither of them accepted that "les lois se taisent parmi le bruit des armes" (*Dg.*, *Disc. prél.*, xxvii, vol. I, p. 17): they held that war is subject to certain rules that govern both its declaration and its conduct. Grotius, appalled by the fact that in "le monde chrétien" "On court aux armes ou sans raison, ou pour de très légers sujets: et quand une fois on les a en main, on foule aux pieds tout droit divin et humain" (*Dg.*, *Disc. prél.*, xxix, vol. I, p. 20), had been one of the first to systematize these rules, which had of course been known since Antiquity. On this question, Montesquieu owes much to the philosophers of natural law, and his views are not original.

He discussed the just causes of war both in the *Lettres persanes* and in the *Esprit des lois*. Usbek claimed that there are only two kinds of just war: those undertaken to repel an invasion, and those to aid an ally (*L.p.* XCV, N. I, iii, p. 188, Pl. I, p. 271). This idea is a commonplace, having been put forward by many writers in Antiquity,[88] as well as by Grotius (*Dg.*, I, ii, 1, vol. I, p. 68 and II, xxv, 4, vol. II, p. 695) and Pufendorf (*Dn.*, VIII, vi, 3 and 14, vol. II, pp. 455–6 and 466–7). In the *Esprit des lois*, Montesquieu added a further, more controversial cause, saying that

le droit de la défense naturelle entraîne quelquefois la nécessité d'attaquer; lorsqu'un peuple voit qu'une plus longue paix en mettrait un autre en état de le détruire; et que l'attaque est, dans ce moment, le seul moyen d'empêcher cette destruction (X, ii, N. I, i, p. 183, Pl. II, p. 377).

Voltaire could not believe that such a Machiavellian doctrine had been put forward by such an enlightened man;[89] indeed, Montesquieu was going against the theorists of natural law, who admitted the right of attack in self-defence only in cases where a state is morally certain of its neighbour's evil intentions.[90] For Montesquieu, on the other hand, the neighbour's power, even unaccompanied by threats, is a sufficient

[88] *Cf.* Levin, *op. cit.*, pp. 135–7.

[89] *Commentaire sur quelques principales maximes de l'Esprit des lois*, *Œuvres complètes*, vol. XXX, p. 412; *Dictionnaire philosophique*, art. 'Guerre', *Œuvres complètes*, vol. XIX, pp. 321–2. The latest study of the attitude of M. to Machiavelli is by Shackleton, *Comparative Literature Studies*, 1964, pp. 1–13.

[90] *Cf.* Grotius, *Dg.*, II, i, 17, vol. I, p. 221; Pufendorf, *Dn.*, VII, vi, 5, vol. II, p. 458; Burlamaqui, *Principes du droit politique*, Amsterdam, 1751, IV, ii, 11, vol. II, pp. 18–19.

ground for declaring war. He was, to say the least, unwise to deal with so delicate a subject in this vague and brief way.

His views on conquest are in some respects more progressive.[91] According to the philosophers of natural law, wars of conquest, unless brought about by one of the "just causes" previously mentioned, are wrong (*Dg.*, II, xxii, 1–12, vol. II, pp. 661–7; *Dn.*, VIII, vi, 5, vol. II, pp. 457–8). In his earlier works, Montesquieu adhered to this belief: in the early editions of the *Lettres persanes*, conquest is condemned completely,[92] as it is in the *Traité des devoirs* (*P.* 1268, Bkn. 617, N. II, pp. 346–8, Pl. I, pp. 1142–3); the *Considérations* are in effect "une démonstration, par l'histoire romaine, de la vanité des grandes conquêtes".[93] However, Montesquieu seems to have changed his mind by 1748, since the *Esprit des lois* apparently contains no outright condemnation of wars of conquest. Indeed, a whole chapter is devoted to describing the 'avantages du peuple conquis', these advantages being principally the ending of corrupt government and tyranny, and the removal of harmful prejudices (*Lois*, X, iv, N. I, i, pp. 186–8, Pl. II, pp. 380–81). We may perhaps see here the result of his belief that he was a descendant of the Germanic conquerors of Gaul, whom he called "Nos pères", and whose treatment of the Gauls he singled out for praise (*ibid.*, iii, N. I, i, p. 186, Pl. II, p. 380).

Nevertheless, Montesquieu's change of attitude did not in fact alter his belief that conquest is often wrong. The maxim that appears in Book X, iii of the *Esprit des lois*, "Du droit de la guerre, dérive celui de conquête [. . .]; il en doit donc suivre l'esprit" (N. I, i, p. 183, Pl. II, p. 378), surely means that wars of conquest, like all other wars, must only be undertaken initially in self-defence.[94] Chapter iv of the same book shows that he was well aware of the evil that conquest can do. The behaviour of the Spanish in South America is an example not to be followed: "Je n'aurais jamais fini", he said, "si je voulais raconter tous les biens qu'ils ne firent pas, et tous les maux qu'ils firent" (N. I, i, p. 188, Pl. II, p. 381). The right of conquest is

> un droit nécessaire, légitime, et malheureux, qui laisse toujours à payer une dette immense, pour s'acquitter envers la nature humaine (*ibid.*).

To mitigate the harm he may do, a conqueror is under certain

[91] *Cf.* Ehrard, *Politique de Montesquieu*, p. 308.
[92] *Lettres persanes*, ed. Vernière, p. 375, n. c, and Pl. I, p. 1593.
[93] Barckhausen, *Montesquieu, ses idées et ses œuvres*, p. 202.
[94] Even though it must be admitted that he did not show that the "Germains" attacked the Roman Empire in self-defence.

obligations, and he is in particular obliged to follow

> la loi de la nature, qui fait que tout tend à la conservation des espèces; la loi de la lumière naturelle, qui veut que nous fassions à autrui ce que nous voudrions qu'on nous fît; la loi qui forme les sociétés politiques, qui sont telles, que la nature n'en a point borné la durée (*Lois*, X, iii, N. I, i, p. 184, Pl. II, p. 378).

So, the conqueror should allow the conquered people to keep their own laws, taking for himself only the "exercice du gouvernement politique et civil" – such at least is the practice "que nous suivons aujourd'hui" (*ibid.*). Here Montesquieu showed himself to be more of a humanitarian than Grotius, for example, who, though he emphasized that wars should be conducted with as little cruelty as possible (*Dg.*, III, xv, 1 and 12, vol. II, pp. 909–10 and 916–7), did not think it the conqueror's duty to allow the people he had conquered to retain their own laws; he did however point out that it is more charitable and even more sensible to do so (*ibid.*, 4–7, pp. 911–14).

If the object of war is peace, as Montesquieu and the philosophers of natural law believed,[95] and if the object of conquest is "la conservation" (*Lois*, X, iii, N. I, i, p. 185, Pl. II, p. 379), then peace treaties, which help to forward both of these aims, are an essential part of the law of nations, and must be scrupulously observed, provided that they are not unjust.[96] Montesquieu endorsed this notion both in the *Esprit des lois* (XXVI, xx, N. I, ii, pp. 153–4, Pl. II, p. 773) and in the later editions of the *Lettres persanes*, where Usbek is made to say that

> Les traités de paix sont si sacrés parmi les hommes, qu'il semble qu'ils soient la voix de la nature, qui réclame ses droits (*L.p.* XCV, N. I, iii, p. 190, Pl. I, p. 272).[97]

This statement, which makes cynics smile – as does Usbek's hopeful remark that if a highly destructive weapon were invented, it would soon be prohibited by "le droit des gens" (*L.p.* CVI, N. I, iii, p. 211, Pl. I, p. 287) – shows how deeply Montesquieu was influenced, in his discussion of international relations, by the doctrine of natural law.[98]

[95] *P.* 1814, Bkn. 390, N. II, p. 538, Pl. II, p. 1100; Pufendorf, *Dn.*, VIII, vi, 2, vol. II, p. 455; Gravina, *Origines iuris civilis*, II, xiv, p. 253; *cf.* Levin, *op. cit.*, pp. 138–9.

[96] Grotius, *Dg.*, III, xx, 27–40, vol. II, pp. 953–9; Pufendorf, *Dn.*, VIII, vii, 2, vol. II, p. 475, and *ibid.*, viii, 1–4, pp. 480–2.

[97] *Cf. Lettres persanes*, ed. Vernière, p. 375, n. c, to p. 197, and Pl. I, p. 1593.

[98] Several points of detail also show this influence. In *P.* 1814, Bkn. 390, N. II, p. 538, Pl. II, p. 1100, M. stated that it is wrong to poison the waters of an enemy country or to assassinate its monarch. These two points had been discussed by Grotius, who implied that it is wrong to poison waters, but that it is not wrong for a king to be assassinated by a man

There is a certain ambiguity in Montesquieu's attitude to international relations. On the one hand, he accepted war as a necessary part of politics. On the other, he believed in a hierarchy of duties that should prevent war. In this matter, it is Voltaire who appears reactionary and Montesquieu who appears progressive. According to Voltaire, "souhaiter la grandeur de son pays c'est souhaiter du mal à ses voisins",[99] whereas Montesquieu believed that "L'esprit du citoyen n'est pas de voir sa patrie dévorer toutes les patries" (*Traité des devoirs*, *P.* 1269, Bkn. 618, N. II, p. 348, Pl. I, p. 1143). In spite of the growing realism of his attitude to war, he expressed cosmopolitan sentiments consistently throughout his life: in the *Traité des devoirs* (N. III, p. 160, Pl. I, p. 110), the *Histoire véritable* (N. III, p. 355, Pl. I, p. 462), the Preface to the *Esprit des lois* (N. I, i, p. lxii, Pl. II, p. 230), and *Pensées* 350 (Bkn. 10) and 741 (Bkn. 11). *Pensée* 350 is less elegant and less often quoted than *Pensée* 741, but it is more significant in that it gives reasons for the view it expresses, while *Pensée* 741 does not:

> Si je savais une chose utile à ma nation qui fût ruineuse à une autre, je ne la proposerais pas à mon prince, parce que je suis homme avant d'être Français (ou bien) parce que je suis nécessairement homme, et que je ne suis Français que par hasard (N. II, p. 140, Pl. I, p. 980).

Such a sentiment has obvious connections with natural law, which is based on a distinction between local positive laws and the more important universal laws derived from man's rational and social nature. To assign one source to Montesquieu's cosmopolitanism is both impossible and unnecessary, for it is clearly the result of personal conviction rather than of reading. Nevertheless, it is instructive to see who among his predecessors had expressed similar sentiments.

There are broadly speaking two currents of cosmopolitanism, religious and secular. Bossuet's was of the first kind, in that he regarded all men as brothers because they are all the children of God.[100] A similar belief is implicit behind Fénelon's cosmopolitanism. In his *Dialogues des morts*, there is a passage that reminds us, both from the

who is not his subject (*Dg.*, III, iv, 16–18, vol. II, pp. 778–83); Pufendorf also thought that such assassination is not wrong (*Dn.*, VIII, vi, 16, vol. II, p. 469). In the *Lois*, M. showed that the rights of ambassadors are governed by the law of nations and not by political law (XXVI, xxi, N. I, ii, pp. 154–5, Pl. II, p. 773); Grotius (*Dg.*, II, xviii, vol. II, pp. 531–47) and Pufendorf (*Dn.*, II, iii, 23, vol. I, p. 215) had spoken in similar terms. In the *L.p.*, Usbek said that "une alliance, faite entre deux nations pour en opprimer une troisième, n'est pas légitime" (XCV, N. I, iii, p. 190, Pl. I, p. 272); Grotius (*Dg.*, II, xxv, 4, vol. II, pp. 695–6) and Pufendorf (*Dn.*, VIII, vi, 14, vol. II, p. 467) again held similar views.

[99] *Dictionnaire philosophique*, art. 'Patrie', *Œuvres complètes*, vol. XX, p. 185.

[100] *Politique tirée de l'écriture sainte*, I, i, 3–4, pp. 313–4.

point of view of style and from that of content, of Montesquieu's *Pensée* 741:

> Un peuple n'est pas moins un membre du genre humain, qui est la société générale, qu'une famille est un membre d'une nation particulière. Chacun doit infiniment plus au genre humain, qui est la grande patrie, qu'à la patrie particulière dans laquelle il est né.[101]

Montesquieu's cosmopolitanism did not, however, have the same strong religious basis as that of Bossuet and Fénelon. He saw love of mankind as the best way to please God, rather than loving mankind through God.[102] His attitude is thus closer to that of the secular-minded School of Natural Law. Cumberland's principle of "la plus grande bienveillance, que chaque agent raisonnable témoigne envers tous" (*Traité philosophique des lois naturelles*, i, 4, p. 47),[103] may have been inspired by religion, but Grotius's principle of international justice (*Dg.*, *Disc. prél.*, xxiii–xxv, vol. I, pp. 15–17), and Pufendorf's principle of "la sociabilité" (*Dn.*, II, iii, 15, vol. I, p. 194–5), are secular doctrines of cosmopolitanism, based on the universality of human nature.

The School of Natural Law, however, lacked Montesquieu's eloquence and perhaps even his conviction. To find both eloquence and conviction in the same writer, one must look either to Fénelon or to one of the Stoic philosophers:

> my nature is rational and civic; my city and country, as Antoninus, is Rome; as a man, the world. The things then that are of advantage to these communities, these, and no other, are good for me.[104]

These lines from Marcus Aurelius would seem to justify the words that Montesquieu wrote in praise of the Stoics, in the *Esprit des lois*:

> Nés pour la société, ils croyaient tous que leur destin était de travailler pour elle: d'autant moins à charge, que leurs récompenses étaient toutes dans eux-mêmes; qu'heureux par leur philosophie seule, il semblait que le seul bonheur des autres pût augmenter le leur (XXIV, x, N. I, ii, p. 90, Pl. II, p. 722).

This essentially humanistic passage would have brought tears to the eyes of Jean-Paul Sartre's Autodidacte; Antoine Roquentin, on the

[101] *Œuvres*, vol. II, p. 567; see Shackleton, *M.*, p. 71, n, 3. for a further parallel between M. and Fénelon.

[102] *Cf. L.p.* XLVI, N. I, iii, pp. 88–9, Pl. I, pp. 194–5.

[103] *Cf.* also Samuel Clarke's "agreeing community of all mankind", *Discourse*, p. 622.

[104] *The Communings with Himself of Marcus Aurelius Antoninus*, VI, xlvi, Loeb edition, pp. 155-7.

other hand, would have read it with a mixture of scorn and amusement. When the words *society* and *humanity* are mentioned, eloquence sometimes leaves sincerity behind, even perhaps in the case of Montesquieu. However, when we think of his defence of the rights of liberty and equality, of his suggestions for making punishments more equitable, of his denouncement of religious persecution, of his plea for charity towards the poor, of his broad vision of cosmopolitanism and his ideas for reducing the oppression so often associated with war, we realize that he has a good title to our respect and admiration when he says:

> C'est en cherchant à instruire les hommes, que l'on peut pratiquer cette vertu générale qui comprend l'amour de tous (*Lois*, Preface, N. I, i, p. lxii, Pl. II, p. 230).

Many of Montesquieu's interpreters have denied that he believed in progress.[105] Their arguments are often rationalistic, rather than empirical: Gilbert Chinard, for example, claims that the *président*'s philosophy of history, where "the march of mankind", which resembles "the swing of a pendulum", precludes any "ascending curve".[106] Montesquieu's philosophy of history is a question too vast to be discussed here; all that need be said is that even if logically it precludes a belief in progress, it did not actually preclude such a belief: the present chapter has shown that he believed in progress in so far as he advocated that many laws and customs in his own country and abroad should be reformed.

Furthermore, Montesquieu did express, on more than one occasion, his conviction that men have become more enlightened. In his discussion of the rights of conquerors, having shown that whereas the Romans tended to exterminate those they had conquered, the modern practice is to allow them to keep their own laws, he commented:

> je laisse à juger à quel point nous sommes devenus meilleurs. Il faut rendre ici hommage à nos temps modernes, à la raison présente, à la religion d'aujourd'hui, à notre philosophie, à nos mœurs (*Lois*, X, iii, N. I, i, p. 184, Pl. II, pp. 378–9).

Among the enlightening influences listed by Montesquieu, we should

[105] For example: Comte, *Cours de philosophie positive*, vol. IV, p. 128; Vaughan, *Studies in the History of Political Philosophy*, vol. I, p. 290; R. Hubert, 'La Notion du devenir historique dans la philosophie de Montesquieu', *Revue de métaphysique et de morale*, 1939, p. 609; G. Chinard, 'Montesquieu's Historical Pessimism', pp. 163–4; Vyverberg, *op. cit.*, pp. 161–9; Crocker, *Nature and Culture*, p. 510; P. Gay, *The Party of Humanity*, Weidenfeld and Nicolson, 1964, p. 271.

[106] *Loc. cit.*

not be surprised to see "la religion d'aujourd'hui". He was not of course blind to the harm which the persecuting zeal of the Church had done: the Jew of the 'Très humble remontrance' showed the Inquisition to be a barbarously anachronistic institution in

un siècle où la lumière naturelle est plus vive qu'elle n'a jamais été, où la philosophie a éclairé les esprits, où la morale de votre Évangile a été plus connue, où les droits respectifs des hommes les uns sur les autres, l'empire qu'une conscience a sur une autre conscience, sont mieux établis (*Lois*, XXV, xiii, N. I, ii, p. 123, Pl. II, p. 748).

Nevertheless, it was above all "la religion d'aujourd'hui", purged of its former anti-social aspects, which he saw as the instrument of the gradual amelioration of humanity. Though he once doubted whether it had really changed "la masse" (*Spicilège* 509, Bkn. *P.* 2173, N. II, p. 829, Pl. I, p. 1565), he claimed that it had given us "de l'équité pour tous les hommes" (*Traité des devoirs*, N. III, p. 161, Pl. I, p. 110), and in particular that it had been responsible for the abolition of slavery in Europe (*Lois*, XV, viii, N. I, i, p. 333, Pl. II, p. 496); he insisted above all on the effect it had had on the behaviour of rulers, and on the way it had eliminated tyrants on the Roman scale.[107] The fact that this enlightenment has not been maintained in our own day should not make us deny that, by eighteenth-century standards, Montesquieu was a cautiously optimistic yet realistic philosopher. If he did not subscribe to any grandiose theory of inevitable progress such as Condorcet was to propose,[108] neither did he have a pessimistic outlook of the sort adopted by Voltaire in his later years.[109] Vyverberg's description of Montesquieu's attitude to history as 'Pessimism in moderation'[110] lays too much stress on its theoretical implications. Optimism in moderation is the keynote of Montesquieu's attitude to the society of his own day.

[107] *Cf. P.* 478, Bkn. 2171, N. II, p. 171, Pl. I, pp. 1564–5; *P.* 551, Bkn. 2172, N. II, p. 187, Pl. I, p. 1565; *P.* 1993, Bkn. 658, N. II, p. 611, Pl. I, p. 1161; *Lois*, XXIV, ii, N. I, ii, pp. 81–2, Pl. II, pp. 715–6.

[108] *Cf.* Vyverberg, *op. cit.*, pp. 66–70.

[109] *Ibid.*, pp. 175–88.

[110] *Ibid.*, p. 155.

CHAPTER 7

MONTESQUIEU'S CONCEPTION OF LAW

How far are the laws that govern the universe a creation of the free will of God, and how far is God Himself dependent on those laws? This is no new problem in philosophy, but it was one that intensely preoccupied the minds of the scientists and moralists of the seventeenth and eighteenth centuries, who lived in a world where man seemed rapidly to be solving many of the mysteries that previous ages had attributed to the unfathomable power of God or nature.

Although Montesquieu's attitude to this question has been studied many times before, it has never been seen in its proper relation to the beliefs of his predecessors. It is the purpose of this chapter to show how far his conception of law was new, and how far it derives from the tradition of natural law. By way of introduction, we shall briefly examine his attitude to God and to natural and revealed religion; this will lead on to a discussion of the new scientific elements and of the traditional moral elements to be found in his conception of law.

I. Montesquieu's Conception of God

In recent years, the religious beliefs of the *philosophes* have at last been treated in a less superficial and prejudiced manner than that which prevailed in the eighteenth and nineteenth centuries. In the case of Montesquieu, no longer can we accept Faguet's statement that the *président* had "l'âme la moins religieuse qui soit",[1] and Peter Gay's remark that "Montesquieu did not believe in the immortality of the soul"[2] seems to echo from the critical attitudes of a bygone age. But the debate still goes on as to the precise nature of Montesquieu's conception of religion. Some scholars say that although he was a deist in

1 *Dix-huitième siècle*, Boivin, [*s.d.*], p. 142.
2 *Op. cit.*, p. 197.

his youth, he later came to accept almost complete orthodoxy;[3] Shackleton, on the other hand, argues very persuasively that he was a deist throughout his life.[4]

Montesquieu's lifelong belief in natural religion is shown partly by his acceptance of many of the traditional proofs of the existence of God – from the rather naïve Ciceronian analogy between God and a watchmaker,[5] and its counterpart the orthodox argument of the First Cause: "il y a un effet; donc il y a une cause",[6] to the more sophisticated but no less ancient theory that blind fate cannot produce intelligent beings.[7] It is also shown by the beautiful phrase,

> Dieu est comme un monarque qui a plusieurs nations dans son empire; elles viennent toutes lui porter le tribut et chacune lui parle sa langue, religion diverse,

which is found both in the *Pensées* and in the manuscript of the *Esprit des lois*.[8]

Those who think that Montesquieu's religion was not particularly unorthodox, sometimes adduce *Pensée* 825 (Bkn. 2110):[9]

> Ce qui me prouve la nécessité d'une révélation, c'est l'insuffisance de la religion naturelle, vu la crainte et la superstition des hommes (N. II, p. 243, Pl. I, p. 1550).

However, this *Pensée*, far from revealing Montesquieu's intimate convictions, simply shows him making an attempt to understand the psychological impulses behind religious belief, as he was to do in the *Esprit des lois* (XXV, ii, N. I, ii, pp. 106–8, Pl. II, pp. 735–7). By the "insuffisance de la religion naturelle", he was not referring, in Pascalian fashion,[10] to the fact that it does not lead to a Redeemer: he was merely implying that it will never be universally recognized. In fact, this *Pensée* is unfavourable to Christianity, since it suggests that if men

[3] Cotta, *Montesquieu e la scienza della società*, pp. 9–67; Vier, *op. cit.*, pp. 140–48.

[4] 'La Religion de Montesquieu', *Congrès*, pp. 287–94; *M.*, pp. 349–54.

[5] *P.* 1096, Bkn. 672, N. II, p. 296, Pl. I, p. 1170 (date uncertain: seems to be 1734–8, but could be fragment of the *Traité des devoirs*); *cf.* Cicero, *De natura deorum*, II, xxxiv; in the Loeb edition, pp. 206–7.

[6] *P.* 2095, Bkn. 2069, N. II, p. 641, Pl. I, p. 1540 (after 1748); *cf. S.t.*, I, Q. 2, A. 3, vol. 1, p. 25.

[7] *Traité des devoirs*, N. III, p. 159, Pl. I, p. 109; *Lois*, I, i, N. I, i, p. 2, Pl. II, p. 232; *cf.* Plato, *Philebus*, 29a–30a; in the Loeb edition, *The Statesman*, *Philebus*, *Ion*, pp. 263–7.

[8] *P.* 1454, N. II, pp. 420–1 (not in Pl.); *cf. P.* 1699, Bkn. 378, N. II, p. 508, Pl. II, pp. 1097–8; see Brethe de la Gressaye, *Lois*, vol. III, p. 437, n. 32, and Pl. II, p. 1549.

[9] *Cf.* Cotta, *Montesquieu e la scienza della società*, p. 43; Dedieu, *Montesquieu*, p. 286.

[10] *Cf. Pensées*, VIII, 556, vol. XIV, pp. 1–7.

were not fearful and superstitious, they could well do without Revelation.

Nevertheless, Montesquieu did on one occasion accept that the Christian religion was established and protected by divine intervention (*P.* 969, Bkn. 2148, N. II, p. 273, Pl. I, p. 1558–9); he did, in the *Esprit des lois*, sincerely appreciate its spiritual aspects (XXIV, xiii, N. I, ii, pp. 91–2, Pl. II, p. 723); and above all, he did, as we saw at the end of the last chapter, believe that it is the best religion from the point of view of morality and public order.

There is not necessarily any deep conflict between the passages which show Montesquieu to be a deist, and those which argue a more fideistic attitude on his part, provided we make allowances for a certain flippancy that he shared with so many of his contemporaries. In our opinion, he believed both in natural religion and in certain aspects of the Christian revelation, though not in the whole of Roman Catholic dogma. The *Défense de l'Esprit des lois* gives an insight into his attitude. "Fait-il bien", he said, referring to his Jansenist critic, "de confondre la religion naturelle avec l'athéisme?" and he continued:

N'ai-je pas toujours ouï dire que nous avions tous une religion naturelle? N'ai-je pas ouï dire que le christianisme était la perfection de la religion naturelle? N'ai-je pas ouï dire que l'on employait la religion naturelle, pour prouver la révélation contre les déistes? et que l'on employait la même religion naturelle, pour prouver l'existence de Dieu contre les athées? (N. I, ii, pp. 452–3, Pl. II, p. 1136).

He had indeed heard these things, though obviously not from Pascal, for whom deism was "presque aussi éloigné de la religion chrétienne que l'athéisme".[11] Religious apologists – St. Thomas himself, Bossuet and Fénelon in France, Samuel Clarke in England – had used the arguments of natural religion to prove the existence of God to the atheists, and then used further, sometimes purely rational arguments to show that Revelation is the logical consequence of natural religion.[12] Clarke, for example, held that "A constant and sincere observance of all the laws of reason, and obligations of natural religion, will unavoidably lead a man to Christianity".[13] Some years after the appearance of the *Esprit des lois*, Christophe de Beaumont, the anti-Jansenist

[11] *Loc. cit.*, pp. 2–3.

[12] *Cf.* É. Gilson on St. Thomas's attitude: "Il y a [. . .] deux théologies qui, si elles ne se continuent pas à la rigueur pour nos esprits finis, peuvent au moins s'accorder et se compléter: la théologie révélée qui part du dogme, et la théologie naturelle qu'élabore la raison" (*La Philosophie au moyen âge*, Payot, 1922, vol. II, p. 18).

[13] *Discourse*, p. 600.

Archbishop of Paris, in his Mandement against Rousseau's *Émile*, claimed that "La religion naturelle conduit [...] elle-même à la religion révélée".[14]

Doubts can of course be thrown on Montesquieu's sincerity in the *Défense de l'Esprit des lois*, but no passage in the *président*'s later works seems to contradict the view that he believed both in natural and in revealed religion, whereas many passages contradict the view that he believed exclusively in one or the other. He had been brought up as a Catholic, and he sometimes accepted Catholic dogma on moral questions, as has been seen in earlier chapters, and even on some spiritual questions; but he certainly did not believe Catholicism to be the only kind of Christianity, or Christianity to be the only kind of religion to lead to an after-life. By the standards of his own day, he cannot be called a Catholic, though in view of his attitude towards the Redemption in Book XXIV, xiii, it does not seem wrong to call him a Christian. Essentially, however, he was a cosmopolitan in religion as well as in ethics.

Those critics who deny that Montesquieu had any strong religious emotions have not seen the whole picture.[15] Nevertheless his belief in God was not usually accompanied by spiritual *angoisse*, by a feeling of privation; rather, it resulted from certain positive convictions. On the personal level, it was born of a simple refusal to believe that his soul would disintegrate entirely at death: "Je suis très charmé de me croire immortel comme Dieu même" (*P.* 57, Bkn. 2083, N. II, pp. 20–21, Pl. I, p. 1543); on the social level, his belief in God was the consequence of his belief in natural law; on the metaphysical level, it was the consequence of his conviction that the laws governing the universe are constant.

Montesquieu's belief in the constancy of the physical and moral laws governing the universe is most strikingly revealed in the opening

[14] Rousseau, *Du Contrat social*, etc., Garnier, 1962, p. 430; *cf. ibid.*, p. 422.

[15] Many critics see M. as a man without deep emotions (see above, pp. 165–6), and some extend this judgment to his religious life too: "le sentiment religieux lui échappa toujours", says V. Giraud, ('Sur l'*Esprit des lois*', in *Moralistes français*, Hachette, 1923, p. 99); *cf.* Sainte-Beuve, *Causeries du lundi*, vol. VII, p. 52; Dedieu, *Montesquieu*, p. 288; Caillois, 'Montesquieu et l'athéisme contemporain', p. 327. They have not seen the whole picture because they have ignored the emotion in *P.* 57 (Bkn. 2083): "je ne suis point si humble que les athées.] [...] je ne veux point troquer [...] l'idée de mon immortalité contre celle de la béatitude d'un jour" (N. II, p. 20, Pl. I, p. 1543); in the *Traité des devoirs* (*P.* 1266, Bkn. 615, N. II, pp. 341–3, Pl. I, pp. 1137–9); and in *P.* 1805, Bkn. 206, N. II, p. 536, Pl. II, p. 1041. They were also unaware of the *Lettre persane* to which É. Cayrol has recently drawn attention ('Des *Lettres persanes* oubliées', *RHLF*, 1965, pp. 15–26), where Hagi Ibbi tells a friend of the intense agony he suffered when he was unable to make his usual prayers to God. According to É. Cayrol, this letter reveals in M. "une certaine effusion de sensibilité religieuse authentique et presque mystique" (*loc. cit.*, p. 21).

paragraphs of the *Esprit des lois*. The work begins with a definition of law: laws governing the universe is most strikingly revealed in the opening

> 'Des lois, dans le rapport qu'elles ont avec les divers êtres'
> Les lois, dans la signification la plus étendue, sont les rapports nécessaires qui dérivent de la nature des choses; et, dans ce sens, tous les êtres ont leurs lois, la divinité a ses lois, le monde matériel a ses lois, les intelligences supérieures à l'homme ont leurs lois, les bêtes ont leurs lois, l'homme a ses lois (N. I, i, p. 1, Pl. II, p. 232).

This definition was received with hostility or bewilderment,[16] and it has generally met with the same reception from later critics. The epithets "vague" and "obscure" are their usual weapons, and they often imply that Montesquieu chose this definition in order to hide his incomprehension or his ignorance.[17] Other critics hold that the definition is incorrect, rather than vague, and seek to propose more satisfactory ones of their own.[18]

The meaning of Montesquieu's definition of law, however unsatisfactory it may be from a philosophical point of view, is fairly clear:[19] the universe is made up of different parts – physical parts such as minerals, vegetables and animals, and immaterial parts such as God and the intelligence of various beings. These parts have different characteristics, or natures, which are constant, and which determine the ways in which the parts act on one another; these ways are constant, that is, they are laws, at least in the case of the physical universe. In a later paragraph Montesquieu showed that although the laws of man are also constant, since they are based on his nature, he does not always follow them because he has free-will (N. I, i, p. 3, Pl. II, pp. 233–4). The difficulty lies not so much in understanding this definition of law as a piece of logic, as in relating it to its historical context. This is what we shall attempt to do in the following pages.

II. Montesquieu and the Laws of Science

In paragraphs four to seven of Book I, i, Montesquieu showed how his definition applied to the world of physical phenomena:

[16] Abbé de La Roche, *Examen critique*, p. 118; La Porte, *op. cit.*, p. 10; Destutt de Tracy, *Commentaire sur l'Esprit des lois*, p. 1.

[17] Sainte-Beuve, *Causeries du lundi*, vol. VII, p. 74; Sorel, *op. cit.*, p. 71; Sir Courtenay Ilbert, 'Montesquieu', Oxford, Clarendon Press, 1904, p. 23; Dedieu, *Montesquieu*, p. 121; Charmont, *op. cit.*, p. 38; P. Martino, 'De Quelques résidus métaphysiques dans l'*Esprit des lois*', p. 237.

[18] Barckhausen, *Montesquieu, ses idées et ses œuvres*, p. 40; Brethe de la Gressaye, 'La Philosophie du droit de Montesquieu', pp. 201–4; G. Vedel in the Seuil edition of M.'s works, p. 8.

[19] For a very clear explanation of M.'s definition of law, see Janet, *Histoire de la science politique*, vol. II, pp. 333–4; Janet unfortunately fails to place the definition in its historical context and embarks instead on speculations about primitive man.

> Dieu a du rapport avec l'univers, comme créateur et comme conservateur; les lois selon lesquelles il a créé sont celles selon lesquelles il conserve: il agit selon ces règles, parce qu'il les connaît; il les connaît, parce qu'il les a faites; il les a faites, parce qu'elles ont du rapport avec sa sagesse et sa puissance.
>
> Comme nous voyons que le monde, formé par le mouvement de la matière, et privé d'intelligence, subsiste toujours, il faut que ses mouvements aient des lois invariables; [...].
>
> Ainsi la création, qui paraît être un acte arbitraire, suppose des règles aussi invariables que la fatalité des athées. [...].
>
> Ces règles sont un rapport constamment établi. Entre un corps mu et un autre corps mu, c'est suivant les rapports de la masse et de la vitesse que tous les mouvements sont reçus, augmentés, diminués, perdus; chaque diversité est uniformité, chaque changement est constance (N. I, i, p. 2, Pl. II, pp. 232–3).

The most obvious feature of these paragraphs, apart from their lyricism, is the idea that God Himself always acts according to the invariable laws of motion that He created.

Although for the orthodox Christian "God necessarily wills His own goodness", and is thus in a sense dependent on moral law, He does not will other things necessarily (*S.t.*, I, Q. 19, A. 10, vol. I, pp. 280–1); hence, He is not subject to fate, and it was by His free-will that He decided that our world should be what it is, for "He could have created another order of things" (*ibid.*, Q. 105, A. 6, vol. V, p. 42).

This voluntaristic attitude to the physical world was undermined in the seventeenth century by the discoveries of scientists such as Descartes,[20] and it is fascinating to see how he struggled with the problem of reconciling God's free-will with the fixed order he saw in the universe. As E. A. Burtt puts it, he hoped that "the whole realm of physics might be reducible to geometrical qualities alone":[21] he showed that the laws of motion are the expression of certain constant proportions between different weights and motions (*Principes*, II, xxxvii–lii, pp. 84–93). If these laws are geometrical, then logically it would seem that they could not, any more than the truths of mathematics, be changed even by God Himself. It was probably in order to avoid these necessitarian consequences of the mathematical universe that Descartes claimed that God could alter the truths of mathematics if He wanted,[22]

[20] On this question see G. Tonelli, 'La Nécessité des lois de la nature au XVIIIe siècle, et chez Kant en 1762', *Revue d'histoire des sciences*, 1959, pp. 224–41; also R. Lenoble, 'L'Évolution de l'idée de nature du XVIe au XVIIIe siècle', *Revue de métaphysique et de morale*, 1953, pp. 108–29.

[21] *Op. cit.*, p. 97.

[22] Letter to Mersenne, 15th April 1630, *Œuvres*, vol. I, p. 145; *Méditations métaphysiques*, pp. 232–3.

and that the essence of things, and hence, by implication, the laws of motion which depend on it, are arbitrary, that is, dependent on the will of God.[23]

Nevertheless, the spirit of Cartesian physics is that the laws of motion are not arbitrary. At the end of the *Principes*, he affirmed, in order to placate the theologians, that God could have produced the world in a variety of ways (IV, cciv, p. 322); but he then showed that since the world is governed by mathematical laws, he had 'une certitude plus que morale' that it was in fact produced in the way he described (*ibid.*, ccvi, p. 324). This necessitarian spirit is reinforced by the fact that Descartes deduced the laws of motion from God's immutable nature (*ibid.*, II, xxxvii, p. 84).

This latent determinism was made patent by Spinoza,[24] and it dogged the thought of Malebranche.[25] It is true that he protested that:

> les volontés de Dieu, quoiqu'éternelles et immuables ne sont point nécessaires: elles sont arbitraires à l'égard des êtres créés. Le monde n'est point une émanation nécessaire de la Divinité.[26]

Such a protest was however ambiguous,[27] and from other places in his work, we have the impression that Malebranche considered the laws of matter to be absolutely necessary. If God, at the creation, "a dû avoir égard", as he puts it, "aux lois de la nature, qu'il voulait suivre constamment, pour faire porter à sa conduite le caractère de ses attributs",[28] then these laws cannot be called arbitrary.

In England, too, scientists tried to avoid the necessitarian implications of their discoveries. Newton affirmed that God's essential attribute is not His reason, but His power,[29] and that the laws of motion are insufficient, without His personal intervention from time to time, to ensure the smooth running of the universe.[30] Similarly,

[23] *Meditationes*, in *Œuvres*, vol. VII, p. 380:
ego non puto essentias rerum, mathematicasque illas veritates quæ de ipsis cognosci possunt, esse independentes a Deo.

[24] *Ethics*, I, xxix, p. 394; *cf.* Tonelli, 'La Nécessité des lois de la nature', pp. 227–8.

[25] For comparisons of Malebranche and Spinoza, see J. Moreau's introduction to Malebranche, *Correspondance avec J.-J. Dortous de Mairan*, Vrin, 1947, pp. 1–98, and Vernière, *Spinoza et la pensée française*, vol. I, pp. 259–70 and 279–86.

[26] *Méditations chrétiennes et métaphysiques*, V, vii, in *Œuvres complètes*, Vrin, 1958–68, vol. X, 1959, p. 49; *cf.* Tonelli, 'La Nécessité des lois de la nature', p. 227, who appears to accept rather uncritically this affirmation by Malebranche.

[27] Because Malebranche did not say that the laws are arbitrary *à l'égard de Dieu* – this would have been in contradiction with the principles of his philosophy – but only "à l'égard des êtres créés".

[28] *Entretiens sur la métaphysique et sur la religion*, X, xvii, p. 247

[29] *Principia*, III, *General Scholium*, pp. 544–6; *cf.* Burtt, *op. cit.*, pp. 290–1.

[30] *Opticks*, III, pp. 375–8; *cf.* Burtt, *op. cit.*, pp. 292–3.

Boyle claimed that the laws of motion are arbitrary,[31] and he criticized Descartes for having made matter independent of God.[32] Clarke followed in the steps of these two scientists.[33]

However, such affirmations did little to stop people drawing the same conclusions from Newton's philosophy as they had from that of Descartes. In a comment that he made in 1732 on Newton's physics, Voltaire said:

> On trouve à chaque pas que l'on fait, que cet univers est arrangé par des lois mathématiques qui sont éternelles et nécessaires.[34]

He also said that the theory that God could alter the truths of mathematics was one of Descartes' "erreurs métaphysiques".[35]

So when Montesquieu stated in the *Lettres persanes* that God "ne peut pas changer l'essence des choses" (*L.p.* LXIX, N. I, iii, p. 146, Pl. I, p. 238)[36] and that the laws of motion are "immuables, éternelles" (*L.p.* XCVII, N. I, iii, p. 193, Pl. I, p. 274), and when in the *Esprit des lois* he again pointed to the constancy and uniformity of those laws, he was repeating a commonplace of the science of his day. As he said in reply to the abbé de La Roche's accusations of determinism, "elles sont invariables, ces règles, et toute la physique le dit avec [l'auteur]" (*Défense*, N. I, ii, p. 438, Pl. II, p. 1124).

How far does the opening of the *Esprit des lois* really show deterministic tendencies on the part of Montesquieu? He did not in fact say that the laws of motion are a necessary consequence of God's nature, only that "elles ont du rapport" with it, and he stressed that they have this relationship with His "puissance" as well as with His "sagesse". However, he also said that the creation is not arbitrary, but that it "suppose des règles aussi invariables que la fatalité des athées", and that it would be absurd to claim that the Creator could govern the world without those rules: thus, according to Montesquieu, God is powerless to create or preserve the world unless He follows the laws of motion. It is also possible that the *président*, in denying that the

[31] *Of The High Veneration Man's Intellect Owes to God*, *Works*, vol. V, pp. 139–40.

[32] *The Excellency of Theology Compared with Natural Philosophy*, *Works*, vol. IV, p. 43; *cf.* Burtt, *op. cit.*, pp. 168 and 187–96.

[33] *Discourse*, pp. 574 and 696–8.

[34] Letter to Maupertuis, no. 516 in *Voltaire's Correspondence*, edited by T. Besterman, Geneva, Institut et musée Voltaire, 1953–65, vol. II, p. 382; *cf.* Y. Belaval, 'La Crise de la géométrisation de l'univers dans la philosophie des lumières', *Revue internationale de philosophie*, 1952, pp. 350–1.

[35] *Lettres philosophiques*, XIV, *Œuvres complètes*, vol. XXII, p. 131.

[36] It is true that this notion seems to be contradicted by *Spicilège* 390, Bkn. *P.* 2070, N. II, p. 787, Pl. I, p. 1541.

creation was "un acte arbitraire", thought that God had to create the world.

To say that the creation was a necessary act would have been heretical (*S.t.*, I, Q. 104, A. 3, vol. V, p. 26), and the abbé de La Roche tried hard to show that Montesquieu was indeed a heretic:

Si la création paraît être un acte arbitraire, et qu'elle ne le soit pas; si Dieu est nécessité à créer; si tous les êtres ont avec lui des rapports si nécessaires, qu'il n'ait pu se dispenser de les créer, et de les créer tels qu'ils sont: voilà donc le monde nécessaire comme Dieu même (*Examen critique*, p. 119).

It is unlikely that Montesquieu meant to imply all that the Jansenist here attributed to him. The logical pattern of paragraphs four, five and six of Book I, i, is that God is Creator and preserver, that the laws of creation and preservation are the same and that they are not arbitrary. So, when he said that the creation is not "un acte arbitraire", it would appear that he was talking of the *laws* that presided at the formation of the universe, and not of God's decision to create. This, at least, is what he claimed in his *Défense* (N.I, ii, p. 438, Pl. II, pp. 1124–5), and it is significant that the Sorbonne did not repeat the abbé de La Roche's accusation. On the whole, the theologians left his metaphysics alone, and concentrated on his theory of social morality: perhaps they remembered the ridicule their predecessors had incurred in the previous century by securing the banning of Descartes' philosophy.

The Jansenist was thus more old-fashioned than the Sorbonne. In accusing Montesquieu of having a Spinozistic conception of law (*Examen critique*, pp. 117–9), he was concentrating his attention on one notorious philosopher, and ignoring the whole trend of natural science in the previous one hundred and twenty years (just as he chose to ignore developments in the philosophy of natural law that had taken place in that period). Oudin's accusation of Spinozism is equally misplaced, as is his assumption that La Roche represents "la doctrine orthodoxe".[37]

Some modern critics – and not only Anglo-Saxon ones – see a Newtonian influence in the opening chapter of the *Esprit des lois*.[38] This may be true in a loose sense, if *Newtonian* simply refers to the idea that the universe is always governed by fixed laws, but this idea is also

[37] *Le Spinozisme de Montesquieu*, pp. 135–47.

[38] Huntington Cairns, 'The Separation of Powers', in *Law and the Social Sciences*, New York, Harcourt, Brace, 1935, p. 132; Starobinski, *op. cit.*, p. 72.

Cartesian, and we would claim that on balance, the opening paragraphs of the *Esprit des lois* are predominantly Cartesian in tone. Firstly, because on external evidence, it is clear that Montesquieu disliked Newton's physics:[39] in this respect he was rather like Fontenelle who maintained a firm disapproval of the ideas of the English scientist even after those ideas were generally accepted in French scientific circles.[40]

Secondly, the paragraphs in question appear to be flavoured with Cartesian terms. It is true that many of the phrases that Montesquieu uses in them are commonplaces of the scientific and philosophical language of the age. Nevertheless, they are particularly reminiscent of the writings of Descartes' disciple, the Oratorian Father Malebranche, especially the phrases "il les connaît puisqu'il les a faites",[41] "sa sagesse et sa puissance",[42] and the words "constance" and "uniformité".[43]

It is at first sight ridiculous to suppose that the Oratorian visionary, author of an abstruse theory that we see and do all things through God, should have influenced the un-theologically minded Montesquieu, who frequently expressed his disapproval of Malebranche's metaphysics.[44] However, Montesquieu had been educated by the Oratorians, and may have made contact with Malebranche's work at that time;[45] like those two anti-metaphysicians Voltaire and Condillac, he admired Malebranche's exposure, in *De la Recherche de la vérité*, of the errors of the senses;[46] in Malebranche, who was a scientist

[39] See above, pp. 24–5.

[40] *Cf.* Brunet, *op. cit.*, p. 340.

[41] *Cf.* Malebranche, *De la Recherche de la vérité* [1674–1712], in *Œuvres complètes*, Vrin, vols. I–III, 1962–4, *X^e^ éclaircissement*, vol. III, p. 152: "Dieu connaît l'étendue puisqu'il l'a faite"; *ibid.*, p. 148.

[42] *Cf. De la Recherche de la vérité*, VI, ii, 4, vol. II, p. 343: "Monsieur Descartes a pensé que Dieu avait formé le monde tout d'un coup. [...] cette pensée est digne de la puissance et de la sagesse de Dieu"; *ibid.*, *XVe éclaircissement*, vol. III, p. 219; Malebranche, *Traité de morale* [1683], II, ii–iii, in *Œuvres complètes*, Vrin, vol. XI, 1966, pp. 157–75; *cf.* Maupertuis in *Histoire de l'Académie royale des sciences, année 1744*, Amsterdam, Mortier, 1750–51, p. 576; Burlamaqui, *Principes du droit naturel*, II, i, 12, pp. 151–2.

[43] *Cf.* Malebranche, *Méditations chrétiennes et métaphysiques*, XI, xiv, p. 121: "Si deux corps se choquent, ils se communiquent mutuellement leur mouvement d'une manière constante et uniforme"; *ibid.*, VI, v, p. 59; *Traité de morale*, I, x, 5, p. 118. For similar phraseology in other writers, see: Clarke, *Discourse*, p. 698; Duverney cited in J. Roger, *Les Sciences de la vie dans la pensée française du XVIIIe siècle*, Colin, 1963, p. 230; Buffon in *Œuvres philosophiques*, p. 27.

[44] See: *P.* 156, Bkn. 2061, N. II, pp. 49–50, Pl. I, pp. 1536–7; *P.* 157, Bkn. 2066, N. II, p. 50, Pl. I, p. 1540; *P.* 1195, Bkn, 2107. N. II, p. 320, Pl. I, p. 1548; *P.* 1946, Bkn. 673, N. II, p. 589, Pl. I, p. 1177; *Geographica*, N. II, p. 955, not in Pl.

[45] On the attitude of the Oratoire to Cartesianism and to Malebranche see: P. Lallemand, *Histoire de l'éducation dans l'ancien Oratoire de France*, Thorin, 1888, pp. 113–39; also Sainte-Beuve, *Port-Royal*, Hachette, 1922, vol. V, p. 396, n. 1.

[46] Such, at least, is the implication of *P.* 305, Bkn. 2108, N. II, p. 131, Pl. I, p. 1549: "Jamais visionnaire n'a eu plus de bon sens que le père Malebranche". *Cf.* Voltaire, *Diction-*

as well as a visionary, he could find a theory of the constancy of the laws of motion corresponding very closely to his own ideas and expressed in elegant, even poetic language: that he appreciated this language is shown by the fact that he called the Oratorian "un écrivain [...] enchanteur" (*Discours sur les motifs*, N. III, p. 226, Pl. I, p. 57), and said he was one of the "quatre grands poètes", together with Plato, Shaftesbury and Montaigne (*P.* 1092, Bkn. 2095, N. II, p. 296, Pl. I, p. 1546).

In his account of the laws of matter at the opening of the *Esprit des lois*, Montesquieu was summing up the outlook of Cartesian science in terms reminiscent of those of a great Cartesian scientist and metaphysician. The same influence is apparent in his concept of law as a relationship, where he linked the physical and moral aspects of the universe.

III. Montesquieu and the Moral Law

"La justice est un rapport de convenance, qui se trouve réellement entre deux choses" (*L.p.* LXXXIII, N. I, iii, p. 169, Pl. I, p. 256); "Les lois [...] sont les rapports nécessaires qui dérivent de la nature des choses". The word *rapport* was so commonly used in the latter part of the eighteenth century that Montesquieu seems merely to have been using a fashionable cliché. For d'Alembert, in 1751, arithmetic is the art of finding "l'expression d'un rapport unique qui résulte de la comparaison de plusieurs autres";[47] for Helvétius, in 1758, "la justesse d'esprit consiste dans la vue nette des véritables rapports que les objets ont entre eux";[48] sometime between 1758 and 1767, Condillac defined a *rapport* as "la ressemblance ou la différence, l'égalité ou l'inégalité qui est entre deux choses".[49] For all these philosophers, the *rapport* is a more or less scientific concept – it is descriptive rather than normative: this usage seems to have its origin in the work of Descartes.[50]

In the case of Montesquieu, however, the *rapport* is a normative as well as a descriptive concept, embracing both moral and physical

naire philosophique, art. 'Idée', *Œuvres complètes*, vol. XIX, p. 396; Condillac, *Traité des systèmes*, in *Œuvres philosophiques*, vol. XXXIII of the *Corpus général des philosophes français*, tome I, pp. 150–1.

47 *Encyclopédie*, *Discours préliminaire*, vol. I, p.v.

48 *De l'esprit*, Durand, 1759, III, ii, p. 192.

49 *Dictionnaire des synonymes* in *Œuvres philosophiques*, tome III, p. 474; for the date of this work, see tome III, p. ix.

50 *Cf. Discours de la méthode*, II, p.20: all sciences based on mathematics are similar in that although the "objets" they study are different, "elles n'y considèrent autre chose que les divers rapports ou proportions qui s'y trouvent".

phenomena, and to find the origin of the normative use of the term we must look elsewhere. A possible source of Montesquieu's conception of law is, as many scholars have noted,[51] Samuel Clarke's *Discourse* of 1704, which was translated into French in 1717. Clarke tells us that by an

> understanding or knowledge of the natural and necessary relations of things, the actions [. . .] of all intelligent beings are constantly directed, (which by the way is the true ground and foundation of all morality:) unless their will be corrupted.[52]

In this passage the word *relations* is clearly used in a normative sense.

However, Clarke was not the first writer to identify law and relationship in a normative sense. Malebranche had already done the same thing twenty years earlier, a fact that has been overlooked by all the scholars who have drawn attention (usually in general terms only) to the similarities between Montesquieu and the Oratorian.[53]

It is true, as Shackleton says, that Malebranche did not, in the *Traité de morale*, call law a relationship: he only called truth a relationship.[54] The *Traité de morale* is not, however, entirely representative of Malebranche's work. To see the true nature of his thought on this matter, we must look at the *Méditations chrétiennes et métaphysiques*, which first appeared in 1683.

Here Malebranche said that there are basically two kinds of relationship: "les rapports de grandeur" – quantitative or descriptive relationships, and "les rapports de perfection" – qualitative or normative relationships. Now,

> il y a cette différence entre les rapports de grandeur et les rapports de perfection, que les rapports de grandeur sont des vérités toutes pures, abstraites, métaphysiques, et que *les rapports de perfection sont des vérités et en même temps des lois immuables et nécessaires*: ce sont les règles inviolables de tous les mouvements des esprits. Ainsi ces vérités font *l'ordre, que Dieu même consulte dans toutes ses opérations.*[55]

[51] T. S. Jouffroy, *Cours de droit naturel*, Prévost-Crocius, 1834–42, vol. II, pp. 369–80; Camille Jullian, *op. cit.*, pp. 10–13; Dedieu, *Montesquieu et la tradition politique anglaise*, pp. 274–5; Brethe de la Gressaye, *Lois*, vol. I, pp. 232–3; Shackleton, *M.*, pp. 245–6.

[52] *Discourse*, p. 571. This quotation comes from the first part of the *Discourse*, *A Demonstration of the Being and Attributes of God*, which Clarke gave as a Boyle lecture in 1704.

[53] Janet, *Histoire de la science politique*, vol. II, p. 330: F. Strowski, *Montaigne*, Alcan, 1906, p. 310; Crisafulli, 'Parallels to Ideas in the *Lettres persanes*', pp. 773–4; Barrière, *Un Grand provincial*, p. 16; Beyer, 'Montesquieu et l'esprit cartesien', pp. 160–1; Shackleton, *M.*, pp. 245–6. It has also been noted that the source of M.'s definition of justice in *L.p.* LXXXIII could be Leibniz' *Théodicée* [1710] (I, 73, in *Œuvres philosophiques*, Alcan, 1900, vol. II, pp. 123–4): *cf.* Crisafulli, *loc. cit.* and *Lettres persanes*, ed. Vernière, p. 174, n. 3.

[54] *M.*, p. 246; *Traité de morale*, I, i, 14, p. 22.

[55] *Méditations chrétiennes et métaphysiques*, IV, viii, p. 39 (our italics).

Malebranche thus did what Montesquieu was to do in the *Esprit des lois*: he identified relationships with laws, and said they apply to God and to man.

Besides this similarity of ideas, there is also a similarity of style. A page or two earlier, Malebranche had said that

Tous les rapports se réduisent à trois genres, aux rapports entre les êtres créés, aux rapports entre les idées intelligibles, et aux rapports entre les êtres et leurs idées.[56]

The first and third of these relationships put us in mind of the phrases used by Montesquieu in the third paragraph of Book I, i, where he talked of the "rapports" between "une raison primitive" and "les différents êtres", and of "les rapports de ces divers êtres entre eux" (N. I, i, p. 2, Pl. II, p. 232).

So far we have established that Malebranche identified normative relationships with laws. Did he also identify descriptive relationships with laws? Not in so many words, because to do so would be to invite the accusation of determinism, but as has been seen in the previous section, he did in fact admit that the laws of motion, which are one kind of "rapport de grandeur", are so unchangeable as to be binding on God Himself: thus he did identify descriptive as well as normative relationships with laws, just as Montesquieu was to do in the *Esprit des lois*.[57]

Shackleton says that since Samuel Clarke not only defined law as a relationship, but also showed that God is bound by His own laws, he is a likely source of Montesquieu's ideas. However, it should be noted that both theories are also found in the work of Malebranche. In view of the stylistic similarities noted in this section and the previous one, we would suggest that Malebranche was more in Montesquieu's mind than Clarke, though the two influences are not of course mutually exclusive, but complementary, since both writers were combating nominalism and voluntarism. For Malebranche, the enemy was Descartes and the Epicureans;[58] for Clarke, it was Hobbes.

When Malebranche identified laws and relationships, he also identified truth and law ("des vérités et en même temps des lois"), that is

[56] *Ibid.*, IV, v, p. 38.

[57] *Cf.* also Bayle's *Continuation des pensées diverses*, clii, p. 409: "Dieu a pu créer *la matière, un homme, un cercle*, ou les laisser dans le néant, mais il n'a pu les produire sans leur donner leurs propriétés essentielles" (our italics).

[58] Malebranche's most forceful attack on voluntarism occurs in the *X^e^ éclaircissement* to *De la Recherche de la vérité*, vol. III, pp. 132–9.

reason and obligation. In so doing, he was merely expressing the traditional teaching of natural law in contemporary terms. Can it therefore be said that Montesquieu's definition of law, based as it seems to be on that of Malebranche, is also in accordance with the tradition of natural law, and that its unusualness is the result of its style and not of its content?

Most scholars would answer in the negative. It is generally assumed that because Montesquieu did not define normative laws as the will of a superior, he was in disagreement with his juristic predecessors.[59] Shackleton's comment is representative of critical opinion on this question:

> This was a surprising attitude to law, and a surprising definition, to come from the pen of one who had been a celebrated magistrate [....]. The jurists of the past, whose example he claimed to be following, had given far different definitions.

Shackleton then cites certain definitions by Grotius, Pufendorf, Burlamaqui, Hobbes and St. Thomas, in order to show that for these philosophers, law is essentially a command.[60] One is prompted to ask whether these particular definitions fully sum up the attitude of the philosophers of natural law.

Grotius did indeed, as Shackleton says, define law as "une règle des actions morales, qui oblige à ce qui est bon et louable" (*Dg.*, I, i, 9, vol. I, p. 47), but he went on to show that this obligation arises not from the command of God, but from the nature of things: natural law consists in "certains principes de la droite raison", and "Les actions à l'égard desquelles la raison nous fournit de tels principes, sont obligatoires ou illicites par elles-mêmes, à cause de quoi on les conçoit comme nécessairement ordonnées ou défendues de Dieu" (*ibid.*, 10, pp. 48–9). He also claimed that natural law would hold true even if God did not exist (*ibid.*, *Disc. prél.*, xi, vol. I, p. 10), just as Usbek was to do in *Lettre persane* LXXXIII. For Grotius as for Montesquieu, law is independent of God's will, being the necessary consequence of the nature of things.[61]

[59] *Cf.* Destutt de Tracy, *loc. cit.*; Seguin in Callot, *op. cit.*, pp. 83–4; Althusser, *op. cit.*, pp. 23–5; Brethe de la Gressaye, 'La Philosophie du droit de Montesquieu', p. 203; D. Oster in introduction to *Lois*, Seuil edition of M.'s works, p.527.

[60] *M.*, pp. 244–5.

[61] *Cf.* Ernst Cassirer, *The Philosophy of the Enlightenment* [1932], translated by F. C. A. Koelln and J. P. Pettegrove, Princeton University Press, 1951, pp. 242–3, and Courtney, 'Montesquieu', p. 36. Cassirer and Courtney are the only scholars to have drawn attention to the similarities between M. and Grotius on this fundamental question.

Though Pufendorf, as Shackleton states, defined law as "une volonté d'un supérieur" (*Dn.*, I, vi, 4, vol. I, p. 89), thus accepting the voluntarist position, he also said that

il suffit que l'on connaisse la volonté du supérieur, de quelque manière que ce soit, même par les lumières seules de la raison, et par des conséquences tirées ou de notre constitution propre et essentielle, ou de la nature de l'affaire dont il s'agit (*Dn.*, II, iii, 20, vol. I, p. 205).

In this passage, at least, the idea of *volonté* is very vague, and is almost replaced by the idea of an obligation derived from the nature of man and society.

If Pufendorf's conception of law was more voluntaristic than that of Grotius, the same cannot be said of Burlamaqui. Shackleton cites the Swiss philosopher's words: "Je définis la loi une règle prescrite par le souverain d'une société à ses sujets" (*Principes du droit naturel*, I, viii, 3, p. 89). But this definition is limited, as the context shows, to civil law, so it cannot be compared with Montesquieu's definition of law in general. In a later section of his work Burlamaqui examined the question of voluntarism, and came to the conclusion that "la raison seule, indépendamment de la loi, suffit pour imposer quelque obligation à l'homme" (*Principes du droit naturel*, II, vii, 8, p. 236). His conception of the laws of nature is very similar to that of Montesquieu:

elles ont leur fondement dans la nature des choses et dans les rapports qui sont entre elles (*ibid.*, v, 10, p. 215).[62]

There can, of course, be no doubt that Hobbes, also quoted by Shackleton, regarded all law, whether human or divine, as the command of a superior: that is why there is no similarity between his conception of law and that of Montesquieu. With St. Thomas, the case is very different. Though, as Shackleton says, he stated that "Law is a rule and measure of acts, whereby man is induced to act or is restrained from acting" (*S.t.*, II, i, Q. 90, A. 1, vol. VIII, p. 2), he did not believe that human law is the result of will, since "the rule and measure of human acts is the reason" (*ibid.*); nor did he believe Divine law to be based simply no God's will. Refuting the unorthodox volun-

62 Is there any possibility of Burlamaqui having influenced M.? The *Principes du droit naturel* appeared in 1747, the *Lois* in 1748, and both works were published by the same firm. M. knew of the existence of Burlamaqui's work (*cf.* Vernet to M., N. III, p. 1136 and Mussard to M., N. III, p. 1092), but it is uncertain whether he ever saw it in full; it does not feature in his catalogue. It is most unlikely to have influenced him at this late date since his conception of law as a relationship is not an after-thought, but inspires the whole of the *Lois*.

tarist position,[63] he said that "the power of God [...] is nothing else but His wisdom" (*S.t.*, I, Q. 25, A. 5, vol. I, p. 356), and, just as Malebranche, Clarke, and Montesquieu were to do, he claimed that "it is impossible for God to will anything but what His wisdom approves" (*ibid.*, Q. 21, A. 1, rep. obj. 2, vol. I, p. 298).[64] In fact, the great majority of philosophers who believe in natural law would accept Socrates' famous dictum that a given action is not just because the gods approve of it, but that the gods approve of it because it is just.[65] As D'Entrèves remarks on the subject of natural law:

> The very condition of its existence is that the identification of law and command be overcome or abandoned.[66]

Montesquieu's definition of law is not therefore "surprising". In saying that moral law arises from the nature of things, he was following the philosophers of natural law. In saying the same thing of political and civil law, he was developing a line of thought initiated by some of these philosophers. In saying the same thing of physical law, he was following the Cartesians. In combining the physical and the moral aspects of law in a single definition, he was again following the Cartesians, who had, in spite of their reluctance to admit the fact, extended the anti-voluntarism of the doctrine of natural law to the world of physical phenomena. Montesquieu's originality lies in the neatness of his formulation of this concept of law, and above all in his working out of its consequences by enumerating the various physical and moral factors that influence the general laws governing man's social and political life.

[63] *Cf.* Bréhier, *op. cit.*, vol. I, pp. 708–30.
[64] *Cf.* É. Gilson, *Le Thomisme*, Vrin, 1927, pp. 281–2.
[65] *Euthyphro*, 10d; in the Loeb edition, *Euthyphro, Apology, Crito, Phædo, Phædrus*, p. 39.
[66] *Op. cit.*, p. 64.

CONCLUSION

In studying the way in which a man reacted to a group of ideas it is all too easy to concentrate on intellectual attitudes and to ignore the human reality behind them. Montesquieu's beliefs about nature may have been complex, even contradictory, but his experience of nature was quite simple. Like another Montaigne, he could say:

> Ma machine est si heureusement construite que je suis frappé par tous les objets assez vivement pour qu'ils puissent me donner du plaisir, pas assez pour me donner de la peine.
>
> [...]
>
> Je m'éveille le matin avec une joie secrète; je vois la lumière avec une espèce de ravissement. Tout le reste du jour je suis content.
>
> Je passe la nuit sans m'éveiller; et, le soir, quand je vais au lit, une espèce d'engourdissement m'empêche de faire des réflexions (*P.* 213, Bkn. 4, N. II, pp. 84–5, Pl. I, pp. 975–6).

He was not averse to personifying this harmony between man and his environment in phrases that make us suspect for a moment that he accepted the physico-theology of a Fénelon; not only in the allegorical story of the Troglodytes: "La nature ne fournissait pas moins à leurs désirs qu'à leurs besoins" (*L.p.* XII, N. I, iii, p. 32, Pl. I, p. 150), but even in the *Esprit des lois*: "La nature est juste envers les hommes" (XIII, ii, N. I, i, p. 286, Pl. II, p. 459). A literary affectation, perhaps, but at the same time, the sign of a deep conviction.

Could it be then that those who accuse Montesquieu of having ignored the principles of natural rights and of morality, and those who praise him for it, are sometimes judging him on the wrong level? His flirtations with certain controversial topics – polygamy, incest, suicide – were conducted on an intellectual rather than a personal level. His marriage may not have been very happy, but he seems to have been content with the usual remedies such as study, prolonged absence or adultery. He had too balanced a temperament to wish to end his life voluntarily, "n'ayant jamais eu de chagrin qu'une heure de lecture ne m'ait ôté" (*P.* 213, Bkn. 4, N. II, p. 85, Pl. I, p. 975).

So, when he discussed these topics in seemingly impartial tones, it could be that he assumed on the part of the reader, as he found within himself, a more or less instinctive moral (or Christian) point of view which he therefore felt it was unnecessary to express. Hence his rather impatient tone in the *Réponses et explications*, each time he felt obliged to add a note or alter a phrase in order to show the reader what moral attitude to adopt: he realized there is nobody so tiresome as a moralizer. If he avoided the moralizing that sometimes mars the work of Rousseau or Diderot, it was not necessarily because he disbelieved in morality.

Like the *philosophes* he was confronted with two seemingly contradictory alternatives: on the one hand, an acceptance of the fact that all knowledge is relative, because it comes from the senses; on the other, a refusal to believe that no absolute values can be derived from the relative, to replace the religious ideals that no longer commanded respect.

In his exploration of the relative, Montesquieu surpassed all his predecessors and all his contemporaries. The *Esprit des lois* stands as a monument not so much to his erudition (which, although it was immense, was sometimes faulty) as to his intelligence, to his ability to see connections between disparate facts and to make human reality comprehensible. In this respect, the work was well in advance of the age in which it was written, and may indeed be seen as the forerunner of present-day comparative jurisprudence and sociological inquiry, even though its basic assumption, that different men need different kinds of government, runs counter to the beliefs of most democrats. Montesquieu may also perhaps deserve some opprobrium for having suggested and sanctioned those methods of manipulating public opinion that in other countries we call brain-washing and in our own, education.

In his attempts to establish an absolute within the relative, Montesquieu takes his place in the series of political and social reformers beginning with the School of Natural Law and leading to the *philosophes* and in particular to the authors of the *Encyclopédie*, who took so much from him.[1]

[1] It has not been our purpose to examine in detail the influence of M. on the men and movements coming after him: such a study deserves a book to itself. Many scholars have dealt ably with the controversial subject of his political influence, among them Eichthal, *op. cit.*, pp. 139–54; Faguet, *La Politique comparée de Montesquieu, Rousseau et Voltaire*, pp. 281–8; R. Carré de Malberg, *Contribution à la théorie générale de l'État*, Sirey, 1920–22, vol. II, pp.

The sources of Montesquieu's work have been the object of several specialized studies. Dedieu has drawn attention to his English predecessors, Carcassonne to his French predecessors, Muriel Dodds and F.Weil to his use of *les récits de voyages*. Hitherto, however, his debt to the philosophers of natural law has been neglected. In the present work, we have shown the considerable extent to which both on questions of principle and in matters of detail he drew on the tradition of natural law in his study of human customs and laws.

We are now in a position to attempt an assessment of what he owed to the various philosophers of natural law whose works have been studied in the preceding pages.

Montesquieu's debt to Descartes appears in the past to have been wrongly stressed. From Cartesianism he took his notion of science and perhaps even his method of studying civil law, but not his conception of natural law, except in so far as he was following Malebranche, who was in turn expressing the age-old idea of natural law in modern terms, and applying it, by implication, to physical as well as to moral phenomena.

In Malebranche, as in other seventeenth- and eighteenth-century philosophers, but above all in Aristotle and Cicero, Montesquieu found support for his belief in a natural law prior to human institutions, a belief that resulted in his lifelong opposition to Hobbes and his acceptance of, though not reliance on, the original contract.

In the *Esprit des lois*, where he attempted to reconcile the eternal law with human diversity, his greatest debt was to Grotius and Pufendorf. When he said "Je rends grâce à Messieurs Grotius et Pufendorf", he was not trying to flatter anyone, but was expressing his sincere thanks for the fact that they had prepared the way for his inquiry. From Grotius, among many other philosophers, he may have taken his anti-voluntaristic conception of law, as well as the basis of his theory of international relations. The Dutch philosopher's empiricism, and in

11–23 and 36–44; Vaughan, *Studies in the History of Political Philosophy*, vol. I, pp. 295–302; Cairns, *op. cit.*, pp. 242–58; Mirkine-Guetzévitch, 'De la séparation des pouvoirs', *Bicentenaire*, pp. 161–84; W. Stewart, 'Montesquieu et l'Angleterre', *IIe Centenaire*, pp. 173–225, and 'Montesquieu vu par les Anglais depuis deux siècles', *Congrès*, pp. 339–48. M.'s influence on humanitarian reform has received less attention: one of the fullest accounts is in Fletcher, *Montesquieu and English Politics*, pp. 185–200 and 228–38. One easily verifiable aspect of M.'s influence is the borrowings made from his work by contributors to the *Encyclopédie*. His discussion of liberty is cited in the anonymous 'Liberté civile' and in Jaucourt's 'Liberté politique' (vol. IX, p. 472). Several of his ideas on the punishment of crime appear in Jaucourt's article 'Peines' (vol. XII, pp. 246–9), as well as in 'Liberté politique'. In Jaucourt's 'Esclavage' we find reminiscences of Pufendorf, Locke, and above all M. (vol. V, pp. 934–9), and he cites M. again in the article 'Égalité naturelle' (vol. V, p. 415).

particular his references to animal instinct, may have guided Montesquieu in his attitude to natural law. But it was above all the more sophisticated empiricism of Pufendorf – with his unmoralistic approach to many controversial problems, and his acceptance of the fact that civil law can, indeed must vary from country to country – which seems to foreshadow Montesquieu's aims in the *Esprit des lois*.

If there is empiricism in the *Esprit des lois*, there is also much evidence of moral attitudes, not least in questions of sexual relations. Here, Montesquieu drew on the religious as well as the secular philosophers of natural law. However, his moral attitude to problems such as slavery and the punishment of crime is not the result of any influence: it came from certain convictions which lead him to rethink the teaching of natural law, and in particular to take to their logical conclusions the concepts of self-defence and equality. However, neither his humanitarianism nor his empiricism would interest us today had they not succeeded in capturing public attention in a way the School of Natural Law had never done, by virtue of his style.

Voltaire, while criticizing both the *Lettres persanes* and the *Esprit des lois* for the frivolity of their style, praised the latter work for its defence of human rights, but he does not seem to have appreciated the serious side of the former work. The more commonly-held view is that Montesquieu gradually evolved away from moral concerns as he grew older. Both views stand in need of revision. Montesquieu's understanding of the relative gradually became deeper, but his belief in certain absolutes, though expressed in different ways in different works, was consistent throughout his life.

INDEX

BIBLIOGRAPHY OF WORKS CITED*

Montesquieu's Works

I. Complete works

Œuvres complètes de Montesquieu, texte présenté et annoté par Roger Caillois, Bibliothèque de la Pléiade, 1949–51, 2 vols.

Œuvres complètes de Montesquieu, ed. Édouard Laboulaye, Garnier, 1875–9, 7 vols.

Œuvres complètes de Montesquieu, publiées sous la direction de M. André Masson, Nagel, 1950–55, 3 vols.

Montesquieu: Œuvres complètes, préface de Georges Vedel, présentation et notes de Daniel Oster, Seuil, 1964.

II. Separate works

Considérations sur les causes de la grandeur des Romains, et de leur décadence, ed. Henri Barckhausen, Imprimerie nationale, 1900.

De l'Esprit des lois, texte établi et présenté par Jean Brethe de la Gressaye, Les Belles Lettres, 1950–61, 4 vols.

Lettres persanes, édition critique avec notes par Antoine Adam, Geneva, Droz, 1954.

Lettres persanes, texte établi, avec introduction, bibliographie, notes et relevé de variantes, par Paul Vernière, Garnier, 1960.

III. Extracts

Montesquieu: choix de textes et introduction, par Paul Archambault, préface de H. Barthélemy, Michaud, 1883.

Montesquieu: introduction et choix, par Bernard Grœthuysen, Geneva and Paris, Éditions des trois collines, 1947.

Montesquieu: livre premier de l'Esprit des lois, accompagné d'un commentaire, par Camille Jullian, Hachette, 1897.

Montesquieu: textes choisis et commentés, par Fortunat Strowski, Plon, 1912.

Politique de Montesquieu, textes choisis et présentés, par Jean Ehrard, Colin, 1965.

* No attempt has been made to given a complete bibliography of the subject of this study.

Primary Sources

i. Antiquity

Aristotle, *Ethics*, Loeb edition, tr. H. Rackham, Heinemann, 1926.

—*Politics*, Loeb edition, tr. H, Rackham, Heinemann, 1959.

Aurelius, Marcus, *The Communings with Himself of Marcus Aurelius Antoninus*, Loeb edition, tr. C. R. Haines, Heinemann, 1953.

Cicero, M. Tullius, *De finibus bonorum et malorum*, Loeb edition, tr. H. Rackham, Heinemann, 1921.

— *De natura deorum*, *Academica*, Loeb edition, tr. H. Rackham, Heinemann, 1933.

— *De Officiis*, Loeb edition, tr. W. Miller, Heinemann, 1928.

— *De republica*, *de legibus*, Loeb edition, tr. C. W. Keyes, Heinemann, 1928.

Herodotus, Loeb edition, tr. A. D. Godley, Heinemann, 1920–24, 4 vols.

Hesiod, *The Homeric Hymns and Homerica*, Loeb edition, tr. H. G. Evelyn-White, Heinemann, 1926.

Justinian I, *Corpus iuris civilis*, ed. T. Mommsen, Berlin, Weidmann, vol. I, 1899.

Lucretius, T. Carus, *De rerum natura*, Loeb edition, tr. W. H. D. Rouse, Heinemann, 1947.

Plato, *Euthyphro*, *Apology*, *Crito*, *Phædo*, *Phædrus*, Loeb edition, tr. H. N. Fowler, Heinemann, 1953.

— *Laches*, *Protagoras*, *Meno*, *Euthydemus*, Loeb edition, tr. W. R. M. Lamb, Heinemann, 1924.

— *Laws*, Loeb edition, tr. R. G. Bury, Heinemann, 1926, 2 vols.

— *The Republic*, Loeb edition, tr. P. Shorey, Heinemann, 1963, 2 vols.

— *The Statesman*, *Philebus*, *Ion*, Loeb deition, tr. H. N. Fowler and W. R. M. Lamb, Heinemann, 1925.

Tacitus, Publius Cornelius, *Dialogus*, *Agricola*, *Germania*, Loeb edition, tr. W. Peterson and M. Hutton, Heinemann, 1946.

ii. Middle ages to eighteenth century

Aguesseau, Henri-François d', *Œuvres choisies*, Didot, 1886.

Aquinas, Thomas, *Summa theologica*, literally translated by Fathers of the English Dominican Province, Burns Oates and Washbourne, 1913–42, 22 vols.

— *Summa totius theologiæ*, Antwerp, ex officina Christophori Plantini, 1585.

Augustine, Aurelius, bishop of Hippo, *On Free Will*, in: *Augustine, Earlier Writings*, Library of Christian Classics, S.C.M., vol. VI, 1953, pp. 113–217.

Barbeyrac, Jean, *Discours sur la permission des lois, où l'on fait voir, que ce qui est permis par les lois, n'est pas toujours juste et honnête*, Geneva, Fabri et Barillot, 1715.

Bayle, Pierre, *Commentaire philosophique sur ces paroles de Jésus-Christ, Contrains-les d'entrer*, in: *Œuvres diverses de Mr. Pierre Bayle*, The Hague, Husson, etc., 1727–31, 4 vols. vol, II, pp. 355– 560.

— *Continuation des pensées diverses*, in: *Œuvres diverses*, etc., vol. III, i, pp. 191–417.
— *Réponses aux questions d'un provincial*, in: *Œuvres diverses*, etc., vol. III, ii.
Beaumont, Christophe de, archbishop of Paris, *Mandement de Mgr. l'archevêque de Paris portant condamnation d'un livre qui a pour titre: Émile, ou de l'éducation*, in: J.-J. Rousseau, *Du Contrat social*, etc., Garnier, 1962, pp. 419–35.
Bodin, Jean, *La Méthode de l'histoire*, traduite et présentée par Pierre Mesnart, Les Belles Lettres, 1941.
— *Les Six livres de la république*, Lyons, Jacques du Puys, 1579.
Bossuet, Jacques-Bénigne, bishop of Meaux, *Discours sur l'histoire universelle*, in: *Œuvres complètes de Bossuet*, Lefèvre, Didot, 1836, 12 vols, vol. X, pp. 131–311.
— *Politique tirée des propres paroles de l'Écriture sainte*, in: *Œuvres complètes*, etc,. vol. X, pp. 312–499.
Boyle, Robert, *The Excellency of Theology Compared with Natural Philosophy*, in: *The Works of the Honourable Robert Boyle*, Johnston, etc., 1772, 6 vols., vol. IV, pp. 1–66.
— *Of The High Veneration Man's Intellect Owes to God*, in *The Works of the Honourable Robert Boyle*, etc., vol. V, pp. 130–57.
Buffon, Georges-Louis Leclerc, *Œuvres philosophiques*, ed. J. Piveteau, in: *Corpus général des philosophes français*, Presses Universitaires de France, vol. XLI, i, 1954.
Burlamaqui, Jean-Jacques, *Principes du droit naturel*, Geneva, Barillot, 1747.
— *Principes du droit politique*, Amsterdam, 1751, 2 vols.
Chesterfield, Philip Dormer Stanhope, *Miscellaneous Works*, Dilly, 1777, 2 vols.
Clarke, Samuel, *A Discourse Concerning the Being and Attributes of God, the Obligations of Natural Religion, and the Truth and Certainty of the Christian Revelation*, in *The Works of Samuel Clarke*, Knapton, 1738, 4 vols, vol. II, pp. 513–733.
Condillac, Étienne Bonnot de Mably de, *Œuvres philosophiques*, ed. G. Le Roy, 3 vols, in: *Corpus général des philosophes français*, Presses Universitaires de France, vol. XXXIII, 1947–51.
Corneille, Pierre, *Cinna*, in: *Œuvres de Corneille*, ed. Marty-Laveaux, Hachette, 1862, 11 vols, vol. III, pp. 359–462.
— *Le Menteur*, in *Œuvres de Corneille*, etc., vol. IV, pp. 117–239.
Cumberland, Richard, bishop of Peterborough, *Traité philosophique des lois naturelles, ou l'on recherche et l'on établit, par la nature des choses, la forme de ces lois, leurs principaux chefs, leur ordre, leur publication et leur obligation*, Amsterdam, Mortier, 1744.
Descartes, René, *Correspondance*, in: *Œuvres de Descartes*, ed. C. Adam et P. Tannery, Cerf, 1897–1910, 12 vols, vols. I–V, p. 612.
— *Discours de la méthode*, in: *Œuvres de Descartes*, etc., vol. VI, pp. 1–78.
— *Meditationes*, in: *Œuvres de Descartes*, etc., vol. VII.
— *Méditations métaphysiques*, in: *Œuvres de Descartes*, etc., vol. IX, pp. 1–224.
— *Principes de la philosophie*, in: *Œuvres de Descartes*, etc., vol. IX, pp. 1–358.
— *Traité de l'homme*, in: *Œuvres de Descartes*, etc., vol. XI, pp. 119–215.

Diderot, Denis, and Alembert, Jean le Rond d', *Encyclopédie, ou dictionnaire raisonné des sciences, des arts et des métiers* [...] *par une société de gens de lettres*, vols. I–VII, Briasson, David, Le Breton, Durand, 1751–7, vols. VIII–XVII, Neuchâtel, Faulché, 1765, reprinted Stuttgart, Frommann, 1966–7.

Domat, Jean, *Les Lois civiles dans leur ordre naturel, le droit public et legum delectus*, Cavelier, 1705, 2 vols.

Fénelon, François de Salignac de La Mothe de, archbishop of Cambray, *Les Aventures de Télémaque*, in: *Œuvres de Fénelon*, Didot, 1857, 3 vols, vol. III, pp. 1–149.

— *Dialogues des morts*, in: *Œuvres de Fénelon*, etc., vol. II, pp. 546–641.

— *Écrits et lettres politiques*, publiés sur les manuscrits autographes par Ch. Urbain, Bossard, 1920.

Filmer, Robert, *Patriarcha and Other Political Works*, ed. P. Laslett, Oxford, Blackewell, 1949.

Gravina, Gian Vincenzo, *Esprit des lois romaines*, tr. Requier, Videcoq et Brière, 1821.

— *Origines iuris civilis, quibus ortus et progressus iuris civilis, ius naturale, gentium et xii. tabulæ legesque ac senatusconsulta explicantur*, Leipzig, Gleditsch, 1708.

Grotius, Hugo, *Le Droit de la guerre et de la paix.* [...] *Nouvelle traduction par Jean Barbeyrac* [...]. *Avec les notes de l'auteur même, qui n'avaient point encore paru en français; et de nouvelles notes du traducteur*, Amsterdam, Pierre de Coup, 1724, 2 vols.

— *Epistolæ quotquot reperiri potuerunt*, Amsterdam, Blaeu, 1687.

Helvétius, Claude-Adrien, *De l'esprit*, Durand, 1759.

Hobbes, Thomas, *Leviathan*, in: *The English Works of Thomas Hobbes*, ed. W. Molesworth, Bohn and Longman, 1839–45, 11 vols, vol. III.

— *Philosophical Rudiments Concerning Government and Society*, in: *The English Works of Thomas Hobbes*, etc., vol. II.

— *The Questions Concerning Liberty, Necessity and Chance*, in: *The English Works of Thomas Hobbes*, etc., vol. V.

— *Tripos* [...] *De corpore politico*, in: *The English Works of Thomas Hobbes*, etc., vol. IV, pp. 77–228.

The Holy Bible.

La Bruyère, Jean de, *Les Caractères de Théophraste, traduits du grec, avec les caractères ou les mœurs de ce siècle*, in: *Œuvres de La Bruyère*, ed. G. Servois, Hachette, 1922, 6 vols, vols. I–III, i.

La Mettrie, Julien Offray de, *L'Homme Machine. A Study in the Origins of an Idea.* Critical edition with an introductory monograph and notes by Aram Vartanian, Princeton University Press, 1960.

Leibniz, Gottfried Wilhelm, *Essais de Théodicée*, in: *Œuvres philosophiques*, ed. P. Janet, 1900, 2 vols, vol. II, pp. 1–442.

Locke, John, *Essai philosophique concernant l'entendement humain, traduit de l'anglais de M. Locke par Pierre Coste*, Amsterdam, Schelte, 1700.

— *Letters Concerning Toleration*, in: *The Works of John Locke*, Strahan, etc., 1777, 4 vols, vol. II, pp. 313–691.

— *Two Treatises of Government*, ed. P. Laslett, Cambridge University Press, 1960.

Malebranche, Nicolas de, *Entretiens sur la métaphysique et sur la religion*, in: *Œuvres complètes de Malebranche*, Vrin, 1958–68, 20 vols, vol. XII, 1965.
— *Méditations chrétiennes et métaphysiques*, in: *Œuvres complètes de Malebranche*, etc., vol. X, 1959.
— *De la Recherche de la vérité*, in: *Œuvres complètes de Malebranche*, etc., vols. I–III, 1962–4.
— *Traité de morale*, in: *Œuvres complètes de Malebranche*, etc., vol. XI, 1966.
Maupertuis, Pierre-Louis Moreau de, 'Accord de différentes lois de la nature', in: *Histoire de l'Académie royale des sciences, année 1744*, Amsterdam, Mortier, 1750–51, pp. 564–76.
Molière, Jean-Baptiste Poquelin de, *Monsieur de Pourceaugnac*, in: *Œuvres de Molière*, ed. E. Despois et P. Mesnard, Hachette, 1921–2, 13 vols, vol. VII, pp. 209–347.
Montaigne, Michel de, *Essais*, ed. J. Plattard, Les Belles Lettres, 1947, 6 vols.
More, Thomas, *Utopia*, tr. R. Robynson, ed. J. Rawson Lumby, Cambridge University Press, 1897.
Morelly, *Code de la nature ou le véritable esprit de ses lois*, ed. G. Chinard, [*s.l.*], 1950.
Newton, Isaac, *Mathematical Principles of Natural Philosophy*, tr. A. Motte, revised F. Cajori, University of California Press, 1947.
— *Opticks, or a Treatise of the Reflections, Refractions, Inflections and Colours of Light*, Innys, 1730.
Pascal, Blaise, *Pensées*, in: *Œuvres de Blaise Pascal*, ed. L. Brunsvicg et P. Boutroux, Hachette, 1908–21, 14 vols, vols. XII–XIV.
— *Préface sur le Traité du vide*, in: *Œuvres de Blaise Pascal*, etc., vol. II, pp. 129–45.
Pope, Alexander, *An Essay on Man*, ed. M. Mack, Methuen, 1950.
Pufendorf, Samuel von, *Les Devoirs de l'homme et du citoyen, tels qu'ils lui sont prescrits par la loi naturelle, traduits du latin de feu M. le baron de Pufendorf, par Jean Barbeyrac. Avec quelques notes du traducteur*, Amsterdam and Luxembourg, Chevalier, 1708.
— *Le Droit de la nature et des gens, ou système général des principes les plus importants de la morale, de la jurisprudence, et de la politique, traduit du latin de feu M. le baron de Pufendorf par Jean Barbeyrac* [...]. *Avec des notes du traducteur; et une préface, qui sert d'introduction à tout l'ouvrage*, Amsterdam, Pierre de Coup, 1712, 2 vols.
Rousseau, Jean-Jacques, *Les Confessions*, in: *Œuvres complètes*, ed. B. Gagnebin et M. Raymond, Bibliothèque de la Pléiade, 1962–9, vol. I, 1962, pp. 1–656.
— *Du Contrat social, ou principes du droit politique*, in: *The Political Writings of Jean-Jacques Rousseau*, ed. C. E. Vaughan, Cambridge University Press, 1915, 2 vols, vol. II, pp. 21–134.
— *Discours sur l'origine et les fondements de l'inégalité parmi les hommes*, in: *The Political Writings of Jean-Jacques Rousseau*, etc., vol. I, pp. 125–220.
— *Émile, ou de l'éducation*, in: *Œuvres complètes*, etc., vol. IV, 1969, pp. 239–868.
Shaftesbury, Anthony Ashley Cooper, third earl of, *An Essay on the Freedom of Wit and Humour*, in: *Characteristicks of Men, Manners, Opinions, Times*, 4th ed., [*s.l.*], 1727, 3 vols, vol. I, pp. 57–150.

— *An Inquiry Concerning Virtue or Merit*, in: *Characteristicks*, etc., vol. II, pp. 5–176.
Spinoza, Benedictus de, *Ethics*, in: *Œuvres complètes*, ed. R. Caillois, M. Francès et R. Misrahi, Bibliothèque de la Pléiade, 1954, pp. 357–652.
— *Tractatus theologico-politicus*, in: *Œuvres complètes*, etc., pp. 653–964.
— *Tractatus theologico-politicus*, in: *Opera*, ed. J. Van Vloten and J. P. N. Land, The Hague, Nijhoff, 1895, 3 vols, vol. II, pp. 1–173.
Voltaire, François-Marie Arouet de, *Dictionnaire philosophique*, in: *Œuvres complètes de Voltaire*, [ed. L. Moland], Garnier, 1877–85, 52 vols, vols. XVII–XX.
— *Lettres philosophiques*, in: *Œuvres complètes de Voltaire*, etc., vol. XXII, pp. 75–187.
— *Le Siècle de Louis XIV*, in: *Œuvres complètes de Voltaire*, etc., vols. XIV and XV, pp. 1–84.
— *Voltaire's Correspondence*, edited by T. Besterman, Geneva, Institut et musée Voltaire, 1953–65, 107 vols.

Secondary Sources

1. Studies on Montesquieu

Actes du congrès Montesquieu, Bordeaux, Delmas, 1956.
Alembert, Jean le Rond d', *Analyse de l'Esprit des lois*, in: *Œuvres complètes de Montesquieu*, publiées sous la direction de M. André Masson, Nagel, 1950–55, 3 vols, vol. I, i, pp. xxxiv–lii.
— *Éloge de Monsieur le président de Montesquieu*, in: *Œuvres complètes de Montesquieu*, publiées sous la direction de M. André Masson, etc., vol. I, i, pp. i–xxxiii.
Alengry, Franck, 'Montesquieu', in: *Essai historique et critique sur la sociologie chez Auguste Comte*, Alcan, 1900, pp. 389–403.
Althusser, Louis, *Montesquieu, la politique et l'histoire*, Presses Universitaires de France, 1964.
André, Désiré, 'Sur les écrits scientifiques de Montesquieu', *Correspondant*, 1880, pp. 1054–81.
Aron, Raymond, 'Montesquieu', in: *Les Grandes doctrines de sociologie historique: Montesquieu, Auguste Comte, Karl Marx, Alexis de Tocqueville, Les sociologues et la révolution de 1848*, Les Cours de la Sorbonne, Centre de documentation universitaire, [1960], pp. 14–55.
Barckhausen, Henri A., *Montesquieu, l'Esprit des lois et les archives de La Brède*, Bordeaux, Michel et Forgeot, 1904.
— *Montesquieu, ses idées et ses œuvres d'après les papiers de La Brède*, Hachette, 1907.
Barrière, Pierre, *Un Grand provincial, ... Montesquieu*, Bordeaux, Delmas, [1946].
— 'L'Humanisme de l'*Esprit des lois*', in: *IIe centenaire de l'Esprit des lois de Montesquieu, conférences organisées par la ville de Bordeaux*, Bordeaux, Delmas, 1949, pp. 31–64.

Barthélemy Saint- Hilaire, Jules, *Préface* to his translation: *Politique d'Aristote*, Dumont, 1848.

Bechard, Ferdinand, 'La Monarchie de Montesquieu et la république de Jean-Jacques', *Correspondant*, 1872, pp. 283–325.

Benrekassa, Georges, *Montesquieu*, Presses Universitaires de France, 1968.

Bérard, Léon, '*L'Esprit des lois* devant la congrégation de l'Index', *Revue des deux mondes*, 1949, pp. 608–33.

Berlin, Isaiah, 'Montesquieu', in: The Proceedings of the British Academy, vol. XLI, Oxford University Press, pp. 267–96.

Bersot, Ernest, 'Montesquieu', in: *Études sur le XVIIIe siècle*, Durand, 1855, vol. II, pp. 297–357.

Beyer, Charles-Jacques, 'Montesquieu et la censure religieuse de l'*Esprit des lois*', *Revue des sciences humaines*, 1953, pp. 105–31.

— 'Montesquieu et l'esprit cartésien', in: *Actes du congrès Montesquieu*, Bordeaux, Delmas, 1956, pp. 159–73.

— 'Le Problème du déterminisme social dans l'*Esprit des lois*', *Romanic Review*, 1948, pp. 102–6.

Boulenger de Rivery, Claude-François-Félix, *Apologie de l'Esprit des lois, ou réponses aux observations de M. de L.P.*, Amsterdam, 1751.

Brethe de la Gressaye, Jean, 'La Philosophie du droit de Montesquieu', *Archives de philosophie du droit*, Sirey, 1962, pp. 199–210.

Brunschvicg, Léon, 'Montesquieu', in: *Le Progrès de la conscience dans la philosophie occidentale*, Alcan, 1927, 2 vols, vol. II, pp. 489–501.

Cabeen, David C., *Montesquieu: A Bibliography*, New York Public Library, 1947.

— 'A Supplementary Montesquieu Bibliography', *Revue internationale de philosophie*, 1955, pp. 409–34.

Caillois, Roger, 'Montesquieu et l'athéisme contemporain', in *Actes du congrès Montesquieu*, Bordeaux, Delmas, 1956, pp. 327–36.

Carcassonne, Élie, *Montesquieu et le problème de la constitution française au XVIIIe siècle*, Presses Universitaires de France, [1927].

Cayrol, Élizabeth, 'Des *Lettres persanes* oubliées', *RHLF*, 1965, pp. 15–26.

Charaux, Auguste, 'Montesquieu', in: *Études franciscaines*, 1909, pp. 601–19.

Cherel, Albert, 'Fénelon et Montesquieu', in: *Fénelon au XVIIIe siècle en France (1715–1820), son prestige, son influence*, Hachette, 1917, pp. 322–6.

— 'Le Président de Montesquieu', in: *De Télémaque à Candide*, Del Duca, 1958, pp. 263–95.

Chinard, Gilbert, 'Montesquieu's Historical Pessimism', in: *Studies in the History of Culture: the Discipline of the Humanities*, Menasha, Banta, 1942, pp. 161–72.

Comte, Auguste, 'Quarante-septième leçon: appréciation sommaire des principales tentatives philosophiques entreprises jusqu'ici pour constituer la science sociale', in *Cours de philosophie positive*, Schleicher, 1908, 7 vols, vol. IV, pp. 118–50.

Condorcet, Jacques-Marie de Caritat de, *Observations sur le vingt-neuvième livre de l'Esprit des lois*, in: Destutt de Tracy, Antoine-Louis-Claude, *Commentaire sur l'Esprit des lois de Montesquieu, suivi d'observations inédites de Condorcet sur le vingt-neuvième livre du même ouvrage*, Desœr, 1819, pp. 399–432.

Cotta, Sergio, *Montesquieu e la scienza della società*, Turin, Ramella, 1953.
— 'Montesquieu, la séparation des pouvoirs et la constitution fédérale des États-Unis', *Revue internationale d'histoire politique et constitutionnelle*, 1951, pp. 225–47.
Courtney, C. P., 'Montesquieu', in: *French Literature and its Background*, ed. J. Cruickshank, vol. III, *The Eighteenth Century*, Oxford University Press, 1968, pp. 30–44.
Crevier, Jean-Baptiste-Louis, *Observations sur le livre de l'Esprit des lois*, Desaint et Saillant, 1764.
Crisafulli, Alessandro S., 'Montesquieu's Story of the Troglodytes: its Background, Meaning, and Significance', *Publications of the Modern Language Association of America*, 1943, pp. 372–92.
— 'Parallels to Ideas in the *Lettres persanes*', *Publications of the Modern Language Association of America*, 1937, pp. 773–77.
Davy, Georges, 'Montesquieu et la science politique', in: *IIe Centenaire de l'Esprit des lois de Montesquieu, conférences organisées par la ville de Bordeaux*, Bordeaux, Delmas, 1949, pp. 127–71.
— 'Sur la méthode de Montesquieu', *Revue de métaphysique et de morale*, 1939, pp. 571–86.
Dedieu, Joseph, *Montesquieu*, Alcan, 1913.
— *Montesquieu*, ed. J. Ehrard, Hatier, 1966 [= *Montesquieu l'homme et l'œuvre*, see next item].
— *Montesquieu l'homme et l'œuvre*, Boivin, 1943.
— *Montesquieu et la tradition politique anglaise en France*, Gabalda, 1909.
Delbos, Victor, 'Montesquieu', in: *La Philosophie française*, Plon, 1921, pp. 169–89.
Desgraves, Louis, (ed.), *Catalogue de la bibliothèque de Montesquieu*, Geneva, Droz, 1954.
— 'Les *Pensées*', in: *Œuvres complètes de Montesquieu*, publiées sous la direction de M. André Masson, Nagel, 1950–55, 3 vols, vol. II, pp. xlv–lxv.
Destutt de Tracy, Antoine-Louis-Claude, *Commentaire sur l'Esprit des lois de Montesquieu, suivi d'observations inédites de Condorcet sur le vingt-neuvième livre du même ouvrage*, Desœr, 1819.
IIe Centenaire de l'Esprit des lois de Montesquieu, conférences organisées par la ville de Bordeaux, Bordeaux, Delmas, 1949.
Dimoff, Paul, 'Cicéron, Hobbes et Montesquieu', *Annales universitatis savariensis*, 1952, pp. 19–47.
— 'La place dans l'œuvre de Montesquieu de l'*Essai touchant les lois naturelles*', *RHLF*, 1957, pp. 481–93.
Dodds, Muriel, *Les récits de voyages, sources de l'Esprit des lois de Montesquieu*, Champion, 1929.
Durkheim, Émile, 'Dans quelle mesure Montesquieu a-t-il contribué à constituer la science des sociétés', *Revue d'histoire politique et constitutionnelle*, 1937, pp. 407–63. [Also entitled: 'Montesquieu: sa part dans la fondation des sciences politiques et de la science des sociétés', this is a translation, by F. Alengry, of Durkheim's thesis of 1892: *Quid Secundatus 'politicæ scientiæ' instituendæ contulerit*].

Ehrard, Jean, 'Les Études sur Montesquieu et l'*Esprit des lois*', *L'Information littéraire*, 1959, pp. 55–66.

Eichthal, Eugène d', 'La Séparation des pouvoirs politiques. Montesquieu et l'Angleterre', in: *Souveraineté du peuple et gouvernement*, Alcan, 1895, pp. 89–154.

Eisemann, Charles, 'L'*Esprit des lois* et la séparation des pouvoirs', in: *Mélanges R. Carré de Malberg*, Sirey, 1933, pp. 165–92.

Étiemble, 'Montesquieu', in *Encyclopédie de la Pléiade, Histoire des littératures*, Gallimard, vol. III, 1958, pp. 696–710.

Faguet, Émile, *La Politique comparée de Montesquieu, Rousseau et Voltaire*, Société française d'imprimerie et de librairie, ancienne librairie Lecène, Oudin, 1902.

Flach, Jacques, 'Platon et Montesquieu, théoriciens politiques', *Revue politique et littéraire* (*Revue bleue*), 1909, pp. 3–7 and 36–42.

Fletcher, F. T. H., *Montesquieu and English politics* (*1750–1800*), Arnold, 1939.

Franck, Adolphe, 'Les Publicistes du XVIIIe siècle: Montesquieu – *L'Esprit des lois*', *Revue contemporaine*, 1858, pp. 49–87.

Giraud, Victor, 'Sur l'*Esprit des lois*', in: *Moralistes français*, Hachette, 1923, pp. 93–104.

Grimsley, Ronald, 'The Idea of Nature in the *Lettres persanes*', *French Studies*, 1951, pp. 293–306.

Gurvitch, Georges, 'La Sociologie juridique de Montesquieu', *Revue de métaphysique et de morale*, 1939, pp. 611–26.

Holmes, Oliver Wendell, 'Montesquieu', in: *Collected Legal Papers*, Constable, 1920, pp. 250–65.

Hubert, René, 'La Notion du devenir historique dans la philosophie de Montesquieu', *Revue de métaphysique et de morale*, 1939, pp. 587–610.

Ilbert, Courtenay, 'Montesquieu'. The Romanes Lecture, delivered in the Sheldonian Theatre, Oxford, June 4, 1904, Oxford, Clarendon Press, 1904.

Jaffray, J., 'La Carrière scientifique de Montesquieu', *La Nature*, 1928, pp. 465–7.

Jameson, R. P., *Montesquieu et l'esclavage. Étude sur les origines de l'opinion antiesclavagiste en France au XVIIIe siècle*, Hachette, 1911.

Janet, Paul, 'Comparaison des théories morales et sociales de Montesquieu et de Jean-Jacques Rousseau', *Revue politique et littéraire*, 1871, pp. 556–61.

— 'Montesquieu', in: *Histoire de la science politique dans ses rapports avec la morale*, Alcan, 1887, 2 vols, vol. II, pp. 322–99.

Koebner, R., 'The Authenticity of the Letters on the *Esprit des lois* attributed to Helvétius', *Bulletin of the Institute of Historical Research*, 1951, pp. 19–43.

La Beaumelle, Laurent Angliviel de, *Suite de la Défense de l'Esprit des lois, ou examen de la réplique du gazetier ecclésiastique à la Défense de l'Esprit des lois*, in: *Œuvres complètes de Montesquieu*, ed. É. Laboulaye, Garnier, 1875–9, 7 vols, vol. VI, pp. 247–312.

Laborde-Milaá, A., 'La Sensibilité de Montesquieu', *Revue des études historiques*, 1908, pp. 333–40.

Laboulaye, Édouard, 'Introduction à l'*Esprit des lois*', in: *Œuvres complètes de Montesquieu*, ed. É. Laboulaye, Garnier, 1875–9, 7 vols, vol. III, pp. i–lxix.

Lanson, Gustave, 'Le Déterminisme historique et l'idéalisme social dans l'*Esprit des lois*', *Études d'histoire littéraire*, Champion, 1929, pp. 135–63.
La Porte, Joseph de, *Observations sur l'Esprit des lois, ou l'art de lire ce livre, de l'entendre et d'en juger*, Amsterdam, Mortier, 1751.
La Roche, Jacques Fontaine de, *Examen critique de l'Esprit des lois*, in: *Œuvres complètes de Montesquieu*, ed. É. Laboulaye, Garnier, 1875–9, 7 vols, vol. VI, pp. 115–37.
— *Réponse à la Défense de l'Esprit des lois*, in: *Œuvres complètes de Montesquieu*, etc., vol. VI, pp. 209–37.
Lemaire, André, 'Les lois fondamentales selon les parlementaires: l'*Esprit des lois*: son influence', in: *Les Lois fondamentales de la monarchie d'après les théoriciens de l'ancien régime*, Fontemoing, 1907, pp. 211–4.
Levin, Lawrence M., *The Political Doctrine of Montesquieu's Esprit des lois: its Classical Background*, New York, Institute of French Studies, [1936].
Loy, Robert J., *Montesquieu*, New York, Twane, 1968.
Martino, Pierre, 'De Quelques résidus métaphysiques dans l'*Esprit des lois*', *Revue d'histoire de la philosophie et d'histoire de la civilisation*, 1946, pp. 235–43.
Masson, André, 'Le *Spicilège*', in: *Œuvres complètes de Montesquieu*, publiées sous la direction de M. André Masson, Nagel, 1950–55, 3 vols, vol. II, pp. lxvii–lxxvi.
Mercier, Roger, 'La Notion de loi morale chez Montesquieu', in: Proceedings of the Sixth Triennial Congress of the International Federation for Modern Languages and Literatures, Oxford, 1954, Oxford, Blackwell, 1955, pp. 184–92.
Meyer, Paul H., 'Politics and Morals in the Thought of Montesquieu', in: *Studies on Voltaire and the Eighteenth Century*, Geneva, Institut et musée Voltaire, vol. LVI, 1967, pp. 845–91.
Mirkine-Guetzévitch, Boris, 'De l'*Esprit des lois* à la démocratie moderne', in: *La Pensée politique et constitutionnelle de Montesquieu, Bicentenaire de l'Esprit des lois*, Sirey, 1952, pp. 11–24.
Oudin, Charles, *Le Spinozisme de Montesquieu*, Pichon et Durant Auzias, 1911.
— *De l'unité de l'Esprit des lois*, Rousseau, 1910.
La Pensée politique et constitutionnelle de Montesquieu, Bicentenaire de l'Esprit des lois, Sirey, 1952.
[Plesse, Pierre-Joseph], *Lettre au P. J. B. sur le livre intitulé l'Esprit des lois*, in: *Œuvres complètes de Montesquieu*, ed. É. Laboulaye, Garnier, 1875–9, 7 vols, vol. VI, pp. 101–13.
Price, E. H., 'Montesquieu's Historical Conception of the Fundamental Law', *Romanic Review*, 1947, pp. 234–42.
Raymond, Marcel, 'L'Humanisme de Montesquieu', in: *Génies de France*, Neuchâtel, La Baconnière, 1942, pp. 124–49.
Risteau, François, *Réponse aux Observations sur l'Esprit des lois*, [Avignon?], 1751.
Roosbroeck, G. L. Van, *Persian Letters Before Montesquieu*, New York, Institute of French Studies, 1932.
Sainte-Beuve, Charles-Augustin de, 'Montesquieu', in: *Causeries du lundi*, Garnier, 3rd. ed., [*s.d.*], 15 vols, vol. VII, pp. 41–84.
Seguin, 'Montesquieu', in: É. Callot, *La Philosophie de la vie au XVIII*^e^

siècle, étudiée chez Fontenelle, Montesquieu, Maupertuis, La Mettrie, Diderot, D'Holbach, Linné, Rivière, 1965, pp. 65–145.
Shackleton, Robert, 'L'*Essai touchant les lois naturelles* est-il de Montesquieu?' in: *Mélanges offerts à Jean Brethe de La Gressaye*, Bordeaux, Bière, [1967].
— 'La Genèse de l'*Esprit des lois*', *RHLF*, 1952, pp. 423–38.
— 'Montesquieu, Bolingbroke, and the Separation of Powers', *French Studies*, 1949, pp. 25–38.
— *Montesquieu, A Critical Biography*, Oxford University Press, 1961.
— 'Montesquieu and Machiavelli: A Reappraisal', *Comparative Literature Studies*, 1964, pp. 1–13.
— 'Montesquieu in 1948', *French Studies*, 1949, pp. 299–323.
— 'Montesquieu: Two Unpublished Documents', *French Studies*, 1950, pp. 313–21.
— 'La Religion de Montesquieu', in: *Actes du congrès Montesquieu*, Bordeaux, Delmas, 1956, pp. 287–294.
— 'Les Secrétaires de Montesquieu', in: *Œuvres complètes de Montesquieu*, publiées sous la direction de M. André Masson, Nagel, 1950–55, 3 vols, vol. II, pp. xxxv–xliii.
Sorel, Albert, *Montesquieu*, Hachette, 1924.
Stark, W., *Montesquieu, Pioneer of the Sociology of Knowledge*, Routledge and Kegan Paul, 1960.
Starobinski, Jean, *Montesquieu par lui-même*, Seuil, 1961.
Stewart, William, 'Montesquieu et l'Angleterre', in: *Actes du congrès Montesquieu*, Bordeaux, Delmas, 1956, pp. 173-225.
— 'Montesquieu vu par les Anglais depuis deux siècles', in: *Actes du congrès Montesquieu*, Bordeaux, Delmas, 1956, pp. 339-48.
Vernière, Paul, 'Montesquieu et le monde musulman d'après l'*Esprit des lois*', in: *Actes du congrès Montesquieu*, Bordeaux, Delmas, 1956, pp. 175–90.
Vian, Louis, *Histoire de Montesquieu: sa vie et ses ouvrages d'après des documents nouveaux et inédits*, Didier, 1878.
— 'Montesquieu et la censure', in: *Œuvres complètes de Montesquieu*, ed. É. Laboulaye, Garnier, 1875–9, 7 vols, vol. VI, pp. 323–30.
Voltaire, François-Marie Arouet de, *Commentaire sur quelques principales maximes de l'Esprit des lois*, in: *Œuvres complètes de Voltaire*, [ed. L. Moland], Garnier, 1877–85, 52 vols, vol. XXX, pp. 405–64.
Waddicor, Mark Hurstone, 'Montesquieu et problème de l'origine des sociétés', *Studi francesi*, 1969, pp. 235-46.
Weil, Françoise, 'Les Lectures de Montesquieu', *RHLF*, 1957, pp. 494–514.
— 'Le Manuscrit des *Géographica* et l'*Esprit des lois*', *RHLF*, 1952, pp. 451–61.
Zévort, Edgar, *Montesquieu*, Lecène et Oudin, 1888.

II. Other studies

Anchel, Robert, *Crimes et châtiments au XVIIIe siècle*, Perrin, 1933.
Barckhausen, Henri A. (ed.), *Statuts et règlements de l'ancienne université de Bordeaux (1441–1793)*, Libourne, Bordeaux, Bouchon, 1886.
Belaval, Y., 'La Crise de la géométrisation de l'univers dans la philosophie des lumières', *Revue internationale de philosophie*, 1952, pp. 337–55.

Blake, R., Ducasse, C., Madden, E., *Theories of Scientific Method*, University of Washington Press, 1960.
Bouillier, Francisque, *Histoire de la philosophie cartésienne*, Delagrave, 1868, 2 vols.
Bréhier, Émile, *Histoire de la philosophie*, Presses Universitaires de France, 3 vols, vol. I, 1926–8, vol. II, 1929–30.
Brunet, Pierre, *L'Introduction des théories de Newton en France au XVIIIe siècle: avant 1738*, Blanchard, 1931.
Bryce, James, *Studies in History and Jurisprudence*, Oxford University Press, 1901, 2 vols.
Buckland, W., *A Textbook of Roman Law*, Cambridge University Press, 1950.
Burtt, Edwin Arthur, *The Metaphysical Foundations of Modern Physical Science*, Routledge and Kegan Paul, 1949.
Cairns, Huntington, *Law and the Social Sciences*, New York, Harcourt, Brace, 1935.
Cassirer, Ernst, *The Philosophy of the Enlightenment*, tr. F. C. A. Koelln and J. P. Pettegrove, Princeton University Press, 1951.
Charmont, J., *La Renaissance du droit naturel*, Chauny et Quinsac, 1927.
Chéruel, A., *Dictionnaire historique des institutions, mœurs et coutumes de la France*, Hachette, 1874, 2 vols.
Coe, R. N. C., 'A la recherche de Morelly', *RHLF*, 1957, pp. 321–34 and 515–23.
Coplestone, Frederick, *A History of Philosophy*, Burns Oates and Washbourne, 1947–60, 6 vols, vol. I, 1947.
Crocker, Lester G., *An Age of Crisis: Man and World in Eighteenth-Century French Thought*, Baltimore, Johns Hopkins Press, 1959.
— 'The Discussion of Suicide in the Eighteenth Century', *Journal of the History of Ideas*, 1952, pp. 47–72.
— *Nature and Culture: Ethical Thought in the French Enlightenment*, Baltimore, Johns Hopkins Press, 1963.
D'Entrèves, A. P., *Natural Law, An Introduction to Legal Philosophy*, Hutchinson, 1957.
Derathé, Robert, *Jean-Jacques Rousseau et la science politique de son temps*, Presses Universitaires de France, 1950.
Ehrard, Jean, *L'Idée de nature en France dans la première moitié du XVIIIe siècle*, S.E.V.P.E.N., 1963, 2 vols.
Esmein, A., *Éléments de droit constitutionnel français et comparé*, Sirey, 1921, 2 vols.
Faguet, Émile, *Dix-huitième siècle*, Boivin, [*s.d.*].
Friedmann, Wolfgang Gaston, *Legal Theory*, Stevens, 1960.
Gay, Peter, *The Party of Humanity. Studies in the French Enlightenment*, Weidenfeld and Nicolson, 1964.
Gilson, Étienne, *La Philosophie au moyen âge*, Payot, 1922, 2 vols.
— *Le Thomisme, introduction au système de Saint Thomas d'Aquin*, Vrin, 1927.
Hampton, John, 'Les traductions françaises de Locke au XVIIIe siècle', *Revue de littérature comparée*, 1955, pp. 240–51.
Havens, G. R., *From Reaction to Revolution. The Age of Ideas in Eighteenth-Century France*, New York, Holt, 1955.

Hazard, Paul, *La Pensée européenne au XVIIIe siècle, de Montesquieu à Lessing*, Boivin, 1946, 3 vols.

Jolowicz, H. F., *Historical Introduction to the Study of Roman Law*, Cambridge University Press, 1952.

Jouffroy, Thomas Simon, *Cours de droit naturel*, Prévost-Crocius, 1834–42, 3 vols.

Jourdain, C., *Histoire de l'université de Paris au XVIIe et au XVIIIe siècle*, Paris, 1862–66, reprint, Brussels, 1966.

Lallemand, P.-J., *Histoire de l'éducation dans l'ancien Oratoire de France*, Thorin, 1888.

Lanson, Gustave, 'Formation et développement de l'esprit philosophique du XVIIIe siècle', *Revue hebdomadaire des cours et conférences*, 1908–9, pp. 357–65, 499–508, 721–36; 1909, pp. 65–75, 211–18, 309–20, 433–42, 549–56, 657–66, 713–20, 796–804, 843–57; 1909–10, pp. 22–32, 106–15, 257–66, 534–44, 734–43.

— 'L'Influence de la philosophie cartésienne sur la littérature française', in: *Études d'histoire littéraire*, Champion, 1929, pp. 58–96.

— 'Origines et premières manifestations de l'esprit philosophique dans la littérature française de 1675 à 1748', *Revue hebdomadaire des cours et conférences*, 1907–8, pp. 289–98, 450–60, 601–13, 721–34; 1908, pp. 1–15, 145–56, 241–54, 409–22, 481–93, 652–37, 738–52, 817–29; 1908–9, pp. 61–74, 113–26, 145–57, 210–23, 259–71.

— 'Le Rôle de l'expérience dans la formation de 'a philosophie du XVIIIe siècle en France. – I. La Transformation des idées morales et la naissance des morales rationnelles de 1680 à 1715', *Revue du mois*, 1910, pp. 5–28.

Leage, R. W., *Roman Private Law*, ed. C. H. Zeigler, Macmillan, 1954.

— *Roman Private Law*, ed. A. M. Pritchard, Macmillan, 1961.

Lenoble, R., 'L'Évolution de l'idée de nature du XVIe au XVIIIe siècle', *Revue de métaphysique et de morale*, 1953, pp. 108–29.

Lovejoy, A. O., Chinard, G., Boas, G., and Crane, R. S., *A Documentary History of Primitivism and Related Ideas*. Vol. I, Lovejoy and Boas, *Primitivism and Related Ideas in Antiquity*, Baltimore, Johns Hopkins Press, 1935.

Maine, H. J. S., *Ancient Law: its Connection with the Early History of Society, and its Relation to Modern Ideas*, Murray, 1930.

Martino, Pierre, *L'Orient dans la littérature française au XVIIe et au XVIIIe siècle*, Hachette, 1906.

McCloy, Shelby T., *The Humanitarian Movement in Eighteenth-Century France*, University of Kentucky Press, 1957.

Mercier, Roger, *La Réhabilitation de la nature humaine (1700–1750)*, Villemonble, La Balance, 1960.

Milhaud, Gaston, *Descartes savant*, Alcan, 1921.

Moreau, Joseph, *L'Âme du monde de Platon aux stoïciens*, Les Belles Lettres, 1939.

— 'Malebranche et le spinozisme', in: Malebranche, *Correspondance avec J. J. Dortous de Mairan*, Vrin, 1947, pp. 1–98.

Nicholas, B., *An Introduction to Roman Law*, Oxford University Press, 1962.

O'Connor, D. J., *Aquinas and Natural Law*, Macmillan, 1967.

The Oxford Dictionnary of the Christian Church, ed. F. L. Cross, Oxford University Press, 1957.

Pollock, Frederick, *Essays in the Law*, Macmillan, 1920.
Proust, Jacques, *Diderot et l'Encyclopédie*, Colin, 1962.
Robson, W. A., *Civilisation and the Growth of Law*, Macmillan, 1935.
Roger, Jacques, *Les Sciences de la vie dans la pensée française du XVIII*e *siècle. La génération des animaux de Descartes à l'Encyclopédie*, Colin, 1963.
Sabine, George H., *A History of Political Theory*, Harrap, 1937.
Sainte-Beuve, Charles-Augustin de, *Port-Royal*, Hachette, 1922, 7 vols.
Schulz, F., *History of Roman Legal Science*, Oxford University Press, 1946.
Sée, Henri, *L'Évolution de la pensée politique en France au XVIII*e *siècle*, Alcan, 1925.
— *Les Idées politiques en France au XVII*e *siècle*, Giard, 1923.
Tonelli, Giorgio, 'La Nécessité des lois de la nature au XVIIIe siècle, et chez Kant en 1762', *Revue d'histoire des sciences*, 1959, pp. 224–41.
Touchard, J., *et al.*, *Histoire des idées politiques*, Presses Universitaires de France, 1959, 2 vols.
Van Tieghem, P., *Le Préromantisme*, SFELT., 1948, 3 vols.
Vartanian, Aram, *Diderot and Descartes, A Study of Scientific Naturalism in the Enlightenment*, Princeton University Press, 1953.
Vaughan, C. E., *Studies in the History of Political Philosophy Before and After Rousseau*, Manchester University Press, 1925, 2 vols.
Vernière, Paul, 'L'Idée d'humanité au XVIIIe siècle', *Studium generale*, 1962, pp. 171–9.
— *Spinoza et la pensée française avant la révolution*, Presses Universitaires de France, 1954, 2 vols.
Vier, Jacques, *Histoire de la littérature française, XVIII*e *siècle*, vol. I, Colin 1965.
Vyverberg, Henry, *Historical Pessimism in the French Enlightenment*, Harvard University Press, 1958.